On Poetry, Painting, and Politics

On Poetry, Painting, and Politics

The Letters of May Morris and John Quinn

Janis Londraville

SUP

Selinsgrove: Susquehanna University Press
London: Associated University Presses

Associated University Presses
440 Forsgate Drive
Cranbury, NJ 08512

Associated University Presses
16 Barter Street
London WC1A 2AH, England

Associated University Presses
P.O. Box 338, Port Credit
Mississauga, Ontario
Canada L5G 4L8

The paper used in this publication meets the requirements of the American National Standard for Permanence of Paper for Printed Library Materials Z39.48–1984.

Library of Congress Cataloging-in-Publication Data

Morris, May, 1862–1938.
On poetry, painting, and politics : the letters of May Morris and John Quinn / [edited by] Janis Londraville.
p. cm.
Includes bibliographical references (p.) and index.
ISBN 0-945636-96-2 (alk. paper)
1. Morris, May, 1862–1938—Correspondence. 2. Women artists—England—Correspondence. 3. Women editors—England—Correspondence. 4. Women dramatists, English—19th century—Correspondence. 5. Quinn, John, 1870–1924—Correspondence. 6. Art patrons—United States—Correspondence. 7. Lawyers—United States—Correspondence. I. Quinn, John, 1870–1924. II. Londraville, Janis, 1949– . III. Title.
CT788.M643A4 1997
941.08'092'2—dc20

96-20004
CIP

PRINTED IN THE UNITED STATES OF AMERICA

To Richard Londraville,
sine qua non

Contents

Acknowledgments

I wish to thank John Quinn's grandnephew, Thomas Conroy, and the New York Public Library's Rare Books and Manuscripts Division: Astor, Lenox, and Tilden Foundations (John Quinn Memorial Collection) for permission to print the correspondence between John Quinn and May Morris; the Society of Antiquaries for permission to publish May Morris's letters; Senator Michael Yeats and Ms. Anne Yeats for allowing me to publish portions of Susan (Lily) Yeats's diaries; the Ashmolean Museum for permission to publish excerpts from May Morris's and John Quinn's letters to Esther Pissarro; the Huntington Library in San Marino, California for providing me with the information on the William Morris manuscripts it received from John Quinn; and Thomas Conroy and the William Morris Gallery for permission to publish the photographs included in this book.

I wish also to thank the Independent Scholars Center of the Associated Colleges of the St. Lawrence Valley, New York, for its support of my work; the research staff at the Crumb Library (Potsdam College, Potsdam, New York) for the many hours of help I received; the Faculty Scholarships and Grants Division of Potsdam College for additional financial support; and the research staff of the Venice Public Library in Venice, Florida.

It is a great pleasure to thank publicly those who have helped me prepare this book. Professor Richard Londraville and Professor Peter Faulkner are due my deepest gratitude. Their help has been both generous and indispensable, and I am deeply indebted to them.

Professor William M. Murphy graciously provided me with excerpts of the typescripts of Susan Yeats's diaries, which he transcribed in Dublin in 1968, and which shed some interesting light on the Morris family business operations; and Mr. Thomas Conroy allowed me access to part of his private collection, Jeanne Robert Foster's typescripts of some of May Morris's letters.

Others who have helped this book become a reality are Dr. Florence Boos, Mr. Frank Sharp, Dr. Jan Marsh, Dr. Norman Kelvin, Dr. Ann Thorold, Dr. Delbert Gardner, Ms. Marilyn Gardner,

Dr. Arthur Wachsler, Mr. Brian Rogers, Mr. David Trithart, Ms. Kathy LaClair, Mr. Mark Samuels Lasner, Ms. Velma Bolyard, and Ms. Lisa McDonough.

Editorial Note

I have used brackets to indicate areas where smudges or tears have made words in the Quinn-Morris letters impossible to read.

On Poetry, Painting, and Politics

Introduction

Even though it was January, it was quite unusual for such a great snowstorm to invade New York City. The young lawyer, exhilarated by the company of his lady friend, decided not to attend the reception at Columbia University for the ambassador of England. Instead, he hired a double-seated horse-drawn sleigh, complete with bells, and toured the city with his charming companion. They rode for hours, obviously enjoying each other's company, both pleased about the decision to skip the party.[1]

It was the beginning of a relationship that was to span eight years. The young lawyer was John Quinn; his companion was May Morris, daughter of poet William Morris.

Quinn (1870–1924) was arguably one of the twentieth century's most important patrons of art and literature. His holdings encompassed, among many others, Manets and Matisses[2] and the manuscripts of Joseph Conrad and T. S. Eliot.[3] His collection, however, received little attention until Aline Saarinen's *The Proud Possessors* was published in 1958.[4] Although that book devotes a chapter to Quinn, it wasn't until the publication of B. L. Reid's Pulitzer Prize-winning biography of Quinn, *The Man from New York* (1968), that Quinn was given the attention he deserved.

Reid was the first to note the connection between Quinn and May Morris (1862–1938), and briefly mentions their friendship, calling it "unequal."[5] Since then, the Quinn-Morris love affair has remained buried in their letters in the John Quinn Memorial Collection of the New York Public Library and in the seven additional letters of their correspondence that were given to my husband by Jeanne Robert Foster, Quinn's companion during the last years of his life.[6]

Not much has been written about May. Jan Marsh's *Jane and May Morris: A Biographical Story* (1986) provides the most detailed picture we have of William Morris's youngest daughter, praising May's artistic and editorial skills.[7] Marsh, however, was unaware of May's eight-year relationship with Quinn, probably because May very likely destroyed Quinn's letters sometime after the liaison ended. Fifty-five letters—twenty-five from May and thirty from Quinn—exist today because Quinn made copies of all his correspondence and kept from people, for the sake of posterity, those that he deemed noteworthy.[8]

May Morris grew up as the daughter of one of the most talented men of the Victorian period, but her position in early-twentieth-century art and literary circles has been little celebrated. Private by nature, she seldom wrote about her relationships with some of the most important people of the time. She never recorded the extent of her friendship with Bernard Shaw, and she mentions Quinn only in passing in her letters to Esther Pissarro, who introduced them.[9] May's own work, among which are numerous embroideries and her 1903 play, *White Lies,* received little attention until recent years. Now, with the discovery of *Lady Griselda's Dream,* May's 1898 one-act play, more interest is beginning to focus on her literary talents.[10] Nevertheless, it is May's role as editor of her father's papers that best secures her place in literary history.

The decisions May made regarding her father's work—what fragments should be kept, how they should be fitted together, how poems should be punctuated, what pieces should be published at all—have influenced our texts of William Morris's works today. Her introductions to the *Collected Works of William Morris* provide us with intimate scenes of the Morris household and with insights into the creative processes of her father. In their 1991 Morris bibliography, David and Sheila Latham refer to May as "the most indispensable scholar on Morris" on the strength of these introductions and her introduction to *William Morris: Artist, Writer, Socialist.*[11]

The psychological aspects of May's development probably contributed to her reasons for devoting so much of her adult life to her father's collected works. William Morris and Jenny, May's older sister, had been very close, and even May agreed that Jenny was "far the more virtuous and amiable child."[12] When Jenny became ill with epilepsy, May tried to take over part of her sister's role, but her father still continued to give most of his time and attention to his firstborn. Lily Yeats, W. B. Yeats's sister, wrote in her diary during the time she worked with the Morris family that Jenny "was the only one of the family that the father took any interest in or showed any affection for, and was playful with her." Although Miss Yeats did not like May and even nicknamed her "the gorgon," she seemed to feel that May suffered some neglect.[13] Whatever the relationship between Morris and his youngest daughter, we do know that May attended political meetings with her father and even acted with him in dramatic productions.[14]

May's mother, Jane Burden Morris, was hardly the typical Victorian parent. She was rescued from a life of poverty by Dante Gabriel Rossetti after he saw her in the audience of a theater production in Oxford, and she quickly became his favorite model. However close their relationship, Rossetti had personal commitments to model, poet, and painter Elizabeth Siddall, whom he later married. Jane ultimately accepted a marriage proposal from William Morris, Rossetti's friend, which seemed at the time the prudent choice.

Jane's position as one of the premiere pre-Raphaelite models may have surprised even her. Jan Marsh reminds us that "those who had known Jane as a child were somewhat astonished at her later elevation into great beauty."[15] Her hair was thick and coarse, and her large hands and feet were not qualities of Victorian beauty. Her dark eyes hinted at a sense of mystery, however, and Rossetti's paint improved her other features. Through the years, Mrs. Morris seemed to take on the demeanor of the woman Rossetti had captured in paint, and even in her old age, one photograph shows her seated on a chair in a long dark gown, posed, as if waiting to inspire his genius.[16]

A few years after Rossetti's death in 1882, Jane began a relationship with Wilfrid Scawen Blunt. Her correspondence with him reveals her pain, her sensitivity, and, as Peter Faulkner says, her "native intelligence," which "helped her to take an equal place in friendship with people like Georgiana Burne-Jones. . . ."[17] In her letters to Blunt, Jane often sounds sorely in need of a rest from the emotional trauma of caring for her chronically ill eldest daughter and, later, from her dismay over May's determination to marry Halliday Sparling, a man that Jane knew her daughter did not love.[18] Morris was often away and Blunt's company probably provided a necessary diversion. Even so, Jane's interest in him would surely have troubled May, who evidently did not like him.[19]

However complicated her relationship with her parents might have been, May must have been interested in their professional talents. She modeled for the central figure of Burne-Jones's "The Golden Stairs" in 1880, when she was only eighteen, and she was becoming proficient in arts and crafts, receiving training from both her father and mother. She attended the South Kensington School of Design, and was, by the age of twenty-three, in charge of running most of the day-to-day operations of the embroidery division of Morris & Co.[20]

We will never know what talent May might have shown if she had decided to commit her time and energies fully to her own art. What work she did complete was impressive. In *A Woman's Touch,* Isabelle Anscombe explains that May's embroidery showed "a lightness and directness distinct from [her father's] patterning,"[21] and Elizabeth Masterman praises May's artistic merits and her original designs for the cover of *Love is Enough* in "May Morris, Some Notes for Book Collectors."[22] As recently as 1993, the Museum of Fine Arts in Boston presented an exhibition of May's work, and the William Morris Gallery in London held another in 1989, indicating a growing interest in May's art.[23]

May's talent was not limited to her art; her critical sense was also acute. In her own chapter, "Embroidery," in A. H. Mackmurdo's book, *Plain Handicrafts,* her discussion of the use of color hints at why painters like Van Gogh and Gauguin appealed to her at the same time they displeased and even disgusted some of her best friends:

> No attempt should be made to faithfully copy on paper a branch of roses, for instance; such a drawing is a *study* and not a design. The student or artist may fill up a certain space with roses of which the branch is the inspiration, but it is seen through his medium, with his individuality stamped on it, a *translation,* not a *photograph,* of nature.
>
> . . . It is almost impossible to say, 'Do not place certain colours side by side,' for the fact is that most colours look well together if, as aforesaid, they are in themselves excellent, and if skillfully arranged. . . . A tree bole or its branch is not brown, but gray and gold and green, and sparkling with light; some flower stems, at first sight brown, are found to be mostly reddish, or pink, and partly green. . . .[24]

To John Quinn, May wrote on 6 December 1910 that the "mad Gauguin" had touched her:

> He seems to have been struggling towards some expression outside the ordinary routine, without having reached. Yet some of his extraordinary experiments have wild snatches of poetry. . . .

Philip Burne-Jones, her own close friend and son of Pre-Raphaelite painter Edward Burne-Jones, had called Gauguin and Van Gogh "hideous and modern iconoclasts,"[25] but as her father had before her, May stood "against the Age"[26] and proved that she was certainly capable of expressing her own ideas—both in art and about art. She understood that every generation has unique artistic impulses and rhythms that succeeding generations must necessarily interrupt to form their own new art. For May, a society's loyalty to living art measured the artistic progression of a nation.[27]

It would seem almost inevitable that the articulate and artistic daughter of William Morris would be attractive to one of her father's greatest admirers, the young Bernard Shaw, who first met May in the 1880s. In *Morris as I Knew Him,* Shaw speaks at length about his mystic betrothal to her, calling May "the beautiful one." Sally Peters explains:

> Shaw found the untouchable May increasingly desirable. One Sunday evening, Shaw turned to say farewell. At that moment May appeared in the hall and, according to Shaw, made a 'gesture of assent with her eyes. I was immediately conscious that a Mystic betrothal was registered in heaven.'[28]

But in 1890 May married Halliday Sparling, a socialist follower of Morris and Secretary of the Kelmscott Press.[29] The marriage lasted only eight years and underwent enormous strain, some of it probably generated by Shaw when he moved in with the Sparlings in 1892 "for a few nights" and stayed three months.[30] Shaw later explained that "May's legal marriage had dissolved as all illusions do and the mystic marriage asserted itself irresistibly. I had to consummate it or vanish." He chose the latter. Then, Shaw explains, "the vengeance of the violated Betrothal consummated itself in a transport of tragedy and comedy. For the husband vanished too!" Shaw apparently had little sympathy for the ineffectual Sparling.[31]

Shortly before May's divorce from Sparling became final, Shaw married Charlotte Payne Townshend. His sister Lucy recorded her feelings about May at the time:

> May made a fool of herself over George and there is no doubt ruined the whole of the romantic side of her life. I believe her only object in divorcing Sparling was to give George the chance of marrying her. She obtained her decree absolute the very day he married.[32]

Lucy's observations might not have been the most objective, and May certainly did not wither away. Over the years she seemed to have acquired strength of will and determination. She exhibited her art; she wrote two plays; and she began editing her father's voluminous works. Whether or not romance had been "ruined" for her, she led a successful and vigorous life.

The decision to take on the task of editing her father's works was not an easy one. Whatever creative impulses May had to put aside, whatever pain she may have felt from failed relationships, she seemed to reconcile the loss by arranging her father's work. The irony is that the work that gave her the greatest fame curtailed her own artistic production. Nevertheless, she eagerly assumed the responsibility as editor of the *Collected Works of William Morris.* Though her decision may have been reasonable, it was nonetheless dearly bought.

The choice made, May had to withstand criticism from her publisher, Charles Longman, who wanted her to work more quickly, and to weigh advice from her father's admirers when it came to making final decisions about publication.[33] In one instance, Morris's official biographer, J. W. Mackail, told May that he did not think she should publish material previously unpublished, that it was not of an appropriate quality and therefore was not suitable for the general readership. On 3 July 1910, he wrote to Sydney Cockerell, one of the Morris estate trustees:

> I expressed myself very strongly against what she is evidently eager to do, that is to print the fragmentary Scenes from the Fall of Troy. I am quite certain that this would be a disastrous mistake.[34]

By this time, May was finding the corroboration she needed from John Quinn, whom she had met in New York in 1909. He wrote to her on 15 July 1910 that "I think that [Morris's] admirers are entitled in a collected edition to have even fragments . . . even though they are not equal to the best of his best." May was certainly grateful to find a friend whose advice she valued. To Quinn, May could write openly about her difficulties with the *Collected Works,* and she often did. In one instance, she complained to him about the Icelandic volumes, which were giving her a "particular source of trouble." Eiríkr Magnússon, who had worked with her father in England on the Volsunga saga and had taught Morris the Icelandic language, insisted at one point on making changes and corrections in her father's text. Distressed over his alterations, May finally decided to reject Magnússon's editing and keep the text in its original form. "I have to write a conciliatory but firm (!) letter," she wrote Quinn on 29 November 1910, "explaining that we have changed our minds. . . ." It was not uncommon at the time for editors to use a free hand in correcting and emending text, and May certainly used hers, especially when she had to piece confusing fragments together, but her integrity as an editor would not allow her to accept Magnússon's changes; she did, after all, wish to preserve her father's works as much as possible in their original form.

When they had first met, May and Quinn were quite thoroughly taken with one another.[35] It had been eleven years since May's relationship with Shaw had ended, and, as far as we know, no one had replaced him. She might have sensed that Quinn was her best and last chance for love. He admired her father's genius, which must have pleased May, but in their weeks together in New York, he showered her with attention, certainly reassuring her that she was the focus of his interest.[36] May was now forty-eight; Quinn thirty-nine.

Quinn had established himself as a powerful attorney and was becoming a force in the Democratic Party. In 1908 he had campaigned at the National Convention for Oscar Underwood, leader of the Democratic Party in the House, and was several times a National and a State Delegate.[37] Much to his displeasure, he was also often referred to as a "Tammany lawyer," but he denied it vehemently.[38] Quinn's reputation was paramount to him; nothing made him angrier than to be accused of shady dealings.

Even though Quinn was a significant figure in the political world, he may be remembered best for his brilliant defense of Joyce's *Ulysses* and for his exceptional art and manuscript collection.[39] He owned several of William Morris's original manuscripts; bought Picassos, Van Goghs, and Gauguins before their value was widely accepted; and he was the patron of many of the leading writers and painters of the early twentieth century, including Henri Gaudier-Brzeska and Georges Braque. He also gave money to Gwen John and James Joyce without expectation of any specific return on his investment; he simply wished that they be allowed to continue their work.[40] Besides the earlier-mentioned Conrad manuscripts, Quinn also owned several by Yeats and Synge, and later bought from Joyce the complete manuscript of *Ulysses*.

May was in the United States in 1909 to give a series of lectures about her work on her father's manuscripts. It was an important trip and stirred up excitement among admirers of both Morris's poetry and his socialist essays. Audiences were delighted, and she was kept busy traveling to New York, Chicago, back to New York, and to Canada until the spring of 1910. At several of her stops, Quinn arranged for people to meet her and to see that she received the kind of treatment due her position as Morris's daughter and editor. When May finally said goodbye to him and sailed for England, she found a bottle of champagne in her stateroom, a gift from her handsome Irish-American friend.[41]

The letters began immediately. May's reveal her perceptions about art, even art that was outside of her own expertise, and show her to possess some of the same talent and intuition her father had. Her interest in politics is similarly reflected in her words to Quinn as she criticizes old friends for their blind perceptions and details plans to relieve human suffering in her own corner of England.[42]

But May's letters to Quinn imply more than an articulate, intellectual exchange between friends preoccupied with the artistic and political turmoil of the twentieth century. She is never shy about revealing to him her deepest secrets or her hopes that she and Quinn will eventually be together, and her words confess a gentle vanity. In one of her first, she thanks him for the bust that he had commissioned Jo Davidson, the sculptor, to do of her: "The few people who have seen it . . . all say it is too haggard, and most are obliging enough to say that it will look more like me in ten years time" (19 May 1910).

The tenor of May's letters to Quinn suggests that there was a sexual liaison between them early on. On 1 June 1910, for instance, she writes:

> I had really forgotten how little interest the folk over here take in my movements. I think if I'd brought home from the other side a baby . . . they would not have been agitated—I wish I had!

It would seem highly improbable that May would write so directly to Quinn had they not been intimate. But as Reid explains, Quinn "kept his letters resolutely platonic from the beginning," and often quoted Dion Boucicault's motto: "Never fornicate through an ink bottle."[43]

By October of 1910, May was lonely. Obviously depressed that Quinn wouldn't allow her to tell her mother about him, she laments in one letter that "I am sorry my dear, you will not let me talk to Mother about you; it would give her so much pleasure to know that at last I had the happiness of loving and being loved" (17 October 1910).

In the existing correspondence, Quinn never responds to such emotional language. His letters, with the exception of very few on which he writes in pen "My Dear," all begin with the formal salutation "Dear Miss Morris," and they give no indication that he would ever marry May. On one occasion (30 December 1910), he does mention that he will write to Jane, but about what he does not say, and there is no evidence that a letter was ever sent.

Even though Quinn did not want a long intimate relationship with May, he enjoyed hearing about her experiences and encouraged her to record them in detail. Responding to his prompts ("It is the kind of writing that I know your father would have liked . . ." [15 November 1910]), May frequently recounts stories about her life at Kelmscott and, in her long letters about her 1913 trip to Mallorca, shares eloquent descriptions of the people she met and the countryside she enjoyed (30 September, 6 October). Although her style is sometimes decorative, her writing is not without poetic talent.

It is perhaps mean-spirited to mention the epistolary flaws of Quinn, but they are easily explained. His rambling style results from his habit of dictating to several secretaries. Modern readers may at first react negatively to his incessant concerns about his business and his health, but it is also evident from Quinn's correspondence with May and others—W. B. and J. B. Yeats, Ezra Pound, Theodore Roosevelt, and Douglas Hyde, to name a very few—that some of the most important people in the literary and political world waited eagerly for news from him. They respected him, considered his opinions important, and worried about his professional and personal difficulties. It may therefore be useful for us to suspend our judgment of his writing style in order to gain hitherto unknown insights about this complex man.

* * *

In 1911 Quinn finally visited May while in England on business. They saw the sights and dined together in the evening. Quinn offered at one point to give May the gift of a pendant watch. She told him she'd prefer a ring and asked, "Make believe it is serious." On 6 September, Quinn left London and, as B. L. Reid relates, "hoped later to return to 'spend more time with his friends.' She pleaded, 'For heaven's sake don't give all your time or spare some of your time—or I'll go crazy.' Quinn commented flatly in his journal: 'The only outbreak she made this time.'"[44] Clinging to John Quinn was not the way to win his favor.

But May persisted. It was difficult for her to understand that Quinn was no longer in love with her. In one letter, dated 23 December 1913, she wrote, "The other night I had a pretty and idyllic dream about us. It was like a sudden vision of some other life . . . a life in another world." Quinn generally responded to such expressions by ignoring them and by asking May how her work on her father's *Collected Works* was going. He seemed unable or unwilling to acknowledge the sincerity of her feelings.

Quinn was a complicated man who faced personal and professional battles with vigor and determination. Born a Catholic, he found it impossible to accept Church doctrine as truth and accused the Church of "repressive intellectual niggardliness."[45] On 23 August, 1907, he wrote to W. B. Yeats saying that the Catholic church

> has made moral cowards out of [the Irish] so that now nine-tenths of the Catholics' chief idea is to cringe their way into heaven on the coat-tails of some priest, and the most unworldly of churches, the follower of Him who said that His kingdom was not of this world, has become autocratic and domineering and grasping.[46]

Quinn saw the results of such "grasping" manifested in the Irish attitude toward art and artists, and especially in J. M. Synge's *Playboy of the Western World.* He wrote to his Irish Catholic friend Frank Hugh O'Donnell on 23 February 1912:

> . . . one may not agree with this particular play of Synge's, but it was the freedom of the theatre, the freedom of an artist, that was at stake. If the Irish are to drive all ideas, all thought out of Ireland . . . then it seems to me that it doesn't make any difference whether the Irish language is revived or not. Thought—fine, high thought—art, literature, poetry, painting, music, the arts generally, will go elsewhere.[47]

Even as Quinn turned away from the Church, though, he carried with him some distrust of the body's passions, a fear instilled in him as a boy. Like Joyce's Stephen Dedalus, Quinn never completely broke from his Catholic upbringing, and his relationships with women were no doubt affected. He admired and loved his two sisters—Clara, a nun; and Julia, a wife and mother—and he enjoyed female companionship generally. But he was always fearful of commitment and appeared to leave relationships before he could be hurt or disillusioned.

Quinn's professional battles revolved around his business associates as much as it did his court adversaries. Much of his correspondence, including that with May Morris, consists of complaints about partners doing slipshod work—or not doing the work at all. He was more than willing to give up his free time to his business and got irritated when others took vacations. In his letters he often protests about having to correct the mistakes of his colleagues, and though his tone gets tiresome on occasion, history has shown that Quinn's legal work was superb and that he often did extend himself in an effort to make certain that anything coming from his law office was of the highest quality. He was obsessive in his desire for exactness, and his choice of a legal career, a profession that demands precision, only emphasized this trait. It is easy to understand why a personal or professional relationship with such a taskmaster would have been difficult.[48]

After May's mother died unexpectedly while on a trip to Bath in 1914, Quinn was quick to write to offer advice for dealing with grief—advice that he had given himself many times at troubling junctures in his own life. He tells her on 10 February that she will be reminded

> every place you turn at Kelmscott of your mother. There is nothing for you to do but to do the work that there is to do. . . . Work is the only thing to do under the circumstances.

These were honest sentiments and the best May could expect from Quinn. Even though he often neglected her, Quinn still understood how hard she was working and encouraged her to persist. On 4 June 1914, he wrote that William Butler Yeats had told him that her introductions to the *Collected Works* "were the best things yet done on your father and his work—even better, [Yeats] added, than Mackail." Such praise must have delighted her.

May was by now in her fifties and depressed over the war and the "blotting out of splendid young life" (7 Oct. 1914). She had great concern for middle-class women caught in the destruction of their ordered society. May never wavered in her belief that creativity was food for the soul, and she hoped fervently that women in particular would realize "the futility of luxury and the value of art" (31 Dec. 1915) as they faced an uncertain future.

These were troubled times for May, and her long-distance, unequal love affair must have made her own future seem even more bleak; she now knew there was little hope for a life with Quinn. In two letters dated 4 June 1915 and 31 December 1915, she vents her frustrations:

> My mother is gone; I never see you; I rarely hear from you. . . ; I think my heart is broken.

> It has not been easy to keep the resolution I had made not to write until I heard—the shortest letter, that might waste five minutes of your time. . . .

Once, in 1916, when Quinn sent her a gift of a book he had personally inscribed, May scolded, "Never again inscribe any books you're kind enough to send, to 'Miss M. M.' or put 'with kind regards'. I *won't* be treated so formally." And on New Year's Eve 1916, one year to the day before May will write her last letter to Quinn, her tone borders on sarcasm: ". . . one could have smiled at the promise 'writing soon'. When? Six months hence?"

Although Quinn did not treat May well, she continued the relationship as long as she did because, at least for several years, she seemed to make allowances for the very real demands made on him. Quinn corresponded with hundreds of people, and his letterbooks for any given year often contain over one thousand pages of typescript. He was always in court or traveling to Washington or Baltimore on legal or political business, and in these ways might have reminded her of her busy father. She may have also forgiven him for his formal letters because she knew that he always dictated his letters and had little time for privacy. Like Morris, Quinn was attentive and kind when he was with May, and though she could not be the center of his life, she loved him. Near the end of their association, however, May became angry when the attention she wanted was denied. The relationship was doomed.

* * *

There are suggestions of Shaw's Ann Whitefield in May Morris, and though she might not have been as direct as the heroine in *Man and Superman,* May's letters to Quinn suggest that she most certainly would have been bolder had not an ocean separated them.[49] Unlike Shaw's Tanner, however, Quinn never succumbed to the institution of marriage: not with Annie Foster, his first love and daughter of his mentor, Ex-Governor Charles Foster, the Secretary of the Treasury for Benjamin Harrison; not with Dorothy Coates, who was his mistress for nearly twenty years; nor with Lady Gregory, with whom he had a brief liaison; not even with Jeanne Robert Foster, the Adirondack poet, the final love of Quinn's life and the woman who was at his bedside when he died in July 1924.[50]

May might have felt with her choice of Quinn, an artist manqué, that at last she had found someone who understood the artistic tradition into which she was born yet would be willing to share her everyday life. But as early as 15 July 1910, Quinn seemed to be intimating that he would not make a permanent commitment:

> . . . the man who succeeds, has I suppose the brains and the imagination to excite the others' interest or imagination so that he will get what he wants from them without in turn committing himself in any way.

B. L. Reid sheds an additional light on Quinn's personality:

> [Quinn] liked being free to order his establishment entirely as he preferred it. His habitual hypochondria and the tense state of his nerves made him see himself as a bad physical risk for any woman. The deaths in his family and his own fear of sickness and death tempted him to keep his intimate circle as small, as little vulnerable, as possible. He had too the Irish tendency to define loyalty and sense of primary obligation to one's parents and siblings. . . .[51]

Quinn did not like the idea of marriage, particularly of pledging promises to another who, years later, could exact financial, social, and even professional punishment. He would have agreed with *Man and Superman's* Don Juan when he explains to Ana the illogic of the "honorable" oath:

> I found that it meant that I desired her continual companionship, counsel, and conversation to the end of my days. . . . I did not object to these conditions because they were exorbitant and inhumane: it was their extraordinary irrelevance that prostrated me.[52]

Quinn seconded the opinion of his good friend, J. B. Yeats, when the painter wrote to him in 1912 that "Marriage is like two mortal enemies (the sexes are enemies) meeting on the scaffold and reconciled by the eminence of the great enemy of both."[53] Yeats seems to argue that it is man's purpose to propagate and move on to propagate again, to spread his seed among as many females as he can; conversely, the female's purpose is to pick the best possible male for her childbearing and do what she must to keep him for nurturing and protection of her young. The two drives are at cross-purposes.

Quinn could not afford someone like May, could not want her natural energy directed toward marriage and family, because it would sap his own strength, that egocentric energy he needed to be successful or, as Quinn himself put it, to "get what he wants." For Quinn, the May Morris descending Burne-Jones's "golden stairs" was a different woman from the one who wrote to him about wanting to have a baby, different from the one who plagued him with requests for letters and demands for his time.

In 1898 May published her own views on the male-female conflict in *Longmans Magazine* in the form of a play. In *Lady Griselda's Dream,* Lady Griselda Fairweather imagines a visit from Eugene Sinclair, an artist Griselda has loved but not seen for ten years. She still harbors the hope that they will one day be together. When Eugene arrives in her dream, a "graver and quieter" man, he tells her he has married, "as many men marry a passing fancy, from a luckless sense of honour." They know they can never be together as man and wife. Eugene falls at Griselda's feet, though, and asks only to visit "sometimes, and be kind to me, that I may go away heartened up, and soothed by the perfume of harmonious graciousness that hangs about you."[54]

Griselda laments, "The passive rôle again! To live beautifully and be admired. Why should some women be doomed to this. Eugene, I could almost envy my little sister, with her intolerable husband and young baby." But Eugene doesn't understand Griselda's distress: "Are you not proud to be the artist's inspiration?"[55] And Griselda doesn't understand that she is trying to entrap Eugene to ensure for herself a fundamental purpose in life.

May demonstrates in her play that the male artist is dangerous, that he can suck life from his muse and leave her "pale and thin," "unwholesomely fragile," and "faded."[56] Written during the year of her divorce from Sparling and Shaw's marriage to Charlotte Payne Townshend, *Lady Griselda's Dream* might have been May's instruction to herself. Although Bernard Shaw was not to publish *Man and Superman* for another five years, it's connection to *Lady Griselda's Dream* is obvious.[57]

The real Eugene Sinclair, portly and rather loud, arrives in the last scene, but he is no longer an artist. He has given up painting, except as an escape from boredom, and has married a rich wife who allows him to play at work. His very existence is Griselda's final defeat. In spite of her accomplishments, there seemed to be but two possible choices in Griselda's life: to be wife and mother or artist's muse. A woman's life alone was empty and useless.

At the end of the play, Griselda takes the red roses from the vase in which she has so carefully arranged them for Eugene's visit, kneels by the glowing hearth, and scatters the flowers on the fire. "In the heart of the fire," she laments, "where they can't decay, or rot, or grow old . . . and the dreams go with them, up into the cold thin air."[58] All of Griselda's "beauty worshipping . . . was not worth a dump as a philosophy of life."[59]

By 1909, eleven years after she had written *Lady Griselda's Dream,* May probably felt that her long-awaited chance for happiness had come. The dashing young lawyer from New York captured her heart. But by 1917, after eight years of corresponding with Quinn, May, like Griselda, knew that one of her most cherished dreams had vanished into that "thin air."

She was fifty-five, but no longer alone. Mary Lobb, a woman sixteen years May's junior, arrived in Kelmscott to work for one Farmer Hobbs as part of the Women's Land Army program, which placed women in agricultural jobs left by men gone to war. But she displeased her supervisor and was dismissed with little hope for another position. May took her in, and the two became close companions.[60] Miss Lobb was an odd-looking friend for May, who had been surrounded all her life by Pre-Raphaelite beauties. Elfrida Manning, daughter of sculptor Sir Hamo Thornycroft, described Miss Lobb as an "enormouse" [*sic*] woman who wore "a tweed jacket and britches and has cropped black hair."[61] But even though Evelyn Waugh called her a "hermaphrodite"[62] and publisher Sir Basil Blackwell called her "androgynous," adding that "a less Pre-Raphaelite character . . . could hardly be imagined,"[63] May had at last found her comrade.

The relationship has raised some speculation, but in light of Quinn's mistreatment of her, it is not surprising that May turned to a safe, female companion. When May Morris and Mary Lobb met, they found themselves in a world just emerging from the insanity and terror of world war, and they responded to such chaos with the healthy impulse to form an intimate bond where support and understanding were unconditionally given.[64] Whether or not the relationship was a lesbian one, both May and Mary Lobb were strong enough to welcome an attachment that was central to their lives.

There is a sense of loss, as Griselda's married sister, Lucy, implies in *Lady Griselda's Dream,* when we deny those energies for which we were created: "If all women demanded as much as you—If I clamoured for poetry and love and all the rest of it . . . Consider, too, what would the future generation be if we *all* went in for the superior sentiments you indulge in."[65] In the end, the final irony of May's life seems to return again to the theme of her own play: a woman who defines her life around what she believes to be a superior male subsumes her own life force. Perhaps May understood this when she wrote to Shaw in the spring of 1936:

> I'm a remarkable woman—always was, though none of you seemed to think so.[66]

She died in October 1938. Five months later, she was joined by her friend Mary Lobb.

The Correspondence between May Morris and John Quinn

1
The Letters of 1910

[Quinn to May Morris, January 1910.]
Dear Miss Morris:

I did not go to Ohio as I expected.

I was glad to receive your special-delivery letter Saturday morning. I am afraid that it was I who made the mistake in giving you my telephone number. My apartment telephone number is 3796 Columbus, and if I gave you the number as stated in your letter, 6397, I was all wrong. It is 3796.

I sent you by mail this afternoon, care of Mrs. Norton, the book by Synge on the Aran Islands and the Henry James short story in one volume that I referred to the other day. The Synge book may remind you of your Orkney Island and the James short story will give you a little insight into one phase of American life which is not uncommon here.[1]

I feel quite sure I shall be able to arrange about Cleveland and also in regard to Buffalo. If you will send me your Pittsburgh address I shall write you there.[2] I hope that you are having good weather in Washington.

I am a little doubtful about arranging for Pittsburgh. I know many men in Pittsburgh but very few women and don't want to take the chance of having you asked to a home where there might be anything uncongenial.

I have been thinking over your not being met at the stations. I suggest that you write to your agent and ask him to make a note, preferably as a postscript, in his letter to the different local bodies or committees somewhat like this:

> "As Miss Morris has with her the slides (or whatever words are the proper ones) for her lectures, she would esteem it a favor if she could be met at the station by some competent person to whom she could entrust the slides for the lecture."

Some such hint as that in a letter would, I am sure, always bring forth the desired attention and would insure your being met so that you would not personally have to be bothered with the slides. A hint of this sort from the manager would save you from this trouble and annoyance.

No, the woman with the caving-in face hasn't haunted me.[3]

I am sorry that we didn't go to the New Theatre that night. A new play called "Don" was given there, a comedy in three acts. It is said to be very good, something like Shaw's "Candida," I think.[4]

I didn't feel that I was obeying any law of hospitality in asking you out, but I know what it is to be in a strange country and away from affection and friends. Douglas Hyde once said to me that it seemed to him that the only really friendly people that he met in America were the negro porters and waiters.[5] What he meant by this was that they seemed friendly to him on the train and at hotels, when the other persons seemed to be frigid and indifferent. Nothing makes one feel the real value of affection and friendship so much as being in a strange country; then one does begin to miss them.

I will write to you in Pittsburgh if you will send me your address there.

I hope the meetings in Washington went off well.

Sincerely yours,

P.S. I sent you a telegram on New Year's Day, as soon as I received your letter, care of Harold Pierce, Haverford, Pa. That was just on the chance that Mr. Pierce lived at Haverford and that the telegram would reach you. I wonder if it did!

* * *

[Quinn to May Morris, 7 January 1910.]

Dear Miss Morris:

I received your special delivery addressed to 97 Central Park West this morning.

I am very sorry that you had such a bad time in Pittsburgh. I think that if you make the suggestion to your agent that I outlined it will save such difficulty. People are often very thoughtless. They mean well enough, but they don't think. But I blame your agent more than anyone. I am perfectly certain that the right kind of a note, a final note or final letter preceding your arrival in a town, directing the attention of the right person to this thing, would save you from this embarrassment, such as "Miss Morris would much appreciate, owing to the fact that she has her slides with her, etc., if she could be met on her arrival at such a station on such a train on such a morning or such an afternoon" and so on. I should urge him to do this.

I wrote to Mrs. Alice Thursby,[6] a friend of mine and the sister of Arthur Brisbane,[7] the editor of the Journal here, to have the Carys, the nicest people I think in Buffalo, ask you to their house. I expected to receive word from Mrs. Thursby that it was settled today. I fully expect to hear from her tomorrow (Saturday) that it is settled, and I shall perhaps telegraph you.

I am leaving tomorrow (Saturday) night at 8 o'clock on the New York Central road for Cleveland, Ohio. I shall arrive there Sunday morning. I shall be in Cleveland on Sunday, the 9th of January, and Monday, the 10th. I shall stop at the Hollenden Hotel. I shall be glad to have a line or telegram from you addressed to me there. My sister expects to enter the hospital there on Sunday and to have an operation on Monday, not of a dangerous or serious but yet of a delicate nature, and I am going to Cleveland to be there, not that I can help her any personally but I can be with her Sunday and help to cheer her up, and perhaps a little while Monday after the operation. I shall leave Cleveland Monday evening, January 10th, at 8:45 and arrive in New York Tuesday morning at 9:15. I wish I had time to stop over in Pittsburgh on Sunday. In fact I thought of leaving here tomorrow (Saturday) night for Pittsburgh, spending Sunday forenoon in Pittsburgh, and going to Cleveland in the afternoon; but in a note which Dr. Humiston, who is to perform the operation, wrote me today he asked me to meet him at the hospital Sunday morning at 11 o'clock. And as I know my sister will be anxious, I have decided to go direct to Cleveland.

I am sending you a book by Synge which I printed here last autumn.[8] It was also printed at the press of the Yeats sisters in Dublin.[9] I printed this edition here at my own expense to save the copyright for Synge's estate. Synge was engaged to be married to a young girl named Molly Allgood, who was in the company in Dublin, and he left her an annuity of some eighty pounds. That is why I printed this book here, in order that the copyright should not be lost. The punctuation in the book published by Miss E. C. Yeats was very poor. I went over the text carefully and corrected it in thirty or forty particulars. Minor points, of course, but they were worth attending to nevertheless. Some of the things in the book were written when Synge knew he was dying and are rather heart-breaking. The book is certainly a curiosity of literature. The prize translations are written in the dialect of the West of Ireland peasants and are, I think, very fine.

Books are rather heavy things to carry around, and if after you have read this and the other books or any books, you are encumbered with them, I suggest that you have them wrapped up and expressed or sent by mail to me at my office and I will keep them here for you pending your return.

I expect to see the Superintendent of Schools in Cleveland, where you are to lecture, on Monday. Dr. Humiston of Cleveland, with whom I talked over the matter, said that the Superintendent was the best one to arrange this matter with. So I hope to be able to telegraph you something definite about Cleveland on Monday. That is why I should like to know whether on Monday, that is January 10th, you are still at the Elmhurst Hotel, Sewickley (an awful name both to pronounce and to spell).[10]

I am glad you got the telegram to Haverford but sorry you didn't get it on time.

Sincerely yours,

* * *

[Quinn to May Morris, 12 January 1910.]
Dear Miss Morris:

I received this (Wednesday) morning a letter from Mrs. Thursby dated Hempstead Monday, January 10th, but postmarked yesterday, January 11th, in which she says:

> "Mrs. Cary and I have written to the Carys in Buffalo asking them to look out for Miss Morris, and also to two other people who would be interested in her. We did not telegraph, as the letter went off immediately and it would have been difficult to have made them understand. I am sure she will receive a great deal of attention and that the Buffalo people will be delighted to know her and will do all they can to entertain her.
>
> "There are many beautiful houses in Buffalo and people are interested in the work that Miss Morris is such an authority on, embroideries, tapestry, etc. The houses are very well decorated, many of them."

In regard to Cleveland: I had hoped that one of the nicest women I know there would entertain you in Cleveland, but she is, I find, now in New York City visiting her daughter, who was married only two months ago. I spoke to Mrs. S. H. Tolles (pronounced as though it were spelled "Toals"), the wife of a lawyer friend of mine, and she will doubtless call on you at the Hollenden. Her address is No. 8321 Euclid Avenue; her telephone number is 17 Doane.

I hope to be able to leave here Saturday night for Cleveland and to be there Sunday morning. I will know definitely in the course of a day or two and will write you care of the Hollenden.

I hope you are having a pleasant time in Buffalo.

The operation on my sister was a very severe one. It lasted an hour. It seemed very hard to put a person who had been enjoying three good meals a day on practically a starvation diet. She was not given anything to eat from Saturday night until Monday, the day of the operation. The operation took place early Monday morning. As late as Monday evening she was not given anything to drink except the moistening of her lips with water. I had two telegrams yesterday (Tuesday), stating that her temperature was normal, her pulse good, and that she was getting along very well. The first forty-eight hours is the crisis. I have no doubt that she will make a rapid and a complete recovery.

I will write you to Buffalo in the course of a day or two.

Sincerely yours,

* * *

[Quinn to May Morris, 17 January 1910.]

Dear Miss Morris:

I have just sent you a telegram as follows:

"Regret exceedingly unable because of professional engagement to be in Cleveland tomorrow. Am writing."

A matter has come up which puts it out of the question for me to leave this evening. I am very much disappointed. I was very much disappointed yesterday at not being able to carry out my plan of leaving for Cleveland Saturday night. I mailed a letter to you and to my sister personally at the Grand Central Station in order to get it on the 8 o'clock train. I hope you received it this morning.

I have received a telegram from my brother-in-law, who got to Cleveland today, telling me that my sister was feeling better and would perhaps be able to sit up toward the end of this week.

I wonder if you had a sleigh ride in Cleveland! I am very sorry I cannot be there tomorrow. I will drop you a note at Detroit.

If you will let me know where you expect to be in Chicago, I will ask my friend Francis Hackett, a most interesting young man, to call and see you. He is the editor of the literary supplement of the Chicago Evening Post.[11]

Sincerely yours,

* * *

[Quinn to May Morris, 13 May 1910.][12]

Dear Miss Morris:

I received your cable and also the letters, which I enjoyed very much. I was in Court the day the cable arrived and it was handed to me late in the afternoon. That evening I was in the office, and about nine o'clock I called up Mrs. Gilman and told her that you had cabled that you had a good voyage and were feeling well. She expressed herself as delighted. She said she would write to you and she hoped that I would come up sometime and take dinner with them. I on the other hand hoped that they would sometime come to the theatre with me, although I have a doubt whether either one of the hopes will ever materialize.

I am delighted that everything went all right. I was a little afraid that the bust might be scratched or injured in that small box. I am glad to know that you are as much pleased with it as you were.[13]

England must be lovely in the spring. I hope that you will find everything pleasant at your mother's. I am certain that she will be delighted to see you back again.

I had rather a severe breakdown two weeks ago yesterday. It came like a shot in the back. The doctor said it was some weakness in the region of the spine. It was very painful for some days; in fact one day, I am sorry to say, I fell down in the office and had to be helped up. However, I have been taking electric-light treatments and every other night I have been taking electric-light baths in a cabinet and a good strong shower of alternate hot and cold water, which is said to be good for the nerves, and a good rub with alcohol. This has helped a great deal. I missed a few days in the office, but I am back in the harness again, although taking things a little easy. The fact is that I had been over-doing my strength and not getting enough rest or let-up from work and things, and anxiety and worry, added to the work I had to do, I suppose brought it on.

I saw in an auction catalogue the other day a copy of Miss Cary's book on your father, and I ordered the dealer to buy it. He bought it and it was sent to me a day or two ago and I have sent it to you.[14] There is nothing original in it. She has written the same kind of a book on Rossetti and another one on Tennyson. Some of the illustrations are rather good, one in particular of your mother, which I thought very charming. If you haven't seen the book, you may be interested in it as a curiosity. If you already have a copy, you may care to pass this one on to Mr. Walker.[15]

Gregg told me a few days ago of a dinner that he had with Davidson at Moquins a day or two before Davidson sailed. There was Davidson, Charley Fitzgerald, the art critic, Gregg, Davidson's sister, and Miss Grigsby. I didn't know that Davidson had any friends on your boat.[16]

* * *

[May Morris to Quinn, from 8 Hammersmith Terrace, 19 May 1910.]

My Dearest—: I meant not to write again until I had heard from you, but you see! I can't keep away from you. I am sitting very close to work, and an hour off with you is a distraction and comfort.

London is dreary beyond words: everyone, to the very poorest,—in mourning (don't you know how the poor simply revel in their funeral pomp and all the outer signs of sorrow!). I am told that the queue of people going to the King's lying-in-state yesterday stretched out to between 6 or 7 miles—exaggeration, doubtless.[17] I go out as little as possible, but yesterday had to go to Paternoster Row for a long sitting with the man who is professionally reading my proofs. Next Monday I quit it all for a fortnight—, taking work and all down to Kelmscott to keep home and keep the maids in hand while Mother goes for a change. I shall be quite alone—not even a cat or a dog for company.

Tonight Fairfax Murray[18] is coming to dinner, and perhaps Emery Walker. I went to talk to Murray about Earthly Paradise, etc, etc, and borrow M.S.S. from him: he has early things and many unpublished scraps. Besides that, he is a most amusing dinner companion, full of racy stories about pictures and dealers and collectors, and Heaven knows what. I must get you to meet him when you come over here.

I don't like this new pen . . .

You know, I am longing to show you my little house: and it will be so good for a lordly person like yourself to come and see "how the poor live" in a poor cheap neighbourhood. It is a ramshackle old house, light and sunny, and set in a bower of grape-vines at the back. It is all most absurdly inconvenient and difficult for one's slave; but they are used to it, I suppose.

I have had no awkwardness in explaining my movements in New York to enquiring friends. They all seem to be absorbed in getting news of their friends whom I have met; and to Walker I talk about the pictures I saw. Also, I've had to tell no fibs about the Bust: they take it quite naturally that I should return laden with a costly bronze! The few people who have seen it—Walker, Buhlig, a New York acquaintance, etc. all say it is too haggard, and most are obliging enough to say that it will be more like me in ten years' time. By the bye, they all think that I'm looking years younger since my wanderings. Thanks to you, my dear, who give me a new lease on life.

I shan't continue to look years younger, though, if I don't hear from you soon! Please, this isn't meant crossly. I suppose the time seems long, and I am idiotically impatient.

Do you know, Augustus John really has a vile reputation with many people: how is it? I was dining with the Richmonds en famille last night, and Sir William, telling a story of which I missed the beginning, made the young lady of whom he spoke (his stories often have a rather unpleasant flavour) say: "But I wouldn't be one of Augustus John's five wives. . . . " Thereat I felt bound to say that I had heard that he had only one at present, and was much attached to her. Then Richmond said: "Oh, if he is a friend of yours, I say no more". I disclaimed friendship of course, but stuck to the point. He then described his art as being distinctly loathsome.[19]

I have just got Douglas Hyde's Literary History of Ireland, but haven't begun to read it yet. I'm reading Dills Roman Society and find it very interesting. I don't think I had realized what huge fortunes people amassed in those days—I did not think it was a possibility, economically, for such 'capitalists' to exist out of our own time.[20]

I wish to be less ignorant of all these things; I wish one had more time (and energy) for reading. . . . do you know, it is principally (or oftenest) when I lay down with a book and feel that I want to discuss it that moment with someone, that I realize what a solitary being I am. I have never had, among all the friends, anyone get-at-able with whom to chat on all matters under the sun—especially literary, and again, things of other-wordly import. The fact is, a woman living alone cannot hope to get much reasonable male companionship, and my women friends are mostly absorbed with Babies.

You, dearest and best, to whom I can talk of everything conceivable (and will, whenever you give me a chance), you are therefore just the perfect Comrade besides all the other delightful things, and if I babble on about a hundred matters, please realize it is the price you pay for being raised to this "good eminence".

Well, my hour of recreation is past, and just as self Discipline I return at once to proof reading and the rest.

When I was a small brat, I used to ornament my letters to Mother with this symbol . . ⊙ . . . Here is a small one for you . . ⊙.

May

Oh, I <u>must</u> tell you this story: when Phil Burne Jones left New York, a lady admirer of his arranged with the stewards that he should find a letter and a present (of some silver object) at his place at breakfast every morning on the voyage—It was all carefully arranged, and when they came in sight of Ireland, that morning's letter said: "You will now be nearing the romantic shores . . . " etc. etc.

So you see, darling, how to do it another time! I confess Pol Roget Champagne seems more natural, but then I have not a soaring mind!

* * *

[Quinn to May Morris, 1 June 1910.]
Dear Miss Morris:

I received your two letters.

You seem indeed to be up to your eyes in work, as an Irishman would put it.

The more new things there can be about the collected edition in the way of introduction, illustrations and any new matter, the more attractive it will be and the better it will be to talk about. I see constant references to the collected or so-called "Memorial" edition of George Meredith. The Scribners are publishing it here.[21] As each of the volumes comes out, or each pair of volumes come out, it is reviewed, etc., and particular attention is drawn to the illustrations or the original illustrations and to the fact that a separate volume will be made of corrections in the text and unpublished matter, etc. A person who is an admirer of a writer naturally wants to have everything that he has written. Where it is a mere re-print, it is not so attractive as it seems to be if there are illustrations or new matter or introductions, and so on. This is badly expressed, but I think you will get my idea.

I have received from Keppel's a copy of the reproduction of the

John drawing of myself. I am sending it to you under separate cover. It is framed and with glass. I hope that the glass won't be broken and that it will reach you safely.[22]

I was amused by what you wrote about Richmond. It is strange that artists hate so fiercely. A person may or may not, an artist may or may not, dislike John's work, but a man who uses the word "loathsome" about any artist's work simply betrays venom or jealousy that is pitiful.

I am sorry that your friends think the bust is too haggard. Of course, to compare a very big man with a young man, Rodin's work in bronze would, I daresay, be considered the same.

Your experience that your friends think you look better is identical with the experience of other friends of mine who have been here. Willie Yeats, for example, went back looking much better.[23] Hyde went back weighing more and looking better and feeling better. They all came here terrified in advance at what they thought were the perils and dangers of the place. All like it; all improved here and went back feeling better.

I am sure you will enjoy Hyde's "Literary History of Ireland." Hyde has packed a tremendous amount of reading into one book. Nowhere is there any book in any language that I know of that comes anywhere near giving as good an idea of the origin and growth of Irish literature as Hyde's book does. Hyde has always been interested in questions about metre. This part of the book was especially interesting to me. It is a perfect storehouse of information, and the notes contain references to practically every accessible book, journal, or periodical containing any Irish text or manuscripts worth looking at or considering, except, of course, the great mass of unedited and uncatalogued manuscripts in Dublin, the British Museum, and other places.

I have changed doctors twice in the last three weeks. The ones I had before were mere tinkerers. I finally went to one of my doctor friends and said that I wanted the best doctor or one of the five best doctors in New York City. He said he thought I exaggerated the number. He gave me a note to an eminent doctor here, and he is a "corker." He didn't jump at conclusions the first five minutes. Neither does he take up my time in telling me tales about the wonderful cures he has performed. He is business from start to finish. I am not in his place over ten minutes at a time. I like that. I wish I could train all my clients in the same way. Life would be much simpler if people only knew when to go and when the matter in hand was over. I take exercises myself which he prescribed for me, and among other things he put me on a starvation diet. I haven't eaten a bit of solid food in ten days and I am going to keep it up for another five or six or seven days. I drink zoolak, a sort of creamy buttermilk prepared, I think, according to the Metchinkoff formula.[24] When I don't get zoolak, I take milk with lacto-bacilline tablets a la Metchinkoff. For the first three or four days I had rather a headache. But I feel much better. For one thing, I don't feel so drowsy. I feel more alert and feel better in the mornings. I still have considerable soreness in the back, but the exercises which I am taking are, I think, the right thing and I am getting much better.

I went out to Ohio last Friday and did not return to the City until yesterday (Tuesday) morning. Monday, the 30th of May, was Decoration Day. That is a holiday with us; by "us," I mean us of the north. That is the day on which the graves of all those who died in war are decorated. Processions are formed; the old soldiers march out; services are held in the churches, stands are erected in the cemeteries, and commemorative addresses are given, songs sung, bands play, etc.; the children are all decorated, they march out with wreaths and flowers, and all the graves are decorated. The friends of those who have died decorate their graves even if they were not soldiers. I went out to the cemetery in the afternoon after the show was over and it was rather pretty to see all the graves decorated with flowers and small American flags standing over the grave of each one that was a soldier, put there by their surviving comrades. Popularly it is called "Decoration Day"; officially it is "Memorial Day."

I enclose for you with this a prospectus of the Viking Club and another prospectus of the Orkney-Shetland Old-lore Series,[25] which, owing to your interest in Orkney, I thought you might be glad to know about. Perhaps you are already a member of the Club. If so, it won't do any harm for me to have sent this, anyway.

It must be pretty up at Kelmscott now and a change to the country will be a good thing after your hard-work in London.

I see that Teddy stood up and gave the English a lot of advice about Egypt. I can imagine Mr. Blunt's feelings when he reads what Roosevelt has said.[26]

* * *

[May Morris to Quinn, from 8 Hammersmith Terrace, 1 July 1910.]

My dearest John:

I must have a few words with you before I go to bed tonight, because I have been working very closely for days and days without intermission and am rather tired. You'd think I had done enough actual writing already this evening, for I've been copying out my Father's Fall of Troy since six o'clock and it is now half-past ten—a quarter of an hour allowed for a hermit-meal in between—My hand is positively aching.

The M.S. is partly in pencil and fragile and I did not wish to have it typed. I am hoping to include a good deal of it: it is very striking, though the execution is often unfinished and rough, so that it would not be right to publish it all. It is in cases like these that Mackail has had the gilt off the gingerbread, as he has quoted the best of it, and given a very able account of all the rest.[27]

Did I tell you last letter that some one has sent me Saintsbury's last volume on English prosody, wherein is a very enthusiastic account of Father's verse.[28] I thought of writing to him. What a queer thing the poetic inspiration is: the poet comes along and shapes his verse—some part of it in a sub-conscious way, I verily believe; then the student comes along and says this is such and such in the science of prosody: and his little scholars sit round and clutch at the internal rhymes and argue over the beat and the stress and the accents, and it is all rather like scraping the bloom off a butterfly's wing to see what it's made of! I say this quite in a friendly spirit because it is all very interesting, and these people are so clever, so clever. . . .

I am sending in another envelope some absurd photographs of this insignificant paper tiger—done long ago. In the biggest you'll see me walking down the garden steps here—Marie Antoinette going to execution someone called it ironically—rather posée [serious], it looks to one now. They may amuse you.

I have sent some photographs of my Father to Jo Davidson.[29] I wonder what he will make of them. My trip to Paris will be quite easy; I had really forgotten how little interest the folk over here take in my movements: I think if I'd brought home from the other side a baby as well as a Bust they would not have been agitated—I wish I had! Excuse my apparent flippancy, my dear: only on the surface, as you know well.

It is high tide and the water is lapping prettily out there among the little fleet of boats below the garden. I am fond of this old river: it is a fool to your magnificent Hudson, but it has charm even here, and in our own upper country it is a dear little jewel of a stream. I look out in the very early morning sometimes, when the light is clear and free from smoke, and it is rather pretty to look down through the trees on all the different little scraps of gardens, fragrant and in flower just now. I have a handsome great bay tree in my garden, and grape vines round all the windows;

and the thrushes sing—sometimes an old heron sails across the water at sundown, homeward to Richmond, and I like his lonely 'squawk'—

I seem rather complacent about my surroundings don't I? (I daresay I've described the whole garden before) Not really though . . . They have always counted for something in my life of course, but one can't enjoy things to order and alone, and I'm a gregarious being—at any rate not the Hermit circumstances have forced me to become; and I sometimes stand in the middle of the room and look round at my belongings with a sort of half affectionate impatience of them, and I want to tell them "oh all of you old friends that I've dusted and taken care of for so long, you know perfectly well that though I'm very fond of you, I'd throw you all over without a moment's hesitation or qualm if someone were able to say 'Come here to me.'" Poor little household gods, how cheap they'd feel suddenly!

Some more Americans are coming on Sunday or tomorrow, I forget which. I'll have 'hundreds and hundreds' of them before long, it would seem.[30]

Dearest dear person, good night. Please think very nice things about your

May

* * *

[Quinn to May Morris, 15 July 1910.]

Dear Miss Morris:

I went down to the seashore yesterday (Thursday), and upon my coming to the office this morning Sadji,[31] who came to take my bag back to the apartment, brought me your two letters of the 4th and 6th. You made a slight slip in the calendar because Sunday evening was July 3d and not July 4th, as your letter stated. I know because I was at Fisher's Island on Monday, July 4th.[32]

You seem to be working very hard and it is a shame that you have to copy out so much yourself. Couldn't you get a copyist or typewriter to do the work and then you devote your time to the correction of the proof in order to see that it is perfectly accurate?

I don't quite understand the stream of Americans calling on you. Each one, almost, of your letters lately has mentioned Americans calling and I really don't know how you can keep up with it or how they can have the cheek to break in on you.

Things do seem to be rather badly muddled in England.

Yes, Mr. Charles D. Norton[33] has got the post of secretary to the President. I don't know him, but I should say that he is not lacking in self-assurance or in self-confidence or in ability to push himself forward. You say that he is "rather a hard man." Did it ever occur to you that most of the men that get along or get to the top, as the phrase is, or become successful men, are hard men, generally ungrateful, men who use others so long as the others are useful and then throw them aside, and that after all it is a matter of brains and intelligence and the hard man, the man who succeeds, has I suppose the brains and the imagination to excite the others' interests or imagination so that he will get what he wants from them without in turn committing himself in any way?

I don't wonder that people are flocking to the other side, it is so dreadfully hot here. This morning as I came across the Brooklyn Bridge the big buildings downtown were wrapped in a gray mist. It looked fine, but I knew that it meant heat. Up in my office on the thirteenth floor with the windows up and the awnings down, it is not so bad. If there is any breath of air stirring, I get it; but on the streets, and particularly from five to eight until the city begins to cool, it is frightful. What it is to those who have to work out in the streets or on the railroads or in the subways or in the shops, real sweat shops in this weather all of the shops are, I should say, it is painful to imagine. Fashionable New York is empty. In fact it is quite unfashionable for anyone to be here now. Middle-class New York has all gone away. All those who can afford it have located their families in the mountains or at the seashore, and the man and his sons employed in the city go out for week-ends. At Fisher's Island, only two hours from New York, it was as cool and comfortable as it would be on an Atlantic liner. I don't think that any city in the world affords the choice or variety of out-of-town or country residences that New York does: there is the Hudson on either bank; Long Island Sound, with Connecticut on the north shore and the north shore of Long Island on the south, with woody hills and valleys and high bluffs and good boating and bathing. Then there is the stretch of the south shore of Long Island for ninety miles from Brooklyn to Montauk Point, with every variety of seashore, bay, sand dunes, and beautiful rolling country in between. Then there is the Jersey coast with the high bluffs, and further down seaside places with fine boating and bathing and golf in the rear. So you see those who make up their mind to stand it are able to temper the heat.

It amuses me to read of the cool weather that you have been

having in London and the rains in torrents. It rained last summer when I was in London in August, day after day.

The name I gave to the building was not the Women's Guild of Arts (and Crafts), but the "Guild of Craft Design." Be sure to get it right. And I think I have the three Kuno Meyer translations from Irish poems,[34] particularly one called "Spring" and I think one called "Summer"; at least I had them when Hyde stopped with me and I think they are somewhere around yet, although it is difficult for me to put my hands on things of that sort since I moved.

If you ever heard Irish poetry beautifully spoken or sung, you would not think it was artificial sounding. It is like the finest and best of Swinburne. Hyde wrote a little miracle play called "The Tinker and the Fairy."[35] Not being able to read Irish, I therefore was able only to read it in the prose translation of Miss Butler. I saw it played here in New York two or three years ago, in Irish, and the little lyrics scattered through the play, which I had only read in blank verse, seemed to me wonderfully beautiful, like a lark pouring forth its melody. I don't think that Hyde over-states the beauty of it, to one who knows the language.

Mrs. Hyde used to think that this was the only country were there were railroad smash-ups. But I don't think, if one takes into consideration the number of passengers and multiplies that by the number of miles travelled, that it will be found that railway travelling here is per mile and per passenger more dangerous than elsewhere. Of course it is not a fair comparison to reckon the number of passengers in a country like England, where the distances are small, or in Belgium or France. The distances here are great and of course on the law of chances the percentage of risk increases as the number of miles travelled increase.

I am sorry to hear about your not being able to sleep properly. I don't want to usurp the functions of a doctor, but I am going to venture to advise you to try some medicine which has done me good. If you would take Boudault's pepsin No. 1 with your meals, I think you will find that you will sleep better. I know that I suffered dreadfully from insomnia. Now that the auto-intoxication and fermentation have stopped, I sleep like a top. With each bottle of the pepsin comes a lead ladle. If you take two ladles (or, if there is no lead ladle, if you take a fairly good teaspoonful) with a meal, I think you would feel better; at any rate, it would do no harm to try it.

The prize-fight really shouldn't have done any harm.[36] If the hypocrite preachers could be abolished, prize-fights could go on in a modest way without doing harm to anybody. If a couple of highly-trained, skillful men want to get to work and attempt to knock each other's heads off, I don't see what harm it can do. Personally, I should like to go to see them if I could, and in the old days I went many a time. It is no worse than many things that were described in Homer or in Virgil. They fight according to rules; they don't hit below the belt; and they don't resort to cowardly tactics. It seems to me the world is becoming very effeminate if it is becoming so good that a couple of highly trained men cannot punch away at each other, especially when they are so well trained that however often they hit each other they are all right in a few hours after the fight. It is the hypocritical preachers that cause the trouble. People have got to have some relaxation, and if the clerks, proof-readers, stenographers, waiters, barbers, and other people that have to work hard, who can't have their clubs, and can't have their automobiles and country places, can't be allowed to read about a prize-fight, it seems to me that after a while, if the people that have country places and have clubs and have automobiles have their way, the world would be so damnably dull that people of the class I have named would go mad from sheer dullness and despair. The prize-fight and the horse-race is really the poor man's excitement and he is entitled to some stimulation and excitement. The next thing they will be abolishing all games except basket-ball and croquet. I think there is too much ladylike attention paid to accidents. They ought to abolish polo because occasionally a neck is broken; make flying in the air a penal offense because occasionally a machine smashes, and so on. The occasional head cracked in polo or man killed in flying in the air is the price which the race pays for vigor, head-ship, and command.

I hope that the man you name will not be named for chief justice.[37] He is a narrow man, and I hope that such a narrow-minded man, without the breadth of view of a real statesman, will not be put in that great office with the mighty power that it wields. He is a round head. That great place ought to be filled by a great statesman and not by a man whose chief claim to fame is that he has suppressed horse-racing during four years of his governorship of New York.

I should like very much to read your introduction to the new edition. Is that to be an introduction to the whole edition, or have you given up the idea of having a short introduction to each volume? Several of the things you have mentioned in your recent letters it seemed to me would go well in the new edition. For example, your statement about the manuscripts that your father didn't revise but threw aside and re-wrote, and about how the manuscripts originally were thrown away until some man made an offer, and then they were given to friends, etc., and statements of that kind are what people are interested in.

It strikes me that the copying out of the Fall of Troy is very hard work. Couldn't you get some good stenographer to read it to, and then do your careful work in seeing that the copying was right. The corrections on typewriting wouldn't be so bad.

I am going to send for Saintsbury's third volume.

As you say, the poet has the poetic inspiration, and then along comes the critic without any poetic inspiration and puts his measure, rule, and tape down, and says that this line is of this kind and that line is of that kind. I happen to know, for example, that Willie Yeats could hardly tell an iambic from a trochaic, although he might be able to recognize a Spenserian stanza. I am perfectly certain that Blake didn't even know the technical terms; and yet along comes the technical chap and fits his measure to it and says it is such-and-such a foot.

I was glad to get the photographs. They look very well, although the one did look a little like Marie Antoinette.

I am as mad as I can be today. I invited a friend of mine and his wife, who have invited me many times to dinner recently without my being able to accept, to dinner tonight. He is a Judge. The last time I dined with them another man and his wife were in the party. The other man and the Judge talked politics and law all during the dinner, and the two women, between whom I sat, talked babies all through the dinner, where this linen could be got, and how Estelle did this and Louise that, until I was nearly mad. It was the wife of the non-judge who dragged the kids in. I swore a mighty oath that I would never dine with that woman and man again. He is a friend of the Judge. Today the Judge called me up and said that he wanted to see the man, that he had a lunch engagement with him, that he could not lunch with him, and wouldn't I ask him to dinner? Of course, there was nothing for me to do but say yes. I called the man on the telephone, and before I could speak he said that the Judge had spoken to him and that he didn't know whether his wife could come or not! This before I had asked him to bring his wife. A little while after that he called me up and said that they would be there at seven o'clock. And there I am!—I paying for the dinner and having to endure for two hours again the same sort of thing that a year ago I swore I would never put up with again.

You will have to do something to stop the calling of these Americans at the same time that you are engaged on your work. You cannot entertain people and work like that, too.

I am glad you liked the Thompson book. I think I told you in the letter I wrote you a week or so ago that he quoted some beautiful lines of your father's in the essay on Pagan poetry.[38]

If your introductions to the different volumes are as well written as parts of your letters, they will be great successes.

Did you really ask so many people to visit you? Visitors from Iowa paying longish calls must be tedious.

In regard to the publication of new matter, it is of course a very delicate question. Nothing should be published that could be called bad, but I don't agree at all that nothing should be published that is not equal to the best. Opinions may differ as to what is best. The unfinished or bad should be avoided. But what Mackail might consider short of the best, I might consider good. A common ground would be to reject what is unfinished, fragmentary, uncraftsmanlike, or bad. But I think that his admirers are entitled in a collected edition to have even fragments, if they are good, even though they are not equal to the best of his best. That is the way the memorial edition of Meredith is going on. A volume has been published of his poems written in early youth, which in his maturity he rejected and did not re-publish.[39] In his lifetime there was published an edition deluxe in thirty-two volumes, and some of the poems written in early youth were not re-published. After his death a volume was brought out of poems written in early youth and that volume will certainly find its place in the memorial edition. And so an unfinished novel of his called "Celt and Saxon" and also a play, I understand, in one act, not finished, will be published. This play, I believe, was acted at one of the subscription performances or repertory theatres in London this last winter.

The page that you sent was very beautifully done. I liked particularly the long line. I don't like too short a line. The type was fine and the paper seemed good.

Talking about dining alone, think of me who haven't eaten a real meal in ten weeks! I think six or seven times I have eaten solid food—two chops, a baked potato, some spinach or asparagus; no soup or fish, coffee, or drink of any kind; no liquid at meals, but water or buttermilk permitted half an hour before a meal or an hour and a half afterwards. My doctor called me on the telephone yesterday to inquire how I was getting along, and as he was about to ring off I asked him to come to dinner with me. He said he wouldn't come to dinner with me until I myself could do the honors and take my own food as generously as he, "which was not yet." As I said, I sleep splendidly—no more insomnia. I get up at seven or half-past seven in the morning; my head is clear; I have caught up with my work, and although I have lost in weight (I was getting a little fat) I am feeling fine. I think I have lost about fifteen pounds, but I don't mind it a bit.

Another good thing to take with meals, especially if one drinks with meals, is the Metchinkoff lacto-bacilline tablets. They come in little glass tubes; eight in a box. Two of these taken with dinner are very fine indeed. I will tell you all about it when I see you.

I enclose you a couple of more clippings about the Meredith edition, a reference to the article in the Oxford and Cambridge magazine and a clipping from the Evening Post where your father, Burne-Jones, and others are mentioned.

I have been cleaning the deck daily and I hope to know shortly when I will be able to get away. I am almost up today. I could practically clean my desk for a month's absence in a day—not for all summer, because cases have to be blocked out, briefed, and depositions taken, and work done during the summer for October, when the courts resume their sessions. But for a month's absence I can, outside of two very vital matters, leave in a day. However, I expect to be able to know within the next ten days just exactly what time I can get away. I will write you again within a week and I hope to know definitely by that time. Please mark your letters "Personal," because when I am away the men in the office open all letters except those which are personal, and when I am away Sadji would of course send letters addressed at the apartment to the office.

Under separate cover I am sending you a volume of essays by William Morton Payne, the editor of "The Dial" in Chicago. I daresay you met him in Chicago. It has rather a good essay on your father, pages 316–348.[40]

I am also sending you under separate cover the third section of the Sunday Sun of July 3d. It has an article by James Huneker,[41] much overdone, I think, because it mentions a good many artists who are not represented in my collection. I gave Huneker a catalogue of the Gallery of Modern Art in Dublin. He mentions the names of several well-known artists. I have fourteen pictures by Hone, twenty-five or thirty pictures by Russell, several by Mr. Yeats, and two splendid Shannons.[42] But to a superficial reader it would look as though I have a small gallery, and I don't like it. In fact, I didn't know he was going to mention my name at all. I wanted him to write something on Mr. Hone's work. Mr. Hone is an old man, seventy-nine or eighty years of age. He has not got much longer to stay here, and the older I get the more I realize the truth of Charles Lamb's saying that a little taffy while one is living is better than any amount of epitaphy after one is dead. I wish to God that I had only realized the truth of this earlier.

* * *

[Quinn to May Morris, 12 August 1910.][43]
Dear Miss Morris:

I got back on Wednesday. It was impracticable for me to cable before that time. I had a hard trip in the west. I hope you got my cable of Wednesday all right. I had a letter partly written and intended to mail it, but was so much rushed when I got back with things that had accumulated while I was away that I simply hadn't a moment to finish your letter in time for the boat.

I received yours of July 31st yesterday.

I was disgusted about having to put off my trip. I never dreamt of such a thing. It has mussed things up dreadfully. There is no use crying over it, but I was bitterly disappointed. I had written to John[44] that I would look in on him before or by this time, and I have just received a letter from him this morning wanting to know when I am coming over. I had written to Shannon[45] that I expected to see him by this time and to my friend T. W. Rolleston[46] in London.

I have not had time to write to John yet.

The matter that kept me here was imperative so far as I am concerned, involving as it did a possible change in the head and control of a concern which is not only one of but which is my chief client and from which over half of my office revenue is derived. The minute the matter was stated to me I saw the impossibility of going away.[47]

It has disarranged things a great deal, including the vacation schedule in the office. Mr. Kieffer,[48] who is my next assistant, is leaving tomorrow accordingly, to be gone for three weeks, so that that can be over.

I hope by the end of the month or early in September to be able to run across, at least for three weeks. I may not be able to be on the other side more than ten clear days, provided I can go on the "Lusitania" or the "Mauretania" or come back on one or the other, being away from New York only a little over three weeks.

The country here is dreadfully in need of rain, and the crops have been rather badly damaged. It is queer that in a letter which I had from Shannon a day or two ago he speaks of their having one summer day in England, whereas we have had nothing but sunshine, hot-weather, heat, and dryness.

Symons' book on the Romantic Movement is a serious, studious, and wonderfully able covering of the ground.[49] It is not often that a poet will put in the time and study and reading necessary to write such a book as that. The writing of that book, Symons told me last summer, helped to break down his health. He would not let anyone do any of the work for him. He read the authors that he criticized personally, and sometimes had to read volumes to write a page or two. Pre-fixed to his essay on each author is a bibliography of the first editions. The book, in my judgment, could be easily used as a university manual, and should be used. It is a scholarly, well-done piece of work. The essay on Blake I particularly liked, and also those on Coleridge, Wordsworth, Shelley, and Byron. If you look at the last volume of Courthope's History of English Poetry, just published, which covers almost this same period, you will see the difference between the dry-as-dust Oxford or Cambridge scholar's way of treating these same poets, and the way of a poet like Symons.[50]

I looked last night for a moment at Mrs. Ritchie's introductions to the thirteen-volume so-called biographical edition of Thackeray's Works, and I was confirmed in my impressions that they were chatty and personal.[51] It seems to me that you have a little exaggerated idea or fear of being too personal. For example, in the introduction to the volume containing "The Virginians," there was a lot of pleasant gossip, talk about her father's visit to America, and page after page of quotations from his letters. I should think you should quote from any of your father's letters referring to the books treated in each introduction, whether the letters have been previously published or not. Whatever a man like William Morris was doing at or about the time he was engaged on the writing of a book is interesting—whether printing or lecturing on socialism or working on designing or weaving or tapestry-making or where he was, or what not.

For example, I know that he was in Dublin at the time he was working on the translation of the Odyssey. I remember reading a short essay in the Bookman Magazine some years ago by a young man who was in Trinity College at that time. Any letters of your father's from Dublin or things about Dublin would be interesting, therefore, in the introduction to the Odyssey.

I think also that you have an exaggerated fear of publishing new stuff. Look at the Meredith case. They have not only published poems written in early youth, but they have republished poems which he had excluded from his collected edition or from the later editions of his early editions. And yet no one objects to these. One cares only for the feelings of a man's admirers, and certainly every admirer of your father would be glad to have everything that he ever wrote. I think the rule should be more relaxed when a man is dead than when he is alive. In other words, one would expect in the case of Meredith to have Meredith be a little more critical judge of the merits of his work than would be the case after his death, when his admirers would be eager for anything of his that they could get.

Not only that, but they are publishing Meredith's unfinished novel "Celt and Saxon," and they are also going to publish in a volume or as part of a volume a list of the changes made in his revisions of his novels.

I wish that I had a chance to look over the introductions. It seems to me that your chief embarrassment would be from not what to say, but how to say little enough, and that you are suffering from a wealth rather than a scarcity of material. I shouldn't hesitate at all to use any letters that Mackail may have published, and, as I wrote, I shouldn't make the test your father's best published, but exclude what was say fragmentary or imperfect or early drafts or bad. But I wouldn't make at all a standard of only the good. It will be published sometime anyway, and you might as well make the definitive edition. Shelley's published works today contain dozens and dozens of poems and letters that Mrs. Shelley never thought of publishing. Perhaps the public wouldn't stand a definitive edition in her day. But the public will enjoy anything now of William Morris, either in prose or verse.

The more intimate and personal you are, it seems to me, outside of purely family matters, the more interesting the introductions will be. Anything in regard to the peculiarities of his writing, his habits of punctuation, etc., would be interesting; about the number of drafts he made of a work, whether he jotted down his thoughts in fragments, as Pater used to, or on slips of paper, whether this work cost him more labor than that, and whether this one was revised but that one not—All these things are interesting to persons who like his work.

Of course, it is uncomfortable to have to do these things in a rush, and I simply wouldn't let them rush you. I would insist upon taking a few weeks more instead of being rushed, because once it is printed you don't want to have regrets about it, and surely you will do it well. But you mustn't think too much about style. People will want to read the introductions because they are written by May Morris, the daughter of William Morris, and because she is talking about her father and his works and writings, his acts and activities, and not because she is a master of style or a Walter Pater or a Robert Louis Stevenson. The more natural and unconsidered your writing is the more personal (not impersonal) it is, the better it will be. Don't let the printers rush you.

I enjoyed your father's joke about Tommy Wise and Tommy Fool, but perhaps Wise was really wise after all.

Mr. Hatch of Scribner's told me that they were going to send back the Jason fragment, and I accordingly bought it for $400 (£80). I really couldn't afford it now, but they told me they would give me all the time I wanted, which means I suppose four to six months. So now I think I have thirteen.

I have been working desperately to clear things up here, but seem to make very little progress, although I am making some progress. The vacation schedule, however, is a trying thing, and now that Kieffer is going away tomorrow, to be gone three weeks, I will be kept here busy every day.

I saw in yesterday's Sun an account of a Latin Bible owned by your father, which I enclose you herewith.

Sincerely yours

* * *

[May Morris to Quinn, from 8 Hammersmith Terrace, 14 August 1910.]

I can't write tonight. But here is an unpublished poem I have copied out for you. It is better than my foolish letters that only talk of one thing. I've been dreaming a great deal lately—radiant dreams but waking is rather a nuisance: the 'realities' seem so un-real for a while.

I'm afraid you must be terribly busy?

Yours with very much love
May

So many stories written here
And none among them but doth bear
Its weight of trouble and of woe!
Well may you ask why this is so
For surely neither sour nor dull

In such a world of fair things full
Should folk be.
                    Ah my dears, indeed,
My wisdom fails at my need
To tell why tales that move the earth
Are seldom of content or mirth;
Yet think if it may come of this—
That lives fulfilled of ease and bliss
Crave not for aught that we can give
And scorn the broken lives we live;
Unlike to us they pass us by,
A dying laugh their history.
But those that struggled sore and failed
Had one thing left them that availed
When all things else were nought
    E'en Love—
Whose sweet voice, crying as they strove
Begat sweet pity, and more love still
Waste places with sweet tales to fill;
Whereby, we living here, may learn
Our eyes toward very Love to turn

And all the pain it bringeth meet
As nothing strange amid the sweet;
Whereby we too may hope to be
Grains in the great world's memory
Of pain endured and nobleness
That life ill-understood doth bless.

Words overgrave and sad for you,
Maybe: but rhyme will still be true
Unto my heart—most true herein
In wishing, dear hearts, you may win
A life of every ill so clear
That little tale for folk to hear
It may be: yet so full of love
That e'en these words your hearts may move
Years and years hence when unto me
Life is a waste and windless sea.[52]

Written by William Morris in Jenny & May's copy of The Earthly Paradise.

* * *

[Quinn to May Morris, 1 September 1910.]
Dear Miss Morris:

I received the two photographs: the one of your father, which is the most interesting and which I am delighted to have but which is not so good of him as the Holyer *[sic]* portrait,[53] and the one by Emery Walker of the group of children, which is very interesting and which I am very happy to have. Thank you very much for sending them to me.

I also read with interest the announcement of the collected edition. It reads very well and I am sure it will be a great success.

But most of all I received your note of August 14th enclosing the poem copied out in your own hand and written by your father in your and your sister's copy of "The Earthly Paradise." I have read it several times. It is perfectly beautiful. You must publish this in your introductory note to the "Earthly Paradise." You ought, it seems to me, to drop entirely the idea that you may be too personal. The next time you go to the British Museum do look at two or three of the volumes of the library edition of Ruskin, edited by Cook and published by George Allen.[54] It has just been finished and is in thirty-seven large volumes. I believe a remaining volume containing the index is to be published. The introductions are practically biographies and bibliographies combined. Introductions are only read by persons who admire a man's work, and to persons who admire and love a man's work everything personal about him is interesting. Reading through these introductions would, I think, give you hints as to similar matters in your father's life that would be interesting to write about.

When it comes to the latter part of his life, it seems to me that you ought to keep in mind, with the dates of the publication of his different books or when he was engaged on them or writing them, his activities as a socialist, etc., and by matching up the dates of his contributions to "Justice" and "The Commonweal" you would know what he was working on, and doing in socialism.

You most certainly ought to include the poem, the copy of which you sent me, written by your father. It is beautiful and almost perfect.

You ought also the next time you are in the Museum to look at several volumes of the "biographical edition" of Thackeray, edited by his daughter, then Mrs. Ritchie (I think now Lady Ritchie). The most intimate and personal things are given there—correspondence, family letters, visits at home, what he was doing, how the family received him, letters from America, and so on. Glancing through these (not of course to copy the style or anything of that sort) would give you hints as to different matters in your father's life, things that would start new ideas or thoughts, and upon tracing them down you would, I am sure, get much interesting matter.

The bibliographies for the different volumes, including perhaps the subsequent editions, it seems to me you ought not to bother with. That is a matter that could be got up by some competent person for the various volumes by consulting Buxton Forman's book and Temple Scott's shorter bibliography.[55]

It seems to me that somewhere you ought to publish in one of these introductions in full your father's short four-page pamphlet "How I became a Socialist." It was published first in "The Commonweal" and is, I think, most interesting.[56]

I think I showed you a book in French entitled "W. Morris et le Mouvement Nouveau de L'art Decoratif" by Jean Lahor, published at Geneva in 1897.[57]

Again coming back to the introductions, it seems to me you cannot be too personal—how your father dressed, family letters, or letters to friends, particularly where they mention writings he is engaged on, any and all letters of a literary kind, for example the one which is in the Life and in which he refers to Swinburne's poetry and says, as I recall, that Swinburne's writings are too literary.

In the preface to Melville's two-volume biography of Thackeray he states that Clement Shorter had taken the introductions out of the thirteen volumes of the biographical edition of Thackeray edited by his daughter and had bound them together and that they practically constituted a complete life of Thackeray.[58] I am sure that if you looked at several of the Ruskin volumes and several of the Thackeray volumes you would get hints about things to put in your introductions. You don't want to make them too condensed. In the Ruskin volumes they gave the books he had, what prints he had, and pictures he had in the different rooms in his house, and so on.

Somewhere you ought, if you can, to re-create the list describing the missals, illuminated books and manuscripts, and other art treasures that your father had, even if you had to send to Mr. Morgan's secretary to have it done or to get descriptions of them. All these things tend to show the manner of man that William Morris was; what books on early printing he had, and so on. There must have been a catalogue of his library before it was sold out and that would perhaps aid you.

In yours of August 21st, received this morning, you do not mention my long letter of August 12th, which I hope you have received long before this. It was a typewritten letter of six pages.

I have been working very hard and have not been out of my office a single day. But I have been going to the dentists in the morning and day before yesterday I had a very severe operation, the two roots on one of the jaw teeth being amputated, no less. After the cocaine had taken effect there was no direct pain, but when the effect wore off toward afternoon and evening I was in great pain and did not sleep the entire night.

I should not let them try to rush you over the introductions, and once you get your hand in and get the swing of them, they will come off all right, I am sure. But don't be carried away with the idea or the fear that you are becoming too personal and don't think anything about style; but just write as though you were telling about your father to some personal friend.

I sent you the early part of the week a copy of Mosher the Portland Maine pirate's edition of "Pilgrims of Hope."[59] It contains a bibliography. I think this ought to be and could be prefixed by a statement that it was not published by your father in his lifetime and it should, it seems to me, be included in the collected edition.

Where your father lived when he was working on his different books, where the family lived, what his activities were, what things he was reading at times, are all interesting things. How he dressed, where he took his vacations, anything by Rossetti, and particularly letters between Rossetti and himself and Swinburne and Burne-Jones, even though they have previously been published. The Icelandic Journal will of course be interesting and it seems to me there ought to be a statement, catalogue, or list of the portraits of your father, including photogravures, half-tones, paintings, or pencil sketches, and their present whereabouts.

Just this morning I received yours of August 24th. From it I infer that when you wrote it you had received my letter of August 12th.

If you can't get the Jason MS. from Buxton Forman and want to reproduce a page in your Jason volume, I should be glad to loan you the Jason manuscript which I recently bought at Scribners. It could be sent quite safely. It is now in a solander *[sic]* case with inside wrappers and it could be sent by registered mail. Please let me know if you care for it, if you don't succeed with Forman.

I have learned from the use of stenographers and assistants in the office that I can treble and quadruple the amount of work I can do by dictation, and it seems to me a pity not to use a stenographer. From the tone of your last two letters it seems to me that you must be overworking, as you allude to "leaden days" and "all you have to keep you going." You remember what Jowett of Baliol[60] used to say, 'four and two are six: six and two are four.'

For real literary work four hours a day is all that one, it seems to me, should do. My work, which is not creative work but which is largely living on the surface of things, or an architect's work or any other kind of work, is different; but a person doing creative work, a writer or a musician, ought not work over four hours a day.

Sincerely

* * *

[Quinn to May Morris, 9 September 1910.]
My Dear [written in]:

I received your letter of August 31st yesterday morning in the apartment, and it surprised and shocked me. I hadn't dreamed that you were worrying about anything or were not feeling well.

As I said many times in the Spring, I am not a free man; I am not a man of independent means or private capital, and every engagement that I make is subject to change or being broken. Had I two or three partners it might be different. I have tried for two or three months to get a partner and some six weeks ago I thought a partnership with three other men might be possible; but it fell through.

I felt positive that I could get away by the middle or toward the end of July. Then a critical situation arose, which it was utterly impossible for me to ignore. I am not going to lay down my troubles or worries at anyone else's door. But the matter was critical and vital so far as I was concerned; it was a professional matter, and to have failed in it would have meant the loss of the major portion of my income, the diminution of my office staff, shrinking of income, and general revolution—too serious a condition altogether for me to neglect for anyone or anything or on any account. I hoped that the situation would improve or be solved in some way, but it is still hanging fire and is still exceedingly critical. I had a hope of being able to get abroad by this time. You know how one goes on hoping, even against one's own better convictions or better judgment.

But your letter shocked me so much that I faced the problem of whether there was any hope of my leaving this month, and it is hopeless. I cabled you today. There is no use going into details about it, but it is a crisis not of my making or seeking, but a matter in which I am most vitally interested and cannot ignore, and I would not have an hour's peace if I were on a boat and running away from it. That would be simply to invite disaster. In fact that would be the end of things, and whatever happens I am going to keep my head and act according to my best judgment. That is what I have had to do and what I am doing now. As I have said, I am not going to put my worries on anybody else, and never have. I have gone through crisis after crisis in my life and no one has ever known it, and I am going through this one in the same way.

It isn't a matter of my wanting a change. I have needed a change for some months. Nor it isn't a matter of my need being greater than anyone on the office staff. It is a matter where I have had to be here, and myself personally. I have cursed and raged about vacations this summer until the word is hateful to me. But vacations for others have not kept me here. Neither has it been business altogether, nor has it been that business to me is a duty. It is a matter of absolute and vital necessity and not duty, business, or anything else. I might as well shut up shop and sink down to becoming a mere employee of some other concern. That is the long and short of it, and I might as well put it bluntly.

At any time in the last six weeks I have been prepared, so far as other things were concerned or office things were concerned, to clear my desk on twenty-four hours' notice and sail. But this thing has kept me here and is keeping me still. Whether it will be settled in September or even October, I cannot say. I hope that early in October it may be settled. If that is true I hope to be able to get away. But please remember that I use the word "hope" in every case. I don't want you to count upon it even in October. If I can, I shall go even in October or in November. But it is only a hope. Everyone says that I need a rest. Only this morning a friend of mine whom I met said that I ought to go away and drop everything. I get that on all sides. But they, like you, think it is only business matters, etc.; where it is not; it is a crisis and critical.

But I cannot do nor will I discuss my affairs with friends.[61]

I am afraid you have been working too hard. You ought to get away with some pleasant and agreeable friends for some days or weeks and not read or write or even think, but just play and talk and eat and sleep.

Personally I have had one day out of the office this summer and also Sundays. That was Monday of this week, which was Labor Day. I was down at the seashore on Sunday and Monday. Sunday I went in bathing, and Monday I rowed a boat for an hour and went in the water again. Then every nerve in my body cried out for a continuation of it for a week or two or three or four—exercise and rest and away from telephones and papers and offices and letters.

I return you with this Buxton Forman's letter. The Jason manuscript which I bought was sold to me as being unique and the only part left. If Forman ever wants to sell his part, I shall be glad to buy it, but I shan't sell mine, and if I live to see Forman's thing sold I will try and buy his "Roots of the Mountains" four volumes. But please don't mention this to him, or he may begin to worry about his health.

I should think you would publish the unpublished "March" poem which was to come between "The Deeds of Jason" and the prologue, or at least include it in your introduction to "Jason" or "The Earthly Paradise."[62]

I am afraid you have been working too hard, keeping too much to yourself, sitting up too late at night and worrying over those introductions, and getting yourself into a state of nerves and brooding. A change will do you good and relieve the intensity and prevent any tendency to become morbid.

I have sworn at vacations, but I don't know what I would have done if I had time to brood this summer. I have been kept busy all the time I have been here, and at night I have been so tired that I haven't felt like doing anything.

I am still on the soured-milk diet and only take a portion of a meal once a day and that usually at dinner time. I haven't had a drop to drink since I started this cure, nor a cup of tea nor a bit of coffee; no soup, no salads, no pastries or pies; nothing of that sort. I have been devoting my time to trying to get myself back in fairly good shape, although it has been a hard job and I haven't recovered the lost ground yet. I am not worrying about it. Worry does no good, and as I cabled it was simply useless.

I wish I could write a more cheerful letter, and perhaps if I had time to sit down and write it out myself it would be more cheerful. But I have just come in from a long conference, and have only time to dictate this so as to catch the mail. It will be delivered to me this evening uptown. I haven't had anything to eat since about one o'clock, and I feel empty and tired out. So that please charge any abruptness in this letter to that and not to my intention.

* * *

[May Morris to Quinn from Kelmscott Manor, Lechlade, 17 October 1910.][63]

My dearest:

How have you been all this long month and what are you doing? I am at Kelmscott still, having been able to bring work here, going about town, when obliged to see printers and others. I go up and back in the day but it is rather tiring. And last time it was the beginning of our three days' gale, and as I had to bicycle to the station, our pony being otherwise engaged, I got wet to the bones, and had to be about town all day, wet and half frozen, keeping all my wits about me during a conference of three of us who were finally arranging the make-up of the first volumes of the Edition. I think riding home from the station in inky darkness, in a tearing wind, my lamp blown out, and no possibility of lighting again—wondering which was ditch and which was road—all this was the best part of the day! Then at the end of it, the kind soft lights of the house among the tossing elms—and groping at the gate in the wall, and stepping into the fragrant quiet garden after that turmoil, and the beautiful picture through the mullion-windows (curtains drawn back to welcome me), with the blazing hearth in a white room, and my mother, all white too, sitting there, waiting—for a second, I put myself "outside myself" and felt how full of wonder and enchantment such an arrival would be if it were new to one,—not part of one's life.

I am sorry my dear, you will not let me talk to Mother about you: it would give her so much pleasure to know that at last I had the happiness of loving and being loved. Imagine, dear John, the contrast between our lives—her and mine: She, married so early, the anxieties and griefs that must come into the happiest of human existences all softened by this atmosphere of measureless love and tenderness: and I—not much to be said, but that I've lived in a desert of loneliness and have set my teeth and endured it with a sort of dogged courage that has sometimes surprised myself. Now, the desert has blossomed, and the dear person who has done this expresses surprise that I'm not quite calm and serene . . . ah, my dear, try to be patient and tender with me over this: your imagination and sympathy, above all, your own feeling for me must help you to understand a hundred things one can't express. I have been expanding under your dear touch, and it is like a new life to get away from the old sad self-repression that so hampers and spoils a person's best years. Well, dearest man, that is enough of serious things, perhaps. Shall I tell you one or two scenes of our life here? For I must write. I do most of the house keeping—coming down in the morning with a key-basket, seeing the cook and the gardener, and so forth, sometimes making a special dish for Mother (Nature intended me for a Cook and housekeeper, and I resent the perversity of things that have so thwarted that intention). Then I settle to work in the Tapestry-room. These are my Father's rooms—in the E. Wing of the house (I sent you the picture of it)—very quiet and isolated from the rest of the house. Mother doesn't get up till late, and I work through the morning with a little girl who comes to copy things. Such a light, gay room, with great mullioned windows—in spite of the Samson tapestry, whose grimness has faded to pleasant harmony of blue and golden browns—A very lovely Persian carpet on the floor—I remember our getting it in Venice: the puzzlement of the Italian dealer at my Father's vehement ways! He was told by an Italian-speaking friend that he was a "grande poeta" and that soothed the gentleman, tho' I don't think it led him to take anything off the account—otherwise!

Mother and I lunch together, and she goes to rest, and I work on, not going out much beyond the garden—a wander by the river or in the church-yard at sunset sometimes. We sit in the parlour at tea and for the evening—a delightful room white paneled, airy and roomy, somehow, tho' not very large. There are jewels of Persian rugs about the floor, a painted settle of Red House days on one side, opposite, my Father's portrait, and his own Iseult picture, D.G.R.'s drawings of "Jenny and May"—[64] And we are lighted not by globes of electric light, my dear, but by modest candles in branches of old Sheffield plate. I occasionally play Bach and Handel on a little old piano, but generally settle to proof-reading. After dinner we play a dreadful game called Patience.

In the old days, all the family used to assemble at night in the Tapestry room. Work was put away, logs in the fire, games played, long talks . . . when the family went to bed, Father often worked. I have waked sometimes and lain watching his [?] at right angles to mine and his figure passing the window; listening to the chanting which accompanied the poetry-making. How the sound seemed wedded to the fragrance of the night in that enclosed garden!

And he is here constantly, John. I never lose the sense of it: at a turn of the garden I hear his footstep on the gravel—and hear it without surprise; the shock is, to come back to the present. Looking up at the windows, I've been conscious of him there in the room, and hear his voice, too—always without surprise. Does it seem strange that I can so write of such poignant things? To no one else, but with you, it is like talking to myself, and a relief in the midst of these long silences.

Did I tell you, my Dear, of the interesting things I want to show you? Very precious, little note books, hurriedly written in pencil the first draft of the Prologue that was discarded, and a good bit of Cupid and Psyche, besides some other E.P. tales. Item, some early sketch books, Item 3 note-books of Iceland Journeys . . . It would all interest if you were less distracted and had leisure to be interested.

I am sending proofs of my first Introduction and the Jason one. You can glance at them or throw them away.

Good-night, my dear dear John; may [you] think of me very often. I wish I might say more. It is very late, but so difficult to stop.

Do you know what happened then! I felt something wriggle nearly at my waist, and Good Heavens, there was a huge mouse inside my clothes! Now a truly sensitive woman would have screamed, but I didn't want to waken the house!

Think of me often, dear John.

Yours

* * *

[Quinn to May Morris, 15 November 1910.]
Dear Miss Morris:

I received your letter of October 24th and enjoyed it very much. I had hoped to be able to answer it by Saturday's steamer, but Mr. Ryan,[65] who returned Friday morning, cabled me to meet him and I had to get up very early to meet him at the boat. His son had been ill for some days with appendicitis and the operation had been delayed pending the father's return. The son, who is a personal friend of mine, was operated on at three o'clock Friday. I spent all day with the father and at the hospital and wasn't in my office all day. Saturday morning I was at the hospital again. He is getting all right now, but the father was much worried. The result was that I was unable to write a letter on Friday for Saturday's boat and I worked all day Sunday, and this letter is being dictated late Tuesday night in the office.

I read through both introductions carefully the night I got them and have re-read parts of them since. I congratulate you on them. I think the introduction to the Defense of Guenevere is if anything a little more interesting than the introduction to the Jason.

I enjoyed your description of your days at Kelmscott very much. It was the kind of writing that I know your father would have liked too, especially your description of the hunt and of the night in the country.

It is a mistake to grow too anxious for perfection. I feel like urging you again not to hesitate too much about using any material, any anecdote, any letter, or any fact stated in Mackail's Life. He got these details either from your mother or from your father's executors or from someone, and they don't belong to him and you have a perfect right to use them. I am sure that the introductions will all go well.

Only it is a mistake to let yourself grow anxious about them or to be hurried in any way. Remember when they are printed and out they cannot be changed, so you ought to take ample time.

Your description of your bicycle ride was rather terrifying and I am glad that you came through it all right.

I received on Monday your card from Rottingdean with a reproduction of the Burne-Jones windows. I hope that you had a good holiday there.

On page xvii of the introduction to Guenevere, about the middle of the page, it strikes me that there is a word omitted, or that the word "so" or "such" should be inserted, so that it would read something like this:

> "Moreover, the Browning Poems are treated with so sweet a seriousness and so direct a simplicity in the attempt to straighten out some of the complicated personalities, that it is scarcely possible to read" etc.

What I mean is that the words "that it is scarcely possible" imply a comparison and that therefore there should be a "so" or a "such" or some word of that sort.

I am angry that a quotation mark ending a quoted passage, not beginning it, struck me as being omitted when I read the proofs, but I have spent half an hour racing through and back and over again the introductions to the two volumes trying to find this, but I cannot do it. I suppose if I didn't feel rushed about the matter I would find it in a moment. But perhaps the printers have caught this.

I particularly liked the introduction to the first volume, especially your treatment of the boyhood of your father and of the building of his house and of his college friendships and early days in London. Again I want to congratulate you. I am sure the introductions will be a success.

I am sorry that you didn't autograph the proofs that you sent me. I hope, if it is not too much trouble, that you will continue to send me the proofs of the different volumes as they come out, each autographed by you, so that when they are out I will have them beautifully bound in vellum and entitled "Notes on the Life and Works of William Morris by May Morris."[66] Your notes together will practically make up your father's life. It seems to me that your only embarrassment is that of the riches of the material that you have to draw from. But you will have the knotty problems of arranging your material, but you will get through with it well, I am sure.

This letter is dictated at the office. It will be brought to me at the Bar Association uptown, where I am working, and I will add a postscript to it and mail it tonight.

I shouldn't hesitate at all when you come to Kelmscott to describe it just as you have written about it. Nor would I hesitate to put in the little episode that you wrote about your father buying the rug in Venice and of your Italian-speaking friend explaining that he was a "grande poeta" and that that seemed to soothe him but that probably it didn't induce him to take anything off the account.

But why should I make these suggestions to you? You know better than anyone else perhaps what to say and what not to say.

A book-dealer who supplies me with books sent me an announcement of the "Collected Works of William Morris" the other day, with a letter asking me if I did not want to subscribe. I want to think about how I can subscribe for a set from the other side, to be sent to me as published, but each volume to be first autographed by you, as Yeats autographed the eight volumes of his collected edition published by Bullen at Stratford. But I will have to think this out and write to you about it again. I don't want to give you any trouble about it.

* * *

[May Morris to Quinn, from 8 Hammersmith Terrace, 29 November 1910.]

My Dearest: I have just left work on "The Hill of Venus" for an hour's gossip with you. Rather a "twister", that, for the printers' copy, even, is very much worked up, and the only other m.s. I have to study is an experimental fragmentary draft, a great part of which he has <u>not</u> used, and the rest twisted about in a manner distracting enough to an unpractised, conscientious Editor. It is very interesting to note how easily some of the poems "flowed from the source", and how others had to be nursed and coaxed. But the poor Editor has got a heavier burthen than this on her shoulders—not so very solid just now. The Icelandic books are giving me a devil of a time and I'll tell you why: Magnússon, joint translator—though of course we all know (entre nous) not the stylist nor writer, has by courtesy to be called into it, and he desires sundry corrections in the text. This was at first conceded (doubtfully by me) after consultation with the trustees. Nemesis follows, and the fun begins: because alterations come one on the heels of another, and at last I see the whole thing is not to be admitted and the text must be kept. I consulted several distinguished scholars about it, and they are very emphatic about leaving Father's text unaltered—notes or explanations afterwards if you will etc. etc. Magnússon, who figures on the title page, and to whom I have to write a conciliatory but firm (!) letter explaining that we have changed our minds, will be unhappy and furious very likely, and I'm going to have a bad quarter of an hour. However, it is all but a matter of courtesy. Only I hate beyond words the prospect of vexing an old acquaintance, and one who is old, and unsuccessful and so forth. This is all very much behind the scenes, but I'm sure you'll sympathise with all these obstacles en route that have to be levelled. All this will be settled before I get your point of view and feeling about it. Meanwhile the press waits, and everyone is slanging me in their hearts, I know. Even the great Longman though as kind and nice as may be has no idea about the Edition just now but Punctuality—quite morbid, I assure you—quality goes for nothing as long as one is up to time. Because, forsooth, they have their silly old Reputation for punctuality to keep up. It worries me in the work, of course, but I do my best not to give way to that. I've been fearfully hindered by having to lie a-bed lately: working in bed does not go so promptly. Can't you get one of your friends onto a good literary notice in one of the New York papers, I wonder? Tell them it is the "last thing" in simple dignified typography and good plain binding, and so forth! You know everybody, and an article might be useful.

I have to write to Bok, the Philadelphia man,[67] but haven't had the energy yet. I've been trying to work the miracle a little over here, as I do want the thing to go in every sense. I must tell you about my "little dissiness" last week. One night was rather special, for I had Clutton-Brock, the Times literary man,[68] and his wife, with Mr. Walker to help and balance. And CB is a dear, and it would have been all very pleasant, only for the first time almost in my career as a housekeeper, the dinner was a hideous failure, as my housekeeper got nervous (nervous when she had two helpers, and only four people to cook a simple meal for!) and spoilt the spoilable things beyond recognition. I was feeling too unwell to want food, and besides being humiliated, was very sorry for my poor dear guests. When the waiting is bad and everyone gets up at once to help me, I am only amused, but I normally manage to give people decent food. The night before, we gave a quite elegant little meal to this good man Sir Herbert Thompson[69] who is helping over the Iceland Journal—a sort of dinner I should not be nervous of offering to a fastidious and delicate person like yourself. If it only had been Yourself sitting there at my right hand, . . . I go dreaming and see such a pretty picture of us two at the round table, and the warm flicker of the wood-fire, and the shaded candles lighting us up; and the whole thing reflected in little and far-off in the dark dark lake of the round mirror.

To return from the poor little dream: would you tell me, when you have time, what I did send you in the way of proofs—Introductions and illustrations; because I kept no record, and if you really mean to do me the honour of binding the same, it might as well be complete. You can check it off from the bound volumes when they arrive. In future I will send the whole bunch of Introduction things. I mean all the illustrations too. There will be some interesting "Month" poems (unpublished) in the next bunch, among other things. You know, I think that Longmans imagine I can reel off an Introduction in two sittings as if it were an advertisement article for Selfridge's Store, whereas I have to think and balance and hunt about, and write letters, and wait and consult folk . . . oh they don't see the work contained in the poor little Introductions as well as in the editing. Yes, I think the "Jason" introduction was thin. But in 24 volumes I can't profess to be equal in quality or in length—oh Lord! Shall I ever find enough to say, all through.

Again yes, you are surely right about that sentence in the introduction to Guenevere p. xcii. I had my misgiving and showed it to one or two, but they said they didn't see it. It is sometimes better to trust to oneself—when one's second self is unhappily not to hand. I shall look for the offending quote marks directly I've got this 4th vol: of E.P. "off my chest". What a good Editor you are; wish I had you here to edit me and give me ideas and generally, to brace me up.

You know, as I fancy I've said before, I don't suppose I could write spontaneously and flowingly about Kelmscott or anything near and dear with the consciousness if it was for the printers. The freshness for whatever it is worth goes when the audience is no longer near and dear, but indefinite and impersonal—even the absurd gossipy things like the Venetian carpet that amused you would not occur to me. But truly, do you imagine a close description of some of the rooms such as I give you and never dreamt of putting down for the public, would have any general interest, or be in place? I am glad enough to lengthen my 'copy' any possible way.

I can see you didn't have those second two Introductions, and will look them up. One is considered quite good. I suppose I was afraid of boring you by sending such an avalanche of printed stuff.

My dear soul, I asked you if you were yet allowed to go back to reasonable human diet. I do want to know. I suppose that was in a later letter. You say nothing about the elections. Did you vote? Did you speak or do anything? It is all so different from us, isn't it? We are Dissolved, and General Elections soon on us. Do you see what Cuckoos some of our women have been? Many of us are getting sick of what they are pleased to call their "Tactics."[70]

Can you bear the length of this? I had many things to add but it is getting near midnight, and I am supposed to be coddling myself still. Like all women, I love being coddled, but can't do it for myself.

John, will you promise me not to go in areoplanes? Please don't.

Yours always
May

I have a lovely D.G.R. of myself in reproduction to send you presently.[71]

* * *

[May Morris to Quinn, from 8 Hammersmith Terrace, 6 December 1910.]

My Dear:

It is some unholy hour of the morning and the wind is racing up the river, and I'm hopelessly wide awake but not yet quite up to working, so I'll victimise you for half-an-hour. I'm not going to apologise for just nonsense gossip letters, because you are supposed to want to know something of my life day by day—monotonous as it is. Yesterday was Sunday, and after working (in bed) from six to eleven a. m. I got up and dusted and tidied and saw things and then a friend from the School of Art at Birmingham where I used to lecture, came to lunch. An accomplished charming woman, and we had great talks. Usually I'm alone all

Sundays and working just as usual). Then two other women came—all of us members of my Woman's Guild—and there we were, talking of the Post-Impressionists, of the last new way of teaching art students; . . . of shop in short: and they were all delighted to meet each other, in this impromptu way. You know, theoretically I don't seek out the society of women particularly, but I must say, it was as fine a little knot of women with an all-round, not self-centered, view of the arts as you could meet anywhere; all comely well-grown creatures, bubbling with vitality and good-humour. Anyway, it is a pleasure to meet women who know their work and are not playing at art. One of them stayed behind and with my little secretary had an absurd supper with me of sandwiches and various fruits. Being women, of course (!) they did not spot the fact that the wine was the best part of the fare, being good of its kind though unpretentious, and warmed to the right temperature! I had intended a long evening's work with the little secretary, but had to be social instead. People very rarely find their way out to me, but when they do—well, they enjoy it.

I am just now working on the last of the Earthly Paradise and am exercised by the Hill of Venus. It gave him a lot of trouble to judge by the various m.s.s. There are some interesting stanzas in all this rejected stuff—sometimes little glimpses of "himself behind", but too wrapt up for me to make use of. I can't be always quoting pieces that are not quite good because there is something in it that appeals to me. I'm afraid I am spending too much time over E. P. poems. After all, I'm not writing a critical essay, and yet one is led on to say more than one set out to say. I expect I'll have to cut down about half of the present notes. You know, dear, it is wonderfully *[sic]* what a genuine story-teller's instinct my Father had. Compare the Venus-Hill story and Wagner's Tannhäuser: My Father would have made no difficulty about piecing a legend together as Wagner does here, but when he found the old legend complete and to his liking he left it. The Holy Elizabeth ending to Tannhäuser is flat indeed compared to the wild mysterious finish of the Hill of Venus which is the old story as we know it.

Well, I suppose I must take up work now.

Good morning, dear, I hope you have slept.

(7th December (Wednesday) The same.)

When I light the lamp by my bedside, your dear face appears gradually out of the dark, as I turn up the light, and that is very pleasant, but oh Lord such a poor substitute for the real thing.

I had to go to town yesterday, and looked in at the Post-Impressionists for a hour. The exhibition has rather fluttered the dove-cotes. Phil Burne-Jones wrote to the Times, I hear, to inform the world that he could not stand such things, and calling on all honest Christians to defend the right, so to speak, and I was at Sir William Richmond's the other day, who was simply furious with them, and expressed his feelings with some picturesqueness: either people declare they stand for everything that is true and deep, and so forth and so forth.[72] It seems to me, who am no critic and not learned in modern pictures (or old ones!) that though they are brutal sometimes, violent—mad, or absurd—anything—yet they are not negligible; and the mad Gauguin rather touched me. He seems to have been struggling towards some expression outside the ordinary routine, without having reached. Yet some of his extraordinary experiments have wild snatches of poetry, even of sentiment. He painted about Martinique and those parts and does the most violent effects of colour—green skies, scarlet trees, purple-brown people, strange dream-like foregrounds with pre-historic wriggling growths, etc. etc.

There is one thing that struck me—if it matters, that the general effect in the exhibition-rooms was far more striking and decorative than the effect of a collection of what one may call sane pictures would be—with their silver tones, their blacks and greys and general discretion and propriety! At the same time, I don't want any one belonging to me to be a Post-Impressionist, and I could not live at close quarters with their work.

I send a vivacious article by Robert Ross in the Morning Post on our Edition.[73] I am disgusted to hear that they will only do a short notice in the Times, because sometime back Clutton-Brock did a long article on my Father when crumpling up that idiot—Alfred Noyes.[74] I am having a worrying time with my Iceland friend, who is restive under my decision not to emend text.[75]

How are you, my dear? Don't let it be quite such a long time between letters, if you can possibly spare me a few minutes. I find it all difficult enough as it is.

Now I must do a little work. It is light now, and everybody is up and about.

I go back for a moment to the pictures: You see how reluctant I am to leave you and get to work! It is after all rather high praise to say that the general impression of an Exhibition is interesting and decorative!

I don't for a moment feel that Gauguin, Cezanne, Gogh, and

all of them are posing when they paint a Christ with scarlet hair and a blue dog with orange eyes. On the contrary, though it may sound absurd, I found Gauguin especially, very sincere. By the bye there are some fine Manet's there.

I'm afraid this is all rank heresy.

Good morning, dear John Quinn.

Yours
M.

* * *

[Quinn to May Morris, 17 December 1910.]

Dear Miss Morris:

I received yours of November 30th and of December 7th. I also received the four beautiful volumes. They are beautifully printed and the binding is quite in keeping with the paper and type and form of the volumes. You ought to be very proud of them. I congratulate you sincerely upon the four volumes published. I noticed in some paper the other day that there are to be published four volumes quarterly. This ought to relieve you from pressure in some degree.

This cannot be an answer to your two letters. Your second letter, the one in which you wrote about the Post-Impressionists show, interested me very much. I had received a catalogue of the show from Knewstub of the Chenil Gallery.[76]

I am sorry I could not have seen the show.

I will of course do, and with great pleasure, what I can to carry out your suggestion in regard to the volumes being noticed here. I think that I will call in at Longmans place on Fifth Avenue some morning on my way downtown. I have bought books of them for years. I think that I will tell them that I know two or three men on the papers here and in Chicago who are friends of mine and inquire whether they have sent copies to them for review, and will indicate three or four papers to which they should in particular be sent. Then I shall write to these men and tell them that the books are likely to come to them or to their editors and to have them look out for them. I had in mind Gregg of the Evening Sun, James Huneker of the morning "Sun," the editor of the Literary Supplement of the New York Times, and Francis Hackett of the Chicago Evening Post. Hackett will give it a full-page review in the Literary Supplement on the first page, and that ought to do a great deal of good in the Middle West and West. I shall also speak to Paul Elmer More, the literary editor of the Evening Post, and that ought to give it a good review. Reviews in the Post are generally re-printed in "The Nation." I will also write to William Morton Payne, the editor of "The Dial," in Chicago.[77]

For the last three weeks I have been continuously engaged in court in the trial of two important cases. For two Sundays I have worked; last Sunday at my apartment beginning at 10 o'clock in the morning, right through to quarter past eight, a pause of about an hour for dinner, and then on till 1:30 Monday morning. I hope to be through with these cases early next week, but what with seeing witnesses, conferring with clients and counsel, actually preparing the cases for other co-defendants and conferring with their counsel, digesting testimony, looking up points of law, and attendance in court, I have had my hands full every moment of the time. Tuesday morning when the boy was telephoning and I was shaving, I went to close my razor to answer the telephone and did it without looking and cut the tip off the thumb on my right hand. I had to get a doctor to dress it and appeared in court at the regular hour, 10:15, that morning. It wasn't so bad that day, but I didn't sleep much all night. I was in court the next day, Wednesday, but in the afternoon I went to the doctor to have him dress it and in taking off the cotton he re-opened the whole thing and I never had such pain in my life for four or five hours. The pain was so severe on Wednesday night that I had to take sleeping powders. It is all right now and has given me no trouble since. But I shan't let that doctor remove the bandage. I will go to another doctor or let it stay on till it falls off.

Most of my letters have therefore gone out unsigned or signed by clerks in my name.

This is only a short note, dictated at quarter to five in the afternoon to catch the "Mauretania," which leaves at six and which will land her mail in London next Friday.

I am instructing Elkin Mathews[78] to send you a set of the memorial edition of Meredith's works. Some twenty-three or twenty-four volumes have been published so far and I think the set is to be twenty-six or twenty-eight volumes, the last volume made up, as is your edition, of previously unpublished matter. I hope that you will receive these before Christmas.

Christmas holidays are a bore to me. It is a child's holiday, anyway. I dislike to have people send me Christmas presents and they generally send the wrong things. Most of the Christmas presents I get I give away. A Judge friend of mine sent me, for example, last year four volumes of "Cathedrals of England," "Cathedrals of France," "Cathedrals of Italy," and "Cathedrals of Spain," which I promptly gave away.

I have had no time to even buy a Christmas present for my little niece, my sister's only child.

I was invited down to Virginia to a house party there a week ago. I could not go then but I promised to go this week and had to put it off on account of these cases. I hope to start the first part of the year with a fairly clean calendar record.

I got the proof of the third volume of the set the other day and it is in my apartment, but I have had only time to look at it. I have not had time yet to read it. I hope sometime next week to have a chance to read it and to answer your letters more fully.

This takes with it my best wishes for a pleasant Christmas for you and yours.

Sincerely yours

* * *

[Quinn to May Morris, 30 December 1910.]
Dear Miss Morris:

I received your telegram on Christmas Day. I have had hard weeks, but never a harder or more vexatious or wearying week than this. There is a regular epidemic of grippe in this vicinity, and my first assistant, who went home for Christmas to Maryland, is ill in bed. I expected him back on Tuesday, but he has telegraphed the doctor will not let him get up. One or two of the other men in the office have been more or less laid up, and with the pressure of things that have to be done before the end of the year in preparation for the beginning of the new year, I have been working every night. I have been to the theatre only once in six weeks, and have dined with friends only once in a month, and even then I dressed in the office and had to leave them soon after dinner. My thumb is much better, but not quite good for writing yet.

I got two copies of a catalogue of the Chicago book publisher before Christmas, the same one who sold the large number of Swinburne manuscripts that Watts-Dunton[79] sold in his hunger for money. At the end of this catalogue is a description of some drawings by Rossetti, and the name of your father and mother is mentioned. I send you under separate cover two copies of this catalogue. I also send you with them a page of the Evening Sun, containing a reprint of an article in the London News on your father's work.

I have had no time yet to step in to Longmans to speak to them in regard to sending out the review copies.

I hope to be able to get away tomorrow (Saturday) to see my sisters in Ohio for a day or two. I expect to reach there Sunday afternoon. Monday, the second, is a legal holiday. I want to stay, if I can, until Wednesday, but I may have to be here on Tuesday. In that event, I shall have to turn around and make the long journey back Monday afternoon, thus traveling over a thousand miles for the purpose of spending one night in my sisters' home.

I have settled down to a regular regime now of no breakfast and no lunch, and one meal a day, and that meal without any drink and without any sweets or coffee. In the morning before I leave my place I take a glass, and sometimes two glasses, of soured milk, and during the day, at intervals of two or three hours, I take a small bottle, containing about a medium sized glass, of soured milk, or a preparation that one gets in a drug store (what you call the chemist's) of Zoolak or Kumyss. It is amazing how much more work I can do on this diet than if I eat a breakfast and a lunch. The important thing is that it must be taken regularly, and that the intervals between glasses be not too long. I save an hour and an hour and a quarter a day which in former times was wasted on lunch, and the drowsy and heavy feeling which used to come along about five or six o'clock no longer appears. I do not recommend this in any sense, and in fact, the soured milk cure should not be taken except under the advice of a doctor. This treatment of mine has almost entirely banished the insomnia from which I used to suffer dreadfully.

There is an account in the Sunday Times of Jo Davidson's work, mentioning his bust of you. I saved the page, but it is up at my apartment, so I cannot send it with the catalogues, but I will send it later.[80]

Christmas was a great bore to me this year. I mean only in this sense: that a lot of friends sent me a lot of junk in the way of presents and books and things that I did not care for and did not want. Among them were three quarto volumes of the life of Columbus by a man named John Boyd Thatcher *[sic]*, who formerly lived at Albany, N.Y.—three gigantic volumes.[81] Imagine three such big books being sent to me who begrudges every available bit of space on my book shelves or book cases, and who does not admit books to the collection that have not some special reason there or do not make some appeal. Cigars, of course, are welcome, and many boxes of them came, and a barrel of delicious apples from Virginia—Albermarle Pippins. Most of these I sent to my sister, as they would not keep in the apartment.

This letter is dictated at eleven o'clock at night to one of the three stenographers, and is to be written out while I am dictating other letters to one of the others so that I can sign it and have it mailed tonight so that it will catch the St. Louis which sails at 6:30 tomorrow morning.

I hope that it will find you well and not worrying over introductions to the succeeding volumes. It seems to me that you are through with the worst of it now.

I will write the letter to your mother early next week on my return.[82] My hand will be better then, and I really haven't had a moment to spare all this week. In fact, it was two o'clock before I got to bed last night.

I hope that you had a satisfactory Christmas Day, and with best wishes for the new year,

Faithfully yours,

* * *

2
The Letters of 1911

[May Morris to Quinn, from 8 Hammersmith Terrace, New Year's Day 1911.]

Last night, I went to bed early, being rather fagged after a close day's work, but was soon disturbed by the clanging of bells all over the city—while I still had in my head the singing of sleigh-bells in the midst of the silent snow! I remembered it was New Year's Eve then. I have to send you the first few words written this year: a letter in the form of a poem of Father's I have pieced together from two different m.s.s.

My love to you: you have my heart in your hand—be kind to it.

May

A sweet garden by the sea
Did my true love give to me;
The All-father's paradise
Was not wrought in fairer wise;
  Ah how lone, how lone it is.

There the birds sing songs for me,
And the murmur of the sea
Do I hear day-long, night long,
Nothing there may do me wrong:
  Ah how lone, how lone it is.

There twixt blossomed trees and sea
He let build a house for me,
Therein is there wealth of gold
Tales on walls and floor are told:
  Ah how lone, how lone it is.

Many a slave he gat for me
On that beach along the sea,
From Mysian land, and Argive land
Did the captive women stand;
  Ah how lone, how lone it is.

Twixt lily-bed and white-crowned sea
Tales of love folk tell to me,
Songs they sing of happy dreams,
But the o'erword ever seems,
Ah how lone, how lone it is.

Sometimes do folk say to me
When the murmur of the sea
At dead ebb is far away,
"Forget him, he died yesterday."
Ah how lone, how lone it is.

Or when west winds make the sea
Mad and loud, they say to me,
"Weeping makes thine eyes less fair
Tomorrow morn shall he be here."
Ah how lone, how lone it is.

When tomorrow comes to me
I shall not hear the unquiet sea,
When today is yesterday
No more shall I weep and say,
"Ah how lone, how lone it is."

W. M. (unpublished)[1]

New Year's Day: 1911.

* * *

[Quinn to May Morris, 3 February 1911.]
Dear Miss Morris:

I have just returned to New York after an absence of ten days and find three of your letters. I have only had a chance to read one so far, as the pressure and accumulation of things is dreadful. In the early part of January I was out of the office a great deal at Albany, New York, and had to do a lot of night traveling. One week I was three nights on the train. After a while one gets used to losing sleep, but one is not worth much during the daytime.

I enjoyed your letter about the Post-Impressionists very much. I also enjoyed your last letter, which was a veritable poem in prose.

One of the companies for which I am attorney was called into a very bad banking situation on Sunday, January 8th. I was called into the matter in the evening and about fifty of us—bankers, directors, lawyers, and others—were kept going Sunday night; in fact I got to bed at quarter past five Monday morning. The Trust Company of which I am attorney took over one of the shaky institutions, and a couple of other big concerns took over the others. This was to prevent failures and for the general benefit of the financial situation. But the amount of work it has plunged me into is enormous. I have had not only to do my current work but to familiarize myself with over twenty complicated matters of the concern which my client took over, some of which are years old and the documents in which are appalling. I haven't been to a theatre in a month. I haven't written a letter in a month. I have only sent a telegram or two to my sister. I have been lucky to be able to get enough sleep, and not always that. I hope soon to have an hour free in my apartment to sit down and write or dictate a private letter. This is only a hastily dictated line to catch the steamer tomorrow. I hope that it will find you well and not worrying over your work.

I received the Burlington from you and enjoyed it very much. I am a regular subscriber to it, but I will keep the copy with your initials and give the regular copy away.[2]

I was especially glad to get the book by Holmes on the Post-Impressionists.[3] I gave this and some catalogues that I received from the Chenil Gallery to James Huneker, the art critic on the New York Sun. He wrote a column or two on the Post-Impressionists, but not having seen the pictures his article was like a half-tone reproduction of an etching—faint and blurred.

I worked so hard during the last few days of 1910 that I fully resolved that in 1911 I wouldn't work so hard. For a day or two I kept the resolution, but suddenly I was plunged into the middle of work and here I am still struggling. However, I am not the only one that is doing it. It seems that everyone in New York who amounts to anything has to work and over-work himself.

I feel as dry in my brain as a door-mat, for I haven't really read a book through in nearly two months, and I have been so tired at nights that even when I have tried to read it was an effort. I have dipped into Hearn's letters and have enjoyed them immensely.[4] He has one wonderful letter about the middle of the book upon Japanese eyelids and colours of various races. As I read it I said to myself, "This fully justifies the Post-Impressionists: for Hearn too saw green eyes and blue skins and purple hair, or at least claimed that such there was." Faithfully yours,

* * *

[May Morris to Quinn, from 8 Hammersmith Terrace, 18 February 1911.]

Such a day, it was yesterday, of pure, serene, unflawed sunshine; a very high tide, all over the banks, the little waves gaily flecked with white, as they went to meet the west wind, and the small fleet of sailing boats out there all curtsying and splashing busily. A Spring day! Do you know all the beauty of the English spring, in the country, John dear? It is the most magical time, where the buds are bursting, and in all the quiet and silence, the busy life showing itself by funny little green things in the soft earth everywhere thrusting off their sheltering roofs, determined to be born. Oh to be wandering with you somewhere in the spring woods, dear John, for a little time of peace and contentment—to be wrapt up in this kind magic of the earth into forgetfulness.

I never meant to write so soon—tho' why should one count, or calculate, in sending love-messages!—but the thrush sang and I had to tell you about it; also it is Saturday morning when I usually write.

There is the mail and my breakfast-coffee, so goodbye, peace—

Good morning, my Dear.
May.

* * *

[Quinn to May Morris, 24 March 1911.]
Dear Miss Morris:

I have just sent a cable to you, that I have not been well for the past ten days. I have had an attack of the grippe and a bad cold, and pains in the abdomen, and haven't felt very happy over it, or in the mood for writing a cheerful letter. It is over now, I hope, and I have been at the office part of the time for three days. It was not very pleasant having to worry over piles of work that I left suddenly and I couldn't help worrying over things. I imagine that I had been going [at] it a little too hard, and I felt very tired a week ago Wednesday, and I suppose nature, or some germ, made up her or its mind that she or it should be noticed. The work is waiting [for] me in the office now in piles, literally, from two to eight inches deep. And I found my old standby stenographer laid up all week and out of the office, and this doubled the time and attention that I have had to give during the last three days to matters large and small. There were two or three epidemics of grippe here in January and February, but aside from a bad cold in January, I escaped them then. Taking it easy for two or three days longer will, I think, bring me around all right.

This letter is dictated at the Bar association in order to catch tomorrow's steamer. I have many things to write about and many things to acknowledge receiving from you. The Gilbert Murray book came yesterday, and the book on war.[5] The Murray book I shall read as soon as I have a couple of hours leisure. The book on War and Peace I shall dip into to get the author's meaning, as one does with such books. I have learned, as you doubtless have, the art of skipping, or of knowing what to skip in reading such books. I enjoyed reading the review of Synge's writings in the Times which you sent me, and I passed it on to Gregg of the Evening sun, who is doing a notice of Synge's last play.[6] Young Hackett, from Chicago,[7] came to see me at my apartment about ten days ago, and I spoke to him about doing a good review, a full-page, signed review, of the collected edition. He said if Longmans' would send him the books he would be glad to do a good review. I wrote to Longmans from my apartment, or rather dictated a letter there, to the manager, and a note came a day or two ago from somebody at Longmans, that the manager was away, but that as soon as he returned, the matter would have his attention. Gregg promised me over three weeks ago that if the books were sent to him he would do a good review for the Evening Sun. And I hope that Paul Elmer More,[8] the literary editor of the Evening Post, and also the editor of the Nation, will do a review of them.[9]

I had been back only four days from a hard trip West, and found an accumulation of work then on my return to the office, almost as great as what is there now. I must have spent nearly one hundred dollars in telegrams and long distance telephone messages while I was away. I hadn't even time on my return to stop off for a day and a night at my sister's place in Ohio, though I hoped to do so and had written her that I would, and though she expected me.

Augustus John wrote me a very funny letter about the young sculptor Gill, whom you wrote about. I couldn't quote from the letter, but you would be amused over it. John seemed to think that Gill did not know too much about the human figure.[10] I dipped into the book by Marie Clair *[sic]*, that you also wrote about. It will of course have its day, as "An English Woman's Love Letters" did, and then it will be forgotten.[11] I can well believe that it was gone over by the literary man that you mention.

Some clients of mine, who are interested in contracts for railroad building in Spain, wanted me very much, about three weeks or four weeks ago, to go to England on the business, and perhaps to Spain, and they would have paid me well for it. But I am sorry to say, it was impossible for me to think of it. I have been looking all winter for a partner or an associate who could assume responsible work and look after critical things in my absence, but so far I have not been able to find the right man, a man whom I could trust and rely on fully. I do get very weary of conducting a post-graduate law school and training men to be lawyers, and at the same time paying them good wages for the training. The expenses of my office amount, including salaries and everything, to over $18,000 a year, (5,600 Pounds.) You may imagine how much work is involved on my part in earning enough from fees and retainers merely to meet these expenses.

But I didn't mean this to be a letter all about myself and my ills and my worries, but I fear it is. I see that the second four volumes of your beautiful and stately edition are announced, and you must take great pride in the work you have done so wonderfully well, and it must be a great joy to your Mother also. I imagine that you are well on with the work on the third set of four volumes by this time.

My edition of Synge's "Deirdre" which was printed months ago, has not been bound yet because I have not had the time or strength to attend to it, though I hope to do so from week to week, but it seems that I have to attend to everybody-else's business but my own.

There is an exhibition of twelve paintings by Manet here at Durand-Ruel's Gallery, nine oils and three pastels. James Huneker is raving about them and has written to me twice to go to see them and to buy one at least as a "foundation for a collection of modern painters." But just at present my exchequer cannot afford a Manet.[12]

But it is 11:15 and I must stop or it will be too late for the letter to catch tomorrow's steamer. A man who knew me some time ago has just said that I "didn't look as fat as I used to," and that I "must be working too hard." I told him that I was never fat, and that as for work I was used to it.

This is not the kind of letter I wanted to write, but I have kept hoping that I would feel in the mood for writing a really cheerful letter. I am going to stay quiet over Sunday, and by Monday I shall feel fit again. The doctor says I am O.K. now.

I hope this will find you quite well and not working too hard, and above all not worrying over your work.

Mrs. Pissarro's friend, Mrs. Wollerson, wrote me inviting me to dinner the day I came back. I had to decline the invitation. I went out to see them for a half an hour on Sunday afternoon. She is a very pleasant woman. They are in an apartment overlooking

Riverside Drive, not far from Mrs. Gilman's place. I promised to call again, but have not called there or anywhere else since.

I asked one of the men to send you a short notice by Huneker on Shaw's last book. The way Shaw lectures the English public is collossal.

This letter will be taken to the sub-station so that it will be sure to catch the mail.

Faithfully yours
[handwritten:]

Your letters have been beautiful. I could not write such letters [?] the word "happy" doesn't sound happy to me these days. But I didn't mean to write this. Good night and pleasant dreams.

John.

* * *

[May Morris to Quinn, from 8 Hammersmith Terrace, 5 April 1911.][13]

I should be disappointed if you did <u>not</u> write about yourself, indeed, dear John.

I am grieved you have been so out of sorts and overworked. But what is to be said? You imagine your dear self "obliged" to give up health and everything that goes to make a reasonable life, for the one thing—business. It is no good expostulating; it is obvious, however precious you are to your friends, they are not precious to you. One knows the terrible exacting impersonal egotism of Business, that sacrifices and belittles everybody, everything.

What sort of meaning has the word "happy" to <u>me</u> now, do you think? I want when this work of mine is finished, to be allowed to die quietly. You brought me to life, and then . . . ? My heart is breaking. It makes no difference, though; think of me loving and blessing you.

Get well, my dear.

May.
My poor letters!

* * *

[Quinn to May Morris, 8 August 1911.]
Dear Miss Morris:
I have just cabled you as follows:

"Writing tonight."

I have been away for the past five days and found your cable of August 2nd, marked "Personal" at my apartment on my return. I am glad you marked the cables personal.

I have been worried about my missing letter. I wrote by the boat sailing Wednesday May 31, or if it missed that boat it should have gone by the next steamer. I know it was properly addressed, because I addressed it myself. My Japanese servant got to be impossible and I had to dismiss him. He had been ill, and, as if I had not enough to do, I had to send him to a hospital. He was away nearly two weeks. About a week after he came back I had to dismiss him for good cause and for two weeks I had no one, but most of that time I was away. Now I have a Chinaman. He seems honest but does not know his way about yet.

I never get any letters at my apartment. When the servant is not in [,] the letters are all left in the hall below on a bench, and anyone could take them easily or they might be mislaid or lie about for days, especially if I am away and the servant not there all the time when I am away. For these reasons, may I suggest that you send any letters to my office, 31 Nassau Street. The managing clerk never opens any letter marked personal. I must repeat in this some of the things I wrote of before. First, the beautiful reproduction of the Rossetti drawing came safely. It is perfectly charming, and I am obliged to you for sending it. Also the 4 Vols. 5 to 8, of the collected edition came and are on my table. The 8 volumes make a fine appearance and the complete set will be a noble one in every way, a worthy monument to your devotion to your father's memory. I am glad also to have the copies of the various reviews that you sent. But for your thoughtfulness I should have seen none of them, because I have not bought for myself a copy of the Saturday or Athenaeum, which I used to see regularly in months.

Alas, as to the new four volumes, I opened (cut) the pages but I have not had the strength or zest to do more than dip into the introductions. I have kept them on the table for the time when I should enjoy reading every word.

I also received the proofs of the introductions to Vols. 7 and 8 and the proofs of the portraits, all in good condition.

And now I come to what I do hate to write about. I wrote you fully after I got out after the attack of grippe, one night at the Bar Association, and your letter in reply to that was pitched in such a key, was so unnecessarily tragic, that I made up my mind not to write about my health again. There is just one thing that annoys me with my sister in the convent, her constant writing and appeals about my health. My other sister knows that I always try to get a good doctor, a specialist, if necessary, and that I act in my own case just as I would in a law case, see that the best counsel is retained and all the facts known, and so she does not annoy one. But to tell a man not to worry, is like telling one not to get mad. I made a mistake after I had the grippe of having to get back to work too soon. The result is still felt in lack of energy, a sense of weariness and fatigue when a certain point is reached, and a state of nerves that at times is hard to control. I have been driven and harassed and annoyed to the limit, and at times almost beyond reason. I don't know when I have felt easy and free: I seemed at times to be like a clock wound up so tight that it could not run. And law work has not let up; illness in the office, personal worries, financial matters, and the loss of my best client, necessitating a complete re-adjustment in my office and the cutting down of expenses—these are a few hints of what I write only to let you know why I have been in no mood to read or enjoy anything.

This is a poor letter to write and I shall be glad if you will let me know that you have torn it up.

As to a vacation, it is all uncertain. As I think I often said to you, I can make no plans, hardly for a dinner engagement. (Do you wonder I ask you to tear this up?) If I can make some arrangement for scaling down expenses here, and dismiss two or three expensive but really inefficient men, and get one good man at two-thirds the salary of the three, I may be able to get away for a few days in the course of the next two or three weeks. If I can't do that (and I am thinking of these things all the time) then I must snatch what rest I can from Fridays to Mondays and hope to get abroad for ten days or so late in October. So far I have not been out of the city a single Sunday for rest, but I have had to do a lot of travelling. Thursday night I leave for Portland, Maine, where I have a law case on Friday and Saturday, and that means all night on the train and all night Saturday returning. Thank God, I will have Sunday here to sleep; but Monday we are in court here on the same matter. Slowly I am beginning to catch up—each day I hope to advance or finish one thing, but interruptions are constant and harassing. Lawyers must all go to heaven when they die, most of them have such a hell on earth.

If there is anything definite about my getting abroad I ought to know it in about two weeks and I shall then write again. But please do not think of altering any plans of yours. I can make no plans.

You ought to be very proud and happy over the splendid reviews your stately volumes have been receiving.

This letter is dictated at my office and it is now 10:30 P.M. It will be brought up town where I am to meet a man, and I will sign it some time after 12 o'clock, but however late, it will go on tomorrow's boat.

I hope this will find you quite well and enjoying the labor of love on your Father's books. Good-night.

Faithfully yours,

* * *

[Quinn to May Morris 19 August 1911.]

Dear Miss Morris:

I received your letter of 4th August the early part of this week.

I have been so dreadfully driven this week that I have had no time at my apartment even to look at the manuscripts, but I will get them out on Monday or Tuesday without fail and will have them carefully packed and perhaps put in a zinc-lined case, so that they would not be injured by water or dampness, and sent to you. I note that you would like the MSS. of the "Aeneid" and also of the "Odyssey" and also of "The House of the Wolfings" and "The Glittering Plain." If I can be certain by the beginning of next week that I am going abroad for even a little while, I might take them with me, although if I go abroad now it will be chiefly because I have to see two clients on two very important matters, one of which will necessarily take me to Paris for two or three days and one to Switzerland for two or three days. I don't care for Paris this time of year, and with the heat that we read about here it must be hot, dusty, dirty, and rotten in the summer time. If the strike is over in England by next week and if I sail, which depends on two cables that I am waiting to receive, I may go on one of the English lines.[14] But I should not think of taking the Cunard or White Star Lines or any of those lines if the strike is still on in England. I don't want to be marooned at Fishguard or Liverpool or any other place. If I sail soon I think I should take one of the German boats or the French boats. But it is all uncertain. If I don't sail next week I shall send the manuscripts.

Mrs. P's[15] remark was as inaccurate, or as accurate, as most women are when they quote a person. Some months ago, two or three months ago at least, she wrote me about something—I have forgotten what; it may have been about her friends the Wollersens—and I recall that among other things she said there was to be an exhibition of her father-in-law's things at the Albert Hall or some other such place in London sometime in July. I sent her a line and in an unguarded moment I said that I hoped to be able to get abroad sometime about the middle or end of July. That is quite different from "she said you (I) had written a while back that you would be here in July." Besides I was quite careful to say to Mrs. P. that I wanted her to keep this in confidence, as my plans were all undetermined and that I had no time to write letters and that it bored me to have to write explaining about delays in coming and that I made no engagements, and so on. It is needless to say that I shall not refer again, ever, in writing to Mrs. P. to any of my plans, expectations or hopes.

You write in your letter about patience. But what's the use? I have been up three nights this week working until nearly two o'clock in the morning, and up again the next morning at 8:30. I was at the office of a friend of mine about ten days ago on a complicated business matter that had caused me a great deal of worry for the last two months and I was damning things and people generally. This man, who is in fact really a patient man but who never talks about it, followed me to the door and said:

> "Don't get angry. Don't let small things worry you. As long as you have your health and are free from pain and those that are dear to you have their health and are free from pain, don't let anything disappoint you or worry you."

This man's wife at that time expected to undergo an operation in a day or two. The operation was had the latter part of last week. She died this morning. He had something to worry about.

Sometime if you are in the British museum I think you would be interested in looking at "The Book-Buyer," a now defunct American magazine. The Volume is Volume XIII. The number is number 10 of Volume XIII. The month and year are November and 1896. It contains a short article on "The Personality of William Morris," only a page and a half. It is by Frederick James Gregg. He gives an account of your father's visit to Dublin and a reference to his lecture and then of how they spent the evenings in Dublin. I quote from the end of the article (page 621) as follows:

> "One remarkable thing about Morris was his method of work. While he was staying in Dublin, he retired to Mr. Walker's conservatory on

> Sunday, with a pipe and a big bag of tobacco, and spent four hours on the Odyssey, which he was then translating. At that time he never wrote any poetry on week days. Sunday was given over to the muse. This is a curious commentary on the theory that poets must wait for inspiration. During the week Morris gave so much time to designing, so much to socialism, and so much to exercise, and so on. It was owing to his methodical ways that he was able to accomplish so much. He looked on his various activities as work, which was to be done honestly and fully. Only in one thing did he seem to be without the gift of self-criticism. He failed to see that his socialistic writings were infinitely below the standard of the rest of his work."[16]

You know of course better than anyone what to think of this. I don't agree with the last two sentences. I cannot agree that "News from Nowhere" or "John Ball" were inferior to the rest of his work. The fact that your father did not re-print or re-publish half of his socialistic writings would seem to be conclusive enough that he did have the gift of self-criticism.

It must be a great pleasure to you to receive so many fine notices about your stately and beautiful edition of your father's works. The books are almost too beautiful to read. The paper is excellent; the type and page are beautiful, and the edition ought to be a success in every way. I am sending you two copies of the New York Evening Post of last week which contained a short reference to your edition.

I enclose you a letter which I received from Longmans Green in March in response to my suggestion that they send review copies to the Nation, Chicago Evening Post, etc. Young Hackett is no longer with the Chicago Evening Post, but he wrote me that if they would send the books to him he would review them.

I shall not know until I hear from the other side by cable or perhaps by letter whether I am going or when. Everything is still uncertain.

Sincerely yours,

* * *

[Quinn's secretary to May Morris, 22 August 1911.]

Dear Madam:

Mr. Quinn asked me to remind him to enclose in his letter to you of Monday a reference to the original Mss. of the "Odyssey" which he bought a few days ago from Messrs. Dodd & Livingston of this city for $700 and which he asked me to put with the other four Mss. which he was going to send you. I forgot to remind him of this. With the other four Mss. he is going to send you the following:

> "The original autograph manuscript of the first draft of Morris' translation of the "Odyssey" about 470 leaves, written on one side only. At the end are nine leaves, containing a translation of a portion of the "Iliad." "

This so far as can be traced has never been printed.

* * *

[Quinn to May Morris: Cable stating that he is sailing 23 August 1911.][17]

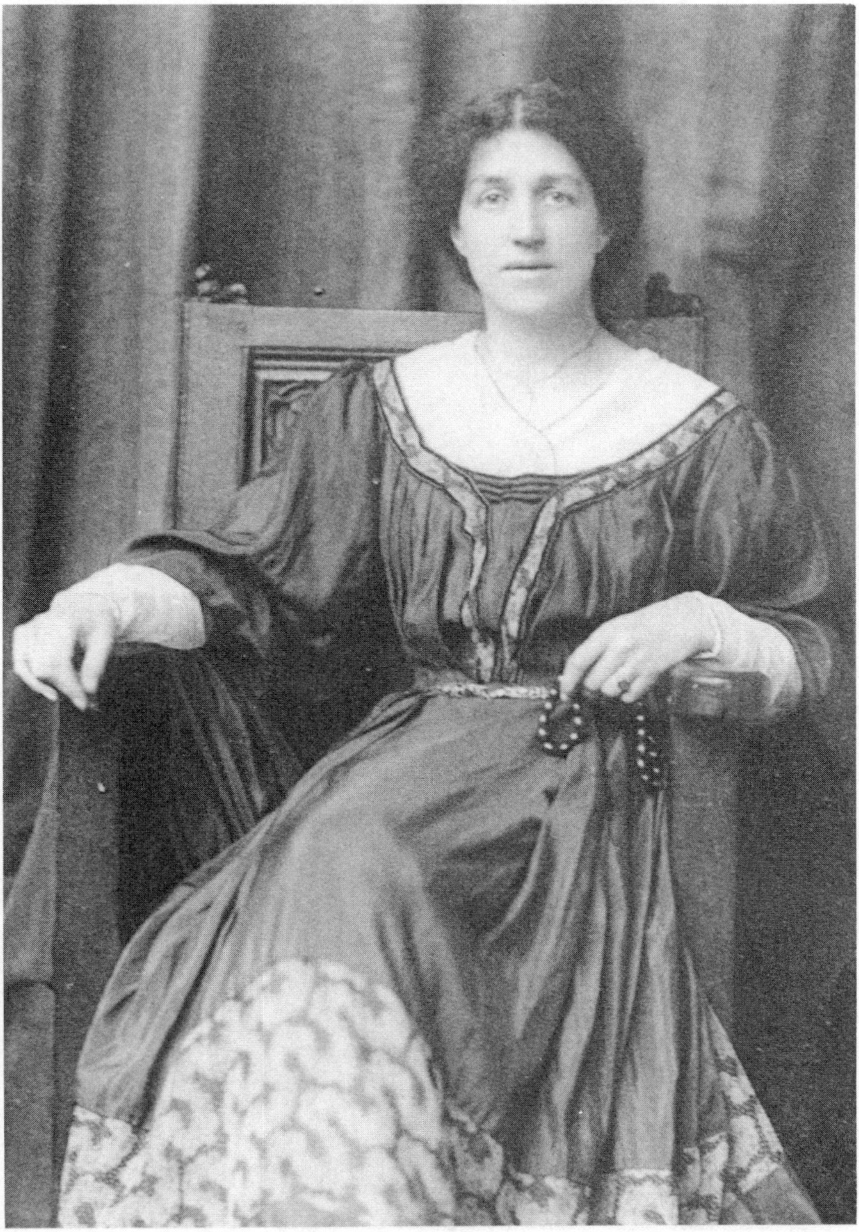

May Morris (1862–1938). This photograph was used on the cover of a leaflet advertising May's U.S. lecture tour. Photograph by G. C. Beresford. Photo used with permission of the William Morris Gallery.

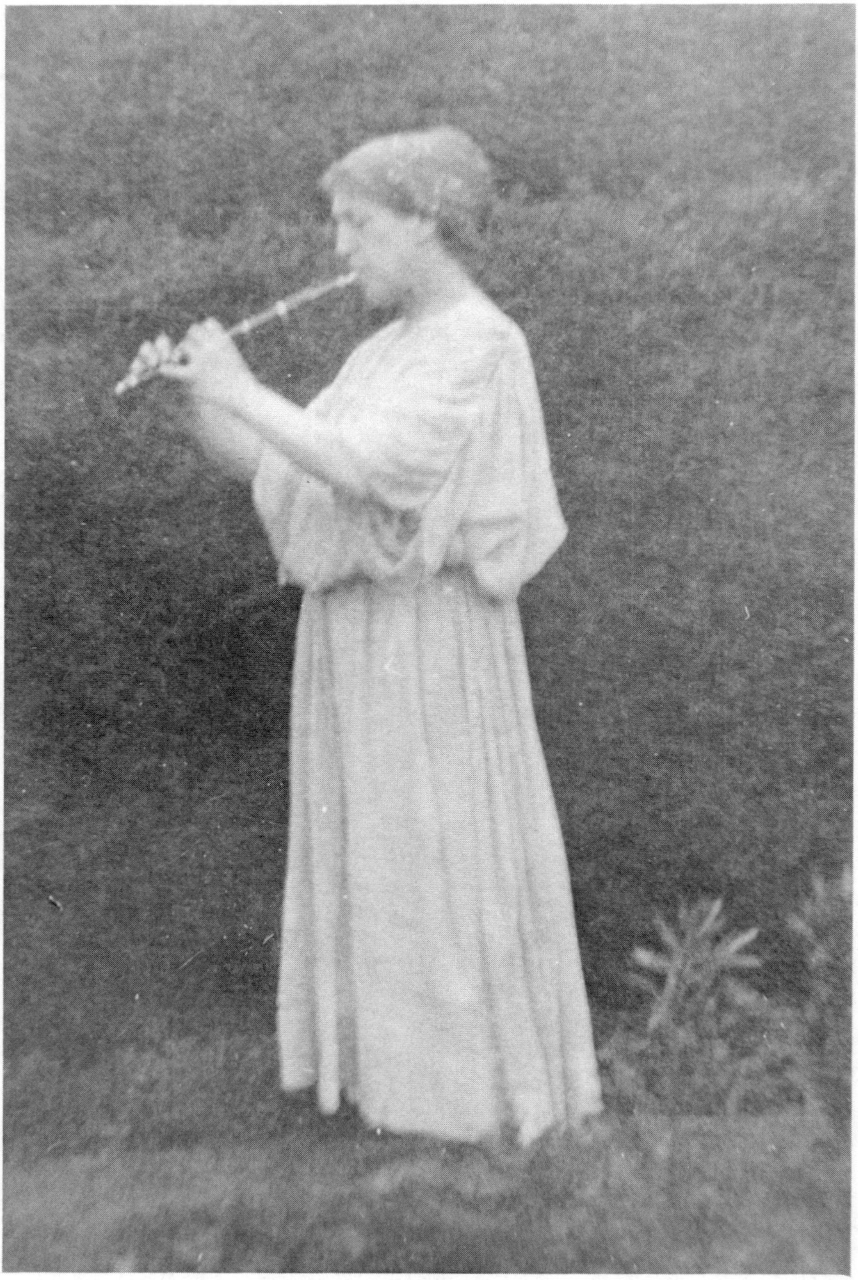

May Morris in classical costume playing a pipe or recorder, at Kelmscott Manor between c 1915–1920. Photograph used with the permission of the William Morris Gallery.

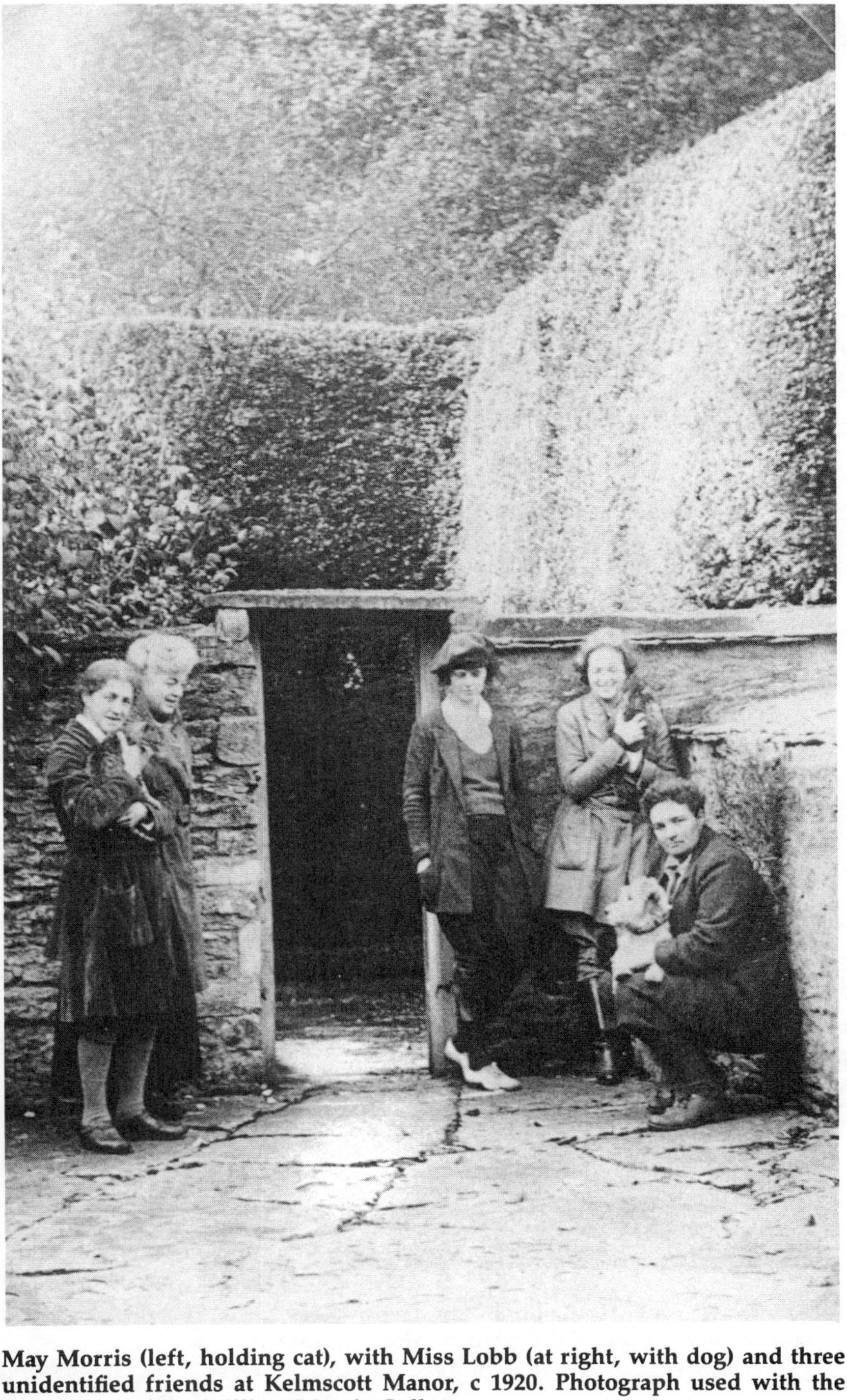

May Morris (left, holding cat), with Miss Lobb (at right, with dog) and three unidentified friends at Kelmscott Manor, c 1920. Photograph used with the permission of the William Morris Gallery.

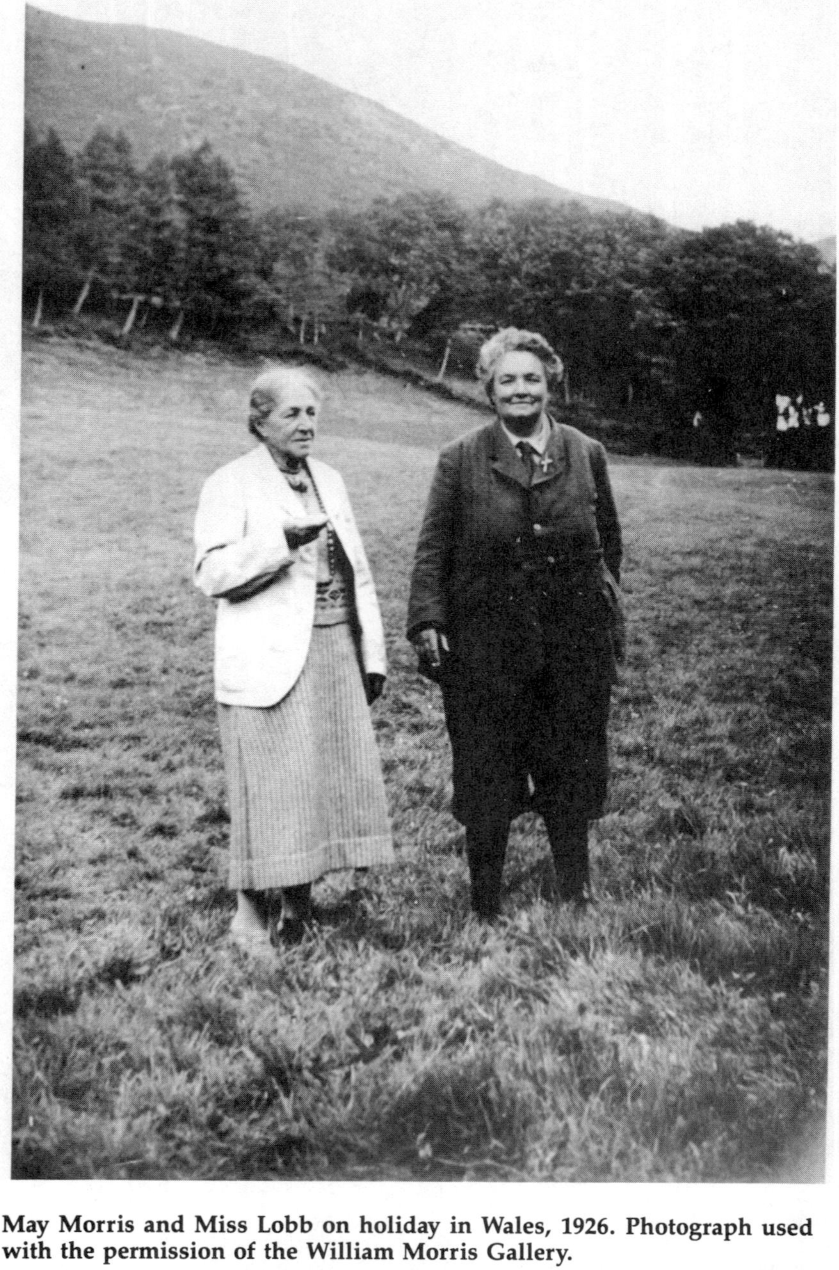

May Morris and Miss Lobb on holiday in Wales, 1926. Photograph used with the permission of the William Morris Gallery.

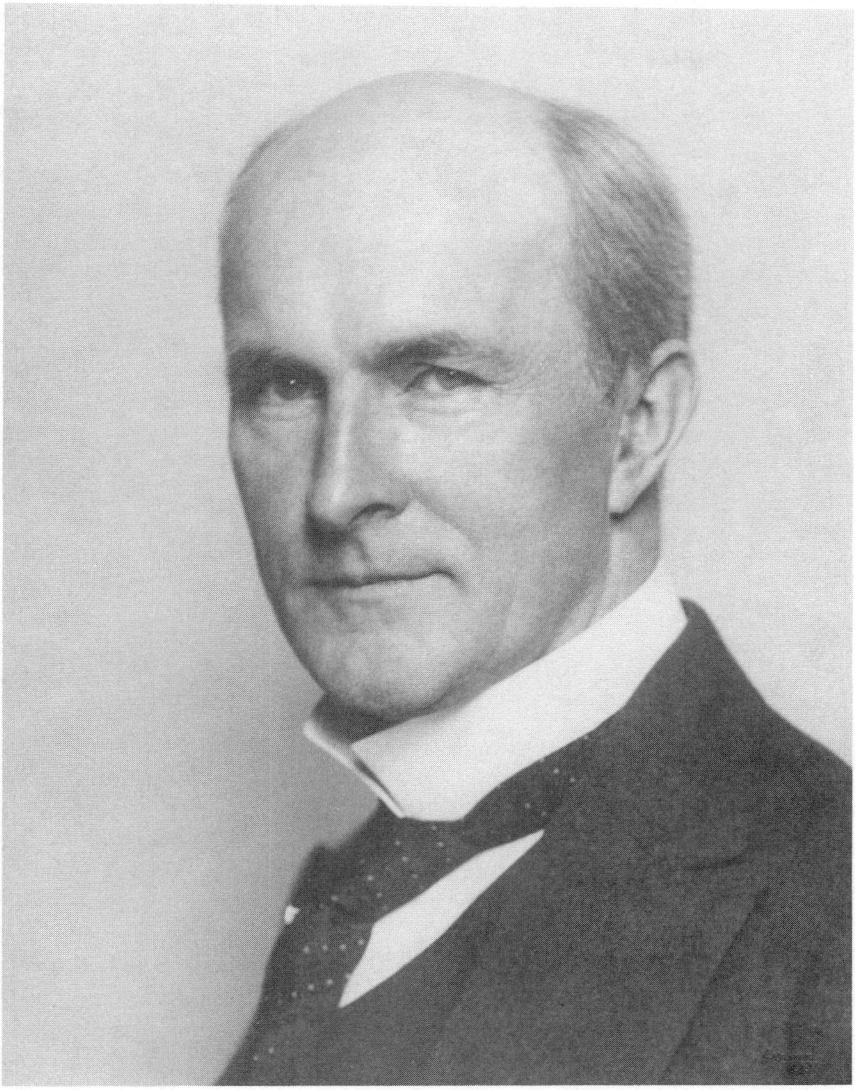

John Quinn. Photograph used with the permission of Thomas A. Conroy, Quinn's grandnephew.

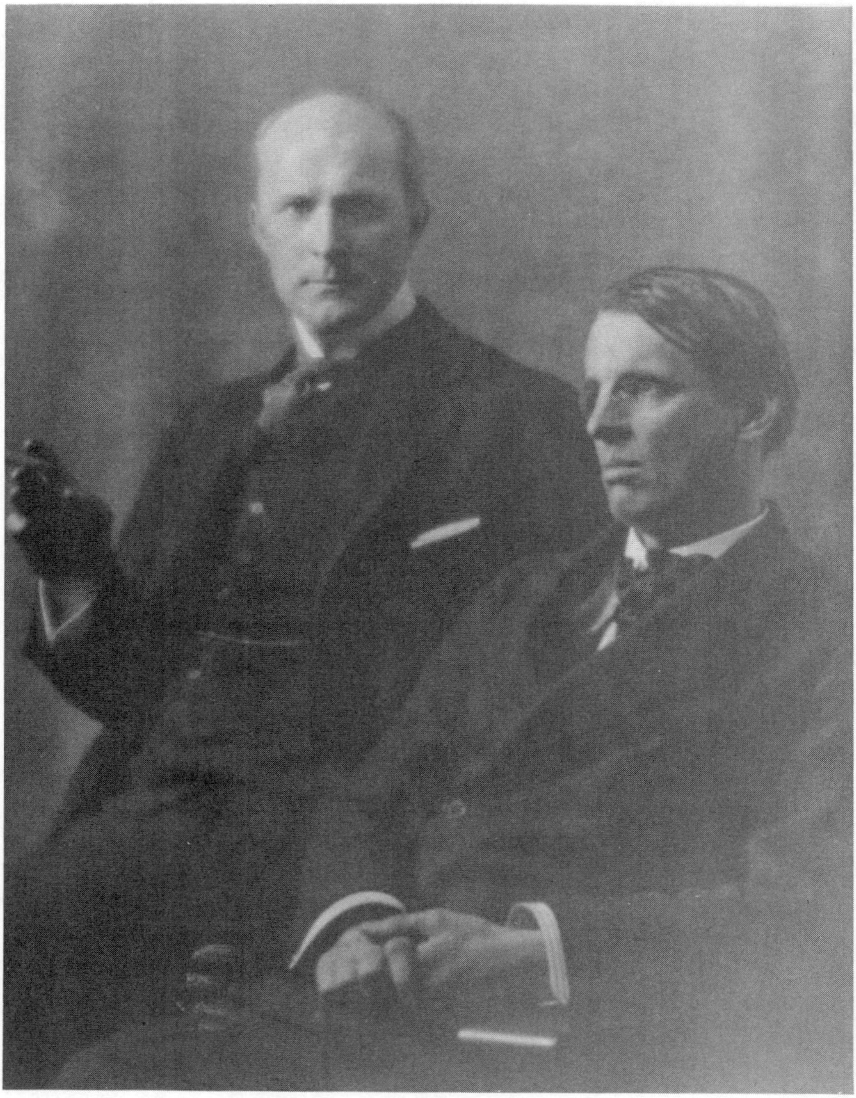

John Quinn and William B. Yeats. Photograph used with the permission of Thomas A. Conroy.

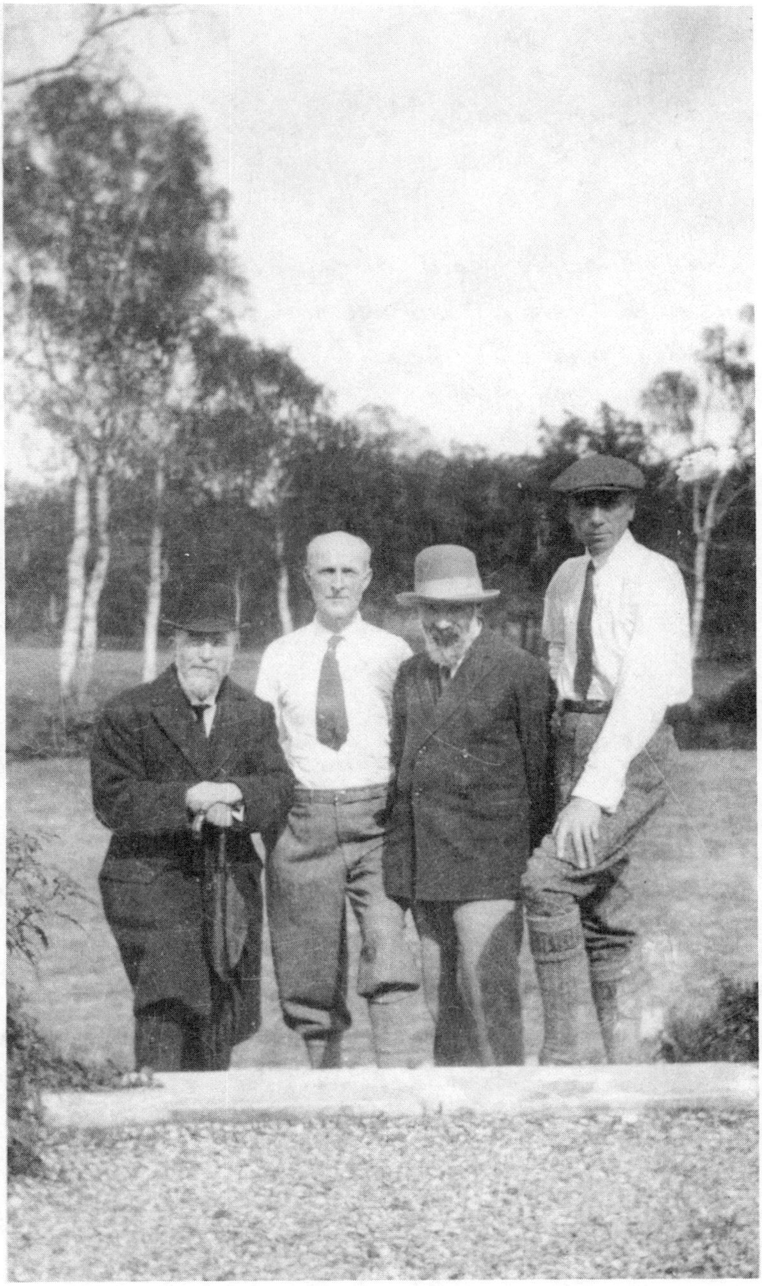

Composer Erik Satie, John Quinn, sculptor Constantin Brancusi, and novelist Henri-Pierre Roché. Photograph used with the permission of Richard Londraville.

Easter: Monday

Kelmscott Manor, Lechlade, Gloucestershire

Beloved

I was thinking hard of you all day yesterday: you just haunted me — and all night I dreamt of you (dear dreams) and this morning there was the blessed surprise of a letter.. And the parcel came too, and I have been admiring it. You know, I saw the book at their place, either finished, or a sheet of it in progress, and wanted to have it, but it was too much of a luxury. So now I have it, and you are a Dear, and needn't be told that it is twice as valuable with your name in it — printed and written. Nor need you be told how the kind inscription touched me — that it was kissed, and cried over, out of the longing to be able to take in mine the dear hand that wrote it. I have had a long close day at work (one of many, straight on) and it is ever so late, but I can't go to bed without a word of greeting and thanks for the Easter gift, as it came at Easter. I'm too tired to write sense, and must stop. I was working early in bed this morning, and can get through a good deal of proof-reading that way. There, now! a glass of milk & a pot of ink dangerously side by side — and I took up the ink-pot! Well perhaps I'll be too sleepy to lie awake in the dark and long for my friend.

Goodnight, my Dear, and bless you, bless you —

A sample of May Morris's handwriting. Collection of the Author.

3
The Letters of 1912

[Quinn to May Morris, 8 March 1912.]
Dear Miss Morris:

I received your letters and have meant to answer long ago, but it is the old story with me. One keeps putting off personal letters that one wants to write fully hoping that there will be more time, then I have so many things to write you about that I don't quite know where to begin.

I received the beautiful little Christmas card of the drawing by Burne-Jones from your father's "Love is Enough."

The four volumes of your collected edition, 9, 10, 11, and 12 were delivered to me by Longmans some three or four weeks ago. I also received the beautiful extra illustrations for those volumes which you sent and also your separate prefaces. I think my prefaces now down to and including volume 12 are complete. I am keeping them all together and when the set is complete I am going to have them all bound as beautifully as they can be bound.

I enjoyed very much your letter from Stratford and am glad to know that you had such a pleasant time there.

The photograph of Stratford, the river and the theatre which you sent with New Year's greeting is post-marked Stratford and the queer thing is your cable is post-marked London. I daresay you had filed the cable before. I am glad to know that you enjoyed the pippins.

Spring must be beginning to show itself at Kelmscott now, and it must be pleasanter for you to be there than in London. Everybody says they have had fearful weather in London this winter, cold and damp and rainy. The news from England about the strike is not very cheering. I suppose it will all come out in the end and there has been so much of that sort of thing lately that one does not think that any fresh strike, no matter what its magnitude, is the beginning of the end.

I presided some three or four weeks ago at a socialist debate at the New Rochelle forum. The debate was between Attorney General Carmody, Attorney General of New York State, and Morris Hilquit, who is perhaps the leading American socialist.[1] It was rather a long debate, lasting over two hours. I got a letter from Mrs. John Sloan, the wife of the artist John Sloan, who is a very zealous socialist, saying that they all thought that I made a good chairman and that I didn't take sides and didn't make speeches.[2]

With me it has been nothing but work and a great deal of traveling. I have been to Washington several times and Chicago and Boston. Each time I thought that when I got away from the office I would have time to write a letter and each time I was so driven that I could not find time to write.

I have got through the winter without a severe cold, with the exception of an attack of rheumatism which laid me up for several days. The only thing that did me any good was hot bags of salt on my chest and good sweating. The pain was very acute in the muscles of the right side. If I had not known something about medicine one night when the pain was very severe I would have thought I had pneumonia. The pains were quite sharp, like pneumonia pains. For two or three days it was hard for me to take a breath and painful to move. The doctor put me on a very wholesome and nutritious diet of half milk and half Vichy. After two or three days the pain went away and although I was a little weak it left no bad effects.

I wanted to write you more fully about your introductions but I can't do it today. I expected to get this letter dictated yesterday but other things came up and prevented. It may seem strange to you but I have worked, or been in conference, or been busy on things every Sunday and every holiday since I came back. I didn't even get out to Ohio for Christmas or New Year. I stopped off at Ohio a day on my way to Chicago but was unable to get away then because I had law business in Cleveland.

I got the Quarterly Review with the splendid article about your father in it.[3] In fact I picked up another copy before you sent yours but that was a copy with the American cover. I have sent the copy with your name on it to the binders to have a slip-case made for it.

It seems to me that as you go on the introductions become richer and better. The illustrations for volumes 9 and 12 are, I think, finer than the earlier ones.

I was very glad to get the catalogue of the John things. John cabled me that he reserved three of the paintings for me at £450. I cabled back that I didn't want them, that I would rather have one of his larger and more important works. I did that because at that time I felt that I could not afford £450, which is $2250. I told you in London that I thought I had secured his large White City painting "The Way down to the Sea." I had seen it in his studio two years ago when he painted my portrait. I told him then that sometime I felt he would carry it further and that I would like to have it. He did carry it further, writing me in the spring that he thought it was very fine and that if I wanted it he would let me have it for £400. I then sent him £100 on account. In justice to him I should say that I owed him more than £400 for some previous work. John inadvertently in sending the picture to the gallery unfortunately put a price of £500 on it and in confidence, Madame Strindberg, the divorced wife, or a divorced wife, or one of the divorced wives of the Swedish dramatist Strindberg sent £100 to the Secretary of the exhibition and secured the picture. John cabled me about it. I was very much upset over it. By all the rules of the game the picture should have been mine. She is nothing but a dealer anyway and is buying it for a profit. Later on John and I got her to relinquish her claim. It is a long story, too long to write. The fact is that she wrote John a letter enclosing a letter to the Secretary of the exhibition relinquishing her claim. Then I thought it was mine for the second time. Later on in December John cabled that the woman had claimed it, that he consulted Marchant of the Chenil Gallery and that Marchant had advised him that she had the prior claim. That disappointed me of course very much. Lately I have had a letter from him saying that he thinks he can get it again. I am rather sorry that I didn't buy two or three of his paintings. They had reserved for me two or three of the drawings in the exhibition that you saw. John has always been praised as a great draughtsman but now he is going towards color. He is a great artist and if he doesn't break down and if he keeps his health he will do bigger and finer things than he has ever done. The very fact that people fight over him shows that he is a real force.[4]

I received the little book of the French Impressionists. I already had a copy of it in the regular series sold here in America, bound in red, but I have kept yours in my bedroom and have been rereading it as a whole. It is one of the best that has been published and the illustration is very good.[5] I saw some beautiful Renoirs in Paris at the apartments of Durand-Ruel.[6] In fact, what I saw of Renoir there was a revelation to me of his wonderful skill as a colorist.

You promised me in one of your earlier letters to send me a

description of your African trip but it has never come. Perhaps you have not had time to write it out. If you have not written it out please don't go to the trouble of doing it now. If you have made a memorandum of it and will send it to me I will be glad to return it after I have read it.

Now I come to something that may shock you, and that is that I am tempted to sell my manuscripts. I mean those that I purchased, nothing that was given to me. In confidence, a dealer who buys for a man who is collecting things to found a library approached me with an offer for the manuscripts. The man is H. E. Huntington, but this is in confidence. He is an uncle or related in some way to Archer Huntington, whom you met here. He is collecting books to found a great library in California and the manuscripts will go into it.[7] I had hoped that the manuscripts would not be sold in my time but for financial reasons I have decided if I get a fair offer for them as a whole I will sell them. Last summer before I went abroad I did not want to run the risk of theft or fire by leaving the manuscripts in my apartment so I had them sent to the Mercantile Safe Deposit Company which was on the ground floor of the Equitable building. The dealer spoke to me about selling them early in December. By the greatest good fortune I had them removed from the safe deposit vault (they were in a big steel box) two weeks before the Equitable fire. You can imagine what my worry and anxiety would have been if they had been in the fire particularly as they were not protected as well as the securities in the steel boxes. Many of those securities, stocks and bonds, were so heated that they were practically worthless and part of the legal work that I have had since has been in connection with the issuance of new securities and stocks and bonds for a Trust Company for which a client of mine acts as transfer agent.

I felt that these manuscripts would be much higher in years to come but I never thought I would sell them. I have a good deal of money locked up in them, particularly some Meredith and Swinburne things that I bought in the last two years, and they are bringing in no income. I told the dealer that five of the manuscripts were on the other side. He asked me to give him a brief description of them. The ones I sent you were "The Glittering Plain," "The House of the Wolfings," "Aeneid of Virgil," "The Odyssey" (the bound volume), and the two slip-cases with the first draft of "The Odyssey" and the "Iliad."

I told him that if you still wanted to keep them I could not sell them except subject to delivery when you were quite through with them. I am having the men in the office go through the files and get out what descriptions I have of the manuscripts so that I can have a typewritten list of the descriptions made. If you have the manuscripts with you at Kelmscott I should be glad if you would let me know the number of pages in the bound volumes and the number of pages in the slip-cases containing the first drafts of the Odyssey.

If anything should happen to me it would be just a chance whether the manuscripts would be well handled or not and whether they would bring decent prices. One or two men only might bid on them and the prices might be slaughtered. If I can persuade the man to let me have the time on the matter I will try to give a little attention to the description of the different manuscripts and then put it in book form and have a little volume printed of the manuscripts in my possession, a little souvenir.[8]

My regret at losing the manuscripts is tempered a little by the fact that they will not be locked up or be the property of any one individual. Huntington is buying to establish a big library in California. They would be safe—safer than they would be in the hands of any one individual.

Please don't mention Mr. Huntington's name to anybody in connection with the matter. If other dealers heard that he was in the market for manuscripts he would be flooded with offers of large and small lots and that might interfere with this transaction.

I have done very little reading of any kind this winter. In fact I have had very little time to read except occasionally late at night when I have read myself to sleep, propped up in bed, which is about the only time I get now to read.

Rothenstein was here and had an exhibition of his things.[9] Between ourselves, he did only fairly well. The same gallery had an exhibition of Conder's work.[10] They sold only two or three things. I had most of Rothenstein's lithographs, bought years ago when they were first published. I dropped in there one morning and bought a few more. I bought eight or nine Conder lithographs which strange to say sold for not much more than I could have bought them for when they were exhibited in the Bond Street gallery in London. These and two small Chinese paintings, which I bought, are the only new things that I have got.

The moving into my new apartment was very expensive. I had to get draperies for the five front windows and the hallway and I learned for the first time what interior decorations might cost. These draperies were very plain but they did cost. Then I got a piano for the middle room. Now I wish I could play it, but alas, my education in many directions has been neglected. It is a Steinway piano, what they call a Grand piano, and I got it with a discount and on easy terms of payment extending over a year and a half.

The Gothic chest came all right. I thought I might use it as a sort of a table for hats and wraps in the hallway-entrance to the apartment, but I found it a little too narrow for that purpose. It is about six feet long, about eighteen inches wide and about two feet and a half high. It really is out of place in an apartment. The apartment originally had four bedrooms. I have one and there is a spare bedroom. The other two bedrooms in the rear I have lined with books and pictures. This I call the study although I am very seldom there. The chest is there but it looks out of place. It is, I think, genuine Gothic and ought really to be in a country house. Would you have room for it at Kelmscott, or would you have room for it in your London house?[11] I should be delighted to send it to you if you would care for it or have a place for it in either place. I could sell it of course but I don't want to do that.

Please don't mention to anybody what I have written about the John White City picture. I may possibly get it yet but if I don't I don't want to have him feel that I have talked or written about it to anyone else.

I will send this letter to Kelmscott as I assume you are still there. I hope it will find you well and not working too hard and not worrying about the work.

Faithfully yours,

* * *

[Quinn to May Morris, 14 March 1912.]
Dear Miss Morris:

I omitted to acknowledge the other day "The Athenaeum" of December 30th, sent by you, containing the review of Volumes IX to XII of your edition of your father's works. I also want to thank you for sending me the Times Literary Supplement of November 16th containing the review of Rolleston's book of Celtic Myths, which he sent me.[12]

In one of Maggs Brothers' catalogues sometime ago, (catalogue No. 272, item No. 660, page 56) there was a description of the original autograph manuscript of "The Story of the Glittering Plain." This is described as

> "Very neatly written in two manuscript volumes and comprising some 179 4to *[sic]* pages, in addition to numerous autograph notes,

etc., written on the reverse of some of the pages. Also (written inside the cover of the first volume) the original autograph manuscript of his Poem, 'The Briar Rose,' comprising some fourteen lines. The two volumes in a morocco case."

The price was £250.

This, I take it, is the first draft by your father of what became the final manuscript, which belongs to me and which you now have, just as the two volumes of the "Odyssey," which you also have from me, were the first draft of the final manuscript which Dodson got and which I sent to you.

I paid £150 to Dodd Mead & Company of this City for the first draft of the "Odyssey." I think £250 is rather high for the first draft of the "Glittering Plain." But if I could have afforded it I would have bought it of them. I daresay it has been sold. It appeared in a catalogue which I got some time in November or December. As it has not appeared in any of the subsequent catalogues, I daresay they have sold it. I have written to them to ask them to let me know whether they have sold it, and if so to whom. If they send me the name of the purchaser I will let you know.

Your ninth, tenth, eleventh, and twelfth volumes have taken their place with the first eight and they look very handsome indeed. I was a little afraid that you were too chary of trenching on Mackail's ground. The description in your introduction to Volume IX of your father's decoration of decorated books and manuscripts was very exciting and interesting, and the description of the manuscripts made by him was new and I think wonderfully well done. I think the introduction to Volume IX is one of the best of the whole series. The introduction to Volume X is interesting, but not so interesting as that to Volume IX. But the description of the visit to the Belgian towns is charmingly done.

The impression that you give in your introduction to Volume XI of the wonderful versatility and tremendous work of your father is, I think, just and very well done and your description of the changes in the firm is to say the least discreet. All of the letters are interesting and the notes of the work done in that single week show what a tremendous genius your father was. All of the descriptions about the ornamentation of his beautiful books are exceedingly interesting and I am sure will be generally enjoyed.

I was especially struck by what you say in your introduction to Volume XII about your father's views of Wagner. The idea does seem absurd of "a sandy-haired German tenor tweedle-deeing over the woes of Sigurd." One has got to forget a good many things though to enjoy opera. Strangely enough, the dragon has always been an absurdity to me, looking to me like the front end of one of our New York subway trains with its two headlights and shrieking and roaring.

I have felt the same way that you write your father felt in regard to Beethoven's and Bach's and Chopin's music being played as an accompaniment to Isadora Duncan's dancing. And I felt the same thing when I heard that Millet's son in Paris some years ago had been making some tableaux of his father's paintings with musical accompaniment.

I used to have time to drop in to the International News Company and get copies of The Athenaeum and The Saturday Review and others. But I have not been able to do that for months now. I used to occasionally have time to read The Saturday Review at the Club. But even that little recreation I have not had time for for some months, and so I feel out of touch with things.

Sincerely yours,

P.S. 4:30 P.M.

This letter was dictated yesterday. There was handed to me in court this morning your cablegram "Please write." It was dated from London but signed "Kelmscott." I dictated on the telephone from the court the following cable "Wrote last week." I sent this to you at Kelmscott, the address of this letter, and hope that you will receive the cable.

I have been very much driven lately because Mr. Shoemaker has been under the weather. He is not in the office today and the man who has been assisting me also happens to be ill.

I have had no time yet to do any work on preparing a description of the manuscripts. The agent who has been to me about the matter is pressing me for the list, stating that if it is not delivered soon the chance will go by.

I was told this morning in leaving my apartment that my servant, a China man whom I have thought to be absolutely honest, was seen taking silver out of the place. I am having a list of the silver made and I will have to have it checked off. If he has been pawning or selling the silver of course I will have to discharge him. It is rather upsetting for one to feel that he has been harboring a thief. One of the stenographers has just told me that when the man came to the office yesterday to get his wages he saw him with a couple of pieces of silver and he asked what he was doing with them and the China man said he was taking them to be repaired.

I think the winter here is at last broken. There has been terrific rains and a lot of railroad wrecks, two the day before yesterday, one the Twentieth Century from Chicago, just above Poughkeepsie. I always urge my friends never to travel in this country except in Pullman cars and always to travel toward the middle or toward the end of the train. The all-steel Pullman cars at any rate do away with one ghastly result of wrecks, that of fire, so that if a person escapes the wreck they generally get out all right.

I hope this will find you well and not working too hard.

Sincerely yours,

* * *

[May Morris to Quinn, from Kelmscott Manor, Lechlade, 26 March 1912.]

My Own Dearest:

I received your first precious letter on the 17th St. Patrick's Day, and the next last Sunday, 24th, my Father's birthday. Bless you, dear; I have no time to purr over you, because I meant to write last night, and behold, a young man—a Birmingham Poet—whom out of sheer good-nature I allowed to come here on pilgrimage, came late, wasted all my time, had to be dry-nursed and shown his way out of the village by moonlight, and then I was what Father would have called 'bed-ripe'. And I had no idea it would take so long to describe your M.S.S. slightly, and if I don't send today from Kelmscott, I shall miss tomorrow's mail. I am sorry, dear. I have only the Wolfings and the rough drafts of Odyssey here. Going through the latter, I thought it was necessary to note the missing bits. Now I haven't time to compare the Iliad fragment with the Greek text, I mean so as to correct the lines, but I suppose this will do for the moment. My Secretary, whom I can trust, was to count the pages etc. of the M.S.S. I left at Hammersmith Terrace, and I should have heard from her this morning, in time for the mail: but you know, we are in a distressingly disorganised state over here, and one doesn't know from day to day what is developing.

I will take the first opportunity of returning the box of M.S.S. but for the moment am so hard-worked that I do not see how I can get to town for the purpose. I always hoped I should bring them back in person, coming over myself. If it is necessary you should have them, cable, dear John, and you may depend upon me for seeing to it without delay. You may be very sure I shall mention nothing about it to Walker or anyone. Besides the fact that according to your request, I am very careful how I mention you at all, I am not likely to mention this impending sale . . . To the people who owe America a grudge for buying so many of our treasures, I have the ready retort, "At any rate, I know folk over there who are not millionaires, who buy, and make some sacrifice to do so, and who never part with their things". . . . I am not going to pretend I am not distressed; it was such a comfort to feel that these precious M.S.S. were in your hands and no one else's. . . . Puzzled, too, because you tell me at the same time of purchases of pictures and so on. Well—let us hope the Museum will not sell to some private individual—and so on, and so on.

I am making enquiries about the G. Plain M.S. you describe—am asking a business-friend of mine who understands M.S.S. old and modern to go to Maggs and report on it if still there. It seems to me it certainly ought to go with the others, but the price is high. I am wondering if I get any definite news of it, if it would be worth while cabling. I shall see.

About cables—I don't care to cable from here, much: one thing it is three miles and we have had floods and torrents day after day, and my messenger is a small boy—but principally because the P.O. people at Lechlade are shocking gossips, and it is simpler to send the cable in a letter to my secretary, who has to know your address, in case I died suddenly (I hope I shall, I'm not going on for ever, so), when she has all instructions as to returning your box of M.S.S. I fear the last cable with its Personal was a worry to you, and very sorry I am it should have annoyed you—but, I'm not going to formally apologize because I refrained from asking for news till the very last moments I could endure much longer really.

I will write a day or two later, but this must go, now. The nice dear kind things you say about my work give me more pleasure than I can say. John, I never longed for anything in life as I long to see you.

Here is a violet for a kiss.

Yes, I should like your chest that we bought together, but surely you can find a place for it. Or why don't you care to sell it, silly?

The mail goes.

Yours Always
May

I'll tell you about work in next letter. Yesterday my birthday.

[Enclosed in May Morris's hand:]
William Morris M.S.S

One of the cases contains a letter from W. M. not important or bearing on the M.S.S.

Draft of Odyssey in two cases:

A)	7 folios foolscap	1 Book I line 1–30	
		2 Book I line 126–170	(recto & verso)
		3 Book II line 97–170	(recto & verso)
		4 Book II line 171–246	(recto & verso)
		5 Book II line 247–282	recto
		line 321–352	verso
		6 Book II line 353–392	recto
		line 283–320	verso
		7 Book II line 393–344	
		Book III line 1–4	
B)	small quarto note book	Book III line 5–end of Book V	
C)	larger quarto note book	Book VI line 1–XI line 144	
D)	larger quarto note book	Book XI line 145–XV 104	

Note: book XIV finishes at line 523 (end of a phrase), book XV lines 1–10 missing.

E)	larger quarto note book	Book XV line 105–XXI 188

Note: book XV line 553–558, book XVI 1–41 missing: equals two leaves gone.

F)	larger quarto note book	Book XXI [?] 209–end of poem

Note: book XXI lines 188–208 missing. Book XXIII 369–373, book XXIV 1–34 missing.

In C there is a very rough sketch on the verso of one page of the White Horse hill, Berkshire near Kelmscott; In E a sketch of the axe with a hole thro' it (XIX 570).

<u>The House of the Wolfings</u> 2 volumes in limp vellum with green ties, in cases.
<u>Vol. I.</u> The poem that appears on the title page
page 1–130
<u>Vol. II.</u> Page 131 (chap. XVI) to end.
All very clean and fresh, except the title page poem which is on inferior paper, and page i, which is slightly dim—not stained.

<u>The Iliad</u> begins right away in volume F. of the note books, without heading or break
9 pages.

* * *

[Quinn to May Morris, 28 March 1912.]
Dear Miss Morris:

I am sending you by registered book post, under separate cover, a little book first published by your friends Mr. and Mrs. Pissarro at their press, from an edition of 125 copies, one of two on Japan paper that is bordered, with colored illustrations and ornaments designed by Mr. Pissarro and engraved by Mrs. Pissarro.[13]

When I ordered the two on Japan paper I meant one of them for you. By an oversight the Pissarros have put my name in both of them, which of course I didn't ask them to do. Mrs. Pissarro wrote me about it hoping that it didn't make any difference and of course there was nothing for me to do but to say it didn't.

I hope the little book will reach you safely.

It must be lovely at Kelmscott now. I wonder if you are still there. I assume you are and will address this letter there and the little book will also go there.

Have you Walter Crane's latest book "William Morris and other essays" published by Bell and Son? I daresay you have seen it. It has a rather good article on your father and one not quite so good on Whistler and some others.[14]

Sincerely yours,

* * *

[May Morris to Quinn, from Kelmscott Manor, Lechlade, Easter Monday 1912.]
Beloved:

I was thinking hard of you all day yesterday: you just haunted me—and all night I dreamt of you (dear dreams) and this morning there was the blessed surprise of a letter. And the parcel came too, and I have been admiring it. You know, I saw the book at their place, either finished, or a sheet of it in progress, and wanted to have it, but it was too much of a luxury. So now I have it, and you are a Dear, and needn't be told that it is twice as valuable with your name in it—printed and written. Nor need you be told how the kind inscription touched me—that it was kissed, and cried over, out of the longing to be able to take in mine the dear hand that wrote it. I have had a long close day at work (one of many, straight on) and it is ever so late, but I can't go to bed without a word of greeting and thanks for the Easter gift, as it came at Easter. I'm too tired to write sense, and must stop. I was working early in bed this morning, and can get through a good deal of proof-reading that way. There, now! a glass of milk and a pot of ink dangerously side by side—and I took up the ink-pot! Well, perhaps I'll be too sleepy to lie awake in the dark and long for my Friend. Goodnight, my Dear, and bless you, bless you—

Thursday night.

I missed Wednesday's mail, my Dear, for I have to send Tuesday from here, and I hadn't a quiet moment to myself all the day. I think I told you I am rather hard-pressed, trying to get this bunch of four volumes out: XIII to XVI, and the folk have a pleasant way of expecting all four Introductions to be got ready in a mighty hurry, as if they were a quite easy mechanical piece of book-making and could be reeled off in a few days to suit their convenience. The great nuisance is having to think of more than one volume at once—to answer questions on one volume when my mind is fixed hard on another—all of which is part of "the day's work", but it is harassing at times, and I know I'm very slow.

I'm just now on Vol. XIV, which is The House of the Wolfings, and I badly want to say something nice about the romances, without seeming to set up for a critic, or any way stepping outside my place as recorder of day to day things . . . I wish you were at hand and that one could talk it all over with you; I know you could give me some suggestions. But I must manage without. Vol. XV is the Roots of the Mountains, where I'll talk about the printing—K.P.[15] etc, and that won't be long, because it is mostly plain sailing, and has all been said. Vol. XVI is the hard one, all about the Socialist times, also Arts and Crafts,[16] and there's a good deal to say, and a good deal to leave out,—about people still alive, Hyndman[17] and so forth. And I particularly want to do that Introduction well, naturally. I'm having all I can do, collecting material, and going through letters and fragments and diaries here, and making extracts, comparing dates, trying to fix dates of certain lectures etc., etc. People wouldn't believe how long all these preliminaries take, and how much time one has to spend in mere consideration. I fancy they think one is taking one's ease, and working about 3 or 4 hours of the day! I have all things around me here, now, and the next thing will be, perhaps, I'll have to migrate back to Hammersmith, because my Mammy must surely be getting tired of London, and want to see her beautiful garden.

I wish <u>you</u> could see it: it is gay with thousands of tulips; and one specially beautiful wild tulip that my Father called the Persian tulip and that he used a great deal in designs, simply runs riot all over the beds. And from one gable window of the Tapestry Room, where I told you I worked, there is a cherry-tree standing out like white foam against a back-ground of the great grey barn in the farm-yard.

I have a guest, who is painting just now, my colleague on the Women's Guild of Arts.[18] She is doing for me a picture of Father's bedroom, and another of this room with me half in the picture, at work—her idea—, and if I like them well enough they are going to you. Indeed they were to be done for your birthday, but may not be ready. I wanted to do them myself, dear, but there is no time, and besides mine would have been but clumsy things.

I must write this in snippets, and finish it early in the morning, perhaps. It is very late now.

I was exceedingly sorry, dear John, to hear from your first letter that you had had rheumatism sharply in the winter. It is no good saying Pray save your precious health by occasional resting. Also to hear of how unsatisfactory your present business-arrangements are. Can one get rid of an unsuitable partner easily, or is it a difficult or embarrassing thing to make a change? Wouldn't a younger man be better.

Good night, dear love. I wish my wishes and prayers could help you.

Friday, near mail time.

I've had a racking time getting off proofs—there's no end to it. I had a day's holiday last week, being quite tired out and wanting fresh air. It may amuse you to hear of our simple country amusements. I think I told you in the winter of a jaunt to Stratford where we learnt Morris-dances and country dances: at Cirencester, a biggish town 15 miles off (Roman, you'll perceive, and having interesting Roman remains about) a sort of Festival or Competition of Dancing was held the other day by the same folk, and a 'team' of dancers from this village went over, and two or three of us 'gentry'. I got my guest, Miss Sloane, up somehow—she is not an early riser—by seven in the morning, and sent her off with friends who were driving, while I started on my cycle. It was a beautiful day, but with a fearful, icy, violent head wind blowing, and I hadn't ridden since last year, to speak of. But there is a sort of primitive pleasure, is there not? in battling with elements especially if one is a bit out of sorts; I got there somehow—rather dishevelled, and left far behind by the carriage-folk, but enjoying the free air, and the wide lonely country. There we were in a biggish hall, all day, watching the different teams of Morris-boys (and girls sometimes), from the villages round. It was so gay and charming: they all had distinctive dress or decoration—some very graceful and just right—others a bit 'arty' or fantastic. But you must understand that they were all villagers from the country round, and the tradition of these dances has barely died out, and has been very readily rekindled, so one felt the whole thing genuine and of the soil.[19] Some of them had plodded from their village in beautiful great yellow wagons, picked out with red, and the front of it, and the huge horses, decked with coloured ribbons—such a pretty sight, these wagon-loads of young things. We sat all day and watched and noted and prizes were given by the local Countess, and we were lunched and tea'd, and I was 'buttonholed' by one and another when discovered to be of Kelmscott; and as it grew dark, we had to break up and start home. Our Kelmscott Kids won many laurels and went back in high feather. Then the beautiful ride home—no wind, a solemn sky and glorious moon, and all down-hill, and I rode on in the serene night with all the aches of the morning ride falling off me, in a sort of pleasant dream, thinking of nothing but nice things, and therefore principally of John.

This must go, but I shall write again soon—more regularly now I know that former letters have reached. I am glad you liked the letters, and that you found them cheerful. I wish I could stretch out my hand and find yours. Here is a Violet for a kiss.

Yours May

* * *

[May Morris to Quinn, from Kelmscott Manor, Lechlade, 25 April 1912.]

Beloved John

There seems so much to say and yet I babble on so about nothing that there never seems time to say anything. No matter.

For the last week I've had frantically close days at work, and not very happy over it owing to Longman's little nagging ways that I told you of. It makes me inclined to fulfil my share of the bargain by bringing out the rest of the volumes without Introductions—which would be just what he would like: but you wouldn't Dear, would you? Oh, and to-day I've been really exasperated by the trustees of Ruskin. I had asked leave to publish 3 or 4 interesting Ruskin letters to Father, rather taking it as a matter of course (in my own mind) that they'd say Yes. Not a bit of it: a nasty, detestable letter from the man Wedderburn, refusing, and expressing surprise I hadn't handed the letters over for the Ruskin "Life" (Cook).[20] I'm all the more annoyed because recently Sally Norton asked leave to publish a letter of my Father's to hers in a

Life she is doing, and the letter is a very important one I ought to have had. I wrote cordially, however, and gave permission (by Mr. Walker's advice) feeling I couldn't well refuse the daughter of an old friend. Well, so it seems that is Quixotic, for the daughter of an old friend of Ruskin's—nearer than Charles Norton—can be refused in curt terms.[21]

We are having some very fine illustrations shortly—a lovely head of mother, another very early one of Father—exquisite—and a wonderful drawing of Philip Webb's of the grave.[22]

Such extraordinary midsummer weather it is here now—ever since the Eclipse—brilliantly hot, yet with all the fresh charm, the jewel-like quality of Spring; the little orchard is a very bower of apple-blossom and to-day I saw the first purple-red rose upon the Tapestry Room wall. I walked with a friend by the river this evening to admire the wild crab-apple blossom in the hedges, and look for the early May. On your birthday, my dear, I found the very first May, and put a spray of it and the first blue-bell beside your portrait as a greeting to you. You know why I love dark grey-blue flowers, don't you?

I am sorry Miss Sloane's Kelmscott drawings were not finished in time to send. I hope you'll like them when they come. They are really rather charming. She is a distinguished artist in her line, and a pleasant-house-mate, quiet and serene and contained. All the same I was glad to get back to my own sunny bed-room, and to be able to work as late as I like, and celebrated the licence by working hard till bed time last night. I have been sleeping in Mother's quarters, a charming blue room, with a big four-post bed hung with old chintz—It is the bed my Father was born in.

I have been looking again, dear, at your plan of the apartment. It was good of you to send it. What a magnificent hermitage! and lots of passage-room which most apartments lack. Will you let me play upon the Steinway Grand some day, John? You strange person, I did not know you had room for music in your life—I mean, enough to want it badly.

I was interested to hear of you presiding over the Socialist debate, and wish I had been there. I think I met Morris Hilquit—if not, heard about him a great deal. I quite agree with you as to the duties of a Chairman—not to take sides, or make speeches: but 'tisn't everyone who is noble enough to sink his little self to that extent!

Sweetheart, I drank your health on the 23rd—in wine made at Kelmscott and very good wine too, though the very thought of it, I daresay, makes a person of your delicate taste in such things, smile! We are quite proud of our vintage.

The other day—Sunday, it was—Miss Sloane and I had an afternoon's holiday, and went with some neighbours to visit the White Horse Hill, which is quite a historic place.[23] It is some 12 miles south from here, and I cycled and got sun burnt, and still have a red nose. I really should not like to have you see me with a scarlet nose, John! The White Horse always seems very much a part of our family life . . . My Father loved the place, and has described it in more than one of his stories. He always paid it a yearly visit, and I have done so ever since—mostly alone on my cycle, in all sorts of weather. On the low ridge of hills south of Thames Valley one can see the wide plain, blue and dreamy, a fine panorama of open country: This is the Vale of the White Horse, and beyond rise up the high chalk hills and on the side of one slope is cut the prehistoric horse, at full gallop. At the bottom of these hills is the old Roman Road, and at the top the ancient British road with a great Camp or Castle with ditches and walls and four entrances. Oh the loneliness and beauty of this ancient grass stronghold, and the remoteness of the wide green road that stretches out into the distance among the low hills! I have lain there looking up at the sky and listening to the wind singing among the bents, and feeling like the one person left alive in the world—or perhaps (according to the mood) like a 'blue Briton' (see Doughty)[24] waiting for a party of my companions to appear climbing up the [?] side with game and Morrisons.[25] I think it is one of the [?] feeling places I know, and casts a spell upon one. I would like to take you there . . . Doubtless, under the spell, you would instantly feel like an ancient Kelt—and call for your Harper. Instead of which, we are reduced to Steinway Grands . . .

Dear John, I must go to bed. I shall finish in the early hours in the morning. Good night, love; sleep well.

Friday: Good morning. Have you slept well? I had an absurdly nice dream, and on waking, lay as still as a Mouse, hoping against hope that it wasn't over yet, and that I could hold on to it a little longer: You suddenly turned up for a short stay, and I was more surprised than one usually is in dreams, and fussed over you and was very content; and you seemed to like it . . . It is queer what a startlingly clear vision I always have of you, for usually my 'personages' in dreams are so blurred and vague. My Father stands out clearly often.

Morocco: Yes I always meant to write an account of it for you, but when no news came, I kept on wondering which of my letters reached and put it off till I heard news of you. Now I keep putting it off till the less busy moment that never comes. I'll turn to before long and send a little sketch of that queer little journey.

I wonder if you happen to be in touch with the Enquiry about the Titanic disaster. I keep resolving to read no more about it, but one goes on.

I must turn on to work now—a long job that would make Longman rage, of hunting through some letters of the '80's that I've already been through, my notes having missed something.

Goodbye, Dearest. I wish you were here wandering by the riverside . . . One can't live on dreams.

More gossip soon
Yours always
May

There! just as I stop, something occurs to my mind to comment on—a pretty book this time . . . Mustn't stop though.

* * *

[May Morris to Quinn, from 8 Hammersmith Terrace, 17 July 1912.][26]

Dearest

When I read about the great Democratic Convention at Baltimore, I thought you would very likely be there. And then came your postcard—written and addressed and all by your own dear hand—which I was glad and interested to get. I hope you are not quite frizzled up by heat, nor too over-whelmed and exhausted. Mind you tell me something next time about Woodrow Wilson and what his chances are of election, and if you <u>want</u> him elected and so forth.

The Americans I am seeing now are some Book-worms and some Artists, and don't seem to follow public affairs much.

Our own public affairs—home-affairs—are rather woeful: the strike at the London Docks still going on, and the distress unspeakable. Private people do what they can, but all we can do is so inadequate to deal with this thing. And it all makes me feel more and more how savage and unfinished and makeshift our precious 'modern civilization' is.

My only dissipation lately (so to call it!) has been 'tea on the Terrace' at Westminster and an hour or so listening to Sir Edward Grey[27] on foreign affairs afterwards. I didn't see many of my M. P.

friends at tea—they were away electioneering—except Cunninghame Graham[28] who was walking up and down the Terrace talking closely with George Lansbury.[29] Graham looked handsome and distinguished as ever, and very little changed since his young days I have just been writing of, when the police mauled him brutally in Trafalgar Square and he and Burns[30] were imprisoned . . .

I hadn't seen our Foreign Minister, Sir Edward Grey, before; and he was just like the impression I had formed of him—he spoke glibly and easily—ably, so unimaginative.

What else have I done outside work (which never changes) since I wrote last? Oh. I went to the Irish Players with my colleague on the Women's Guild; I particularly wanting to see 'The Countess Kathleen'. We were both rather impecunious, so went to the shilling Gallery, which at these plays is very intellectual—all the women in loose flowing gowns and the men with broad thoughtful brows . . . And I'm sure in between they don't munch Rumpelmayer chocolates but nut-sandwiches and various brain foods. This is flippant, but, John dear, they were solemn! The Countess Kathleen I like as much as ever; it struck me as fresher and closer knit than later things. It was rather prettily staged as far as I could see from a wretched seat, but the words weren't spoken with much distinction or enjoyment. It suffered from the appearance of the actress, who misses being pretty by a pinched little mouth and queer underhung jaw—remarkably unromantic.[31]

By the bye my enjoyment was marred by an unpleasant, odious experience—quite unexpected in that 'intellectual' atmosphere: in the middle of the play, being very much absorbed, I became aware that a man in front who had been leaning against my knee (I indulgent and maternal thinking, oh well the poor beggar has perhaps had a long day at an office stool and is tired; let him lean!) was curling his beastly hand round my ankle. That's all I got for being as I thought human and amiable: he thought I was encouraging him. Never; never will I go to a backless gallery again. Well, in the entr'acte the Beast went out, and coming back stepped over and into, my one precious and only summer hat, which is delicate and choice and almost worthy of walking out with my dear John—or was till the Beast left his heel-mark on it; and after saying some casual word barely an apology, to which I paid no heed at all, would you believe it, when the next play came on, he began his sickening game again—or tried to. But of course I was alive and kicking then, and exceedingly angry and nauseated. When I told my friend afterwards, she said why hadn't I got an attendant to come: but Scum of the Earth like that are not easy for a woman to deal with, and I didn't see how to make a fuss without being put very much out of countenance. Ugh! I had to wash all over with rose-water when I got in—and think hard of you and what a dear you are—before I could feel clean and comfortable again.

Longmans are issuing a cheap News from Nowhere—3/, 2/- and 1/- I'm sending a copy of the shilling one to show you what a neat little volume it is. You can give it away to someone. Also a copy of Ker's English Literature in the new Home University series, which has some good volumes.[32] Ker is always brilliant and very human too and witty. I wish he would write a book a year. This is my copy I've just finished reading; and I send love in it. I may also send if I can get it for tomorrow's mail, a series of essays on the "Great State", H. G. Wells and others;[33] it may be worth glancing at, and then chucking. I haven't read it.

I had an amusing visit yesterday from a young man I may have mentioned in the winter, who was war-correspondent in Tripoli with the Arabs, and wrote home rather brilliant articles in the Daily Express. He finished his work there with Typhus-fever which all but finished him, but has turned up in London full of zest and youth and confidence. He is a good story-teller, and favoured me with some blood-curdling experiences. He brought with him an atmosphere of open-air and devil-may-care life that was refreshing to a hot person mewed up in four walls of a London house. It is hot: I sit this evening airily dressed in almost nothing, with strict orders that no visitor is to be brought up direct to me.

Now, dear, I'll finish up with two or three little scraps about Father that won't be published, I don't suppose.

The scene is Kelmscott House after a Sunday evening lecture and supper—those evenings that people who shared them remember so vividly—and Bruce Glasier, a Scottish Socialist friend was staying in the house and went to bed. To his room, up came my father very wakeful and lively, with Huck Finn in his hand, saying he was going to read it to him. But before settling to it, he asked Glasier if he had been to the New Gallery and what he thought of Burne-Jones's Mermaid ("In the depths of the Sea") which was shown there. Glasier unwarily replied some such obvious thing as a non-connoisseur if frank would say, that it was interesting but seemed to him archaic—or some such expression. Then a thunderclap of anger—Huck Finn flung to the corner of the room, and an eloquent flow of words that resounded thru' the slumbering house, about people who didn't deserve to live if they didn't see the beauty of Burne-Jones's work; and little Bruce Glasier hunched up in a corner of his bed, bowing his head to the storm . . . Next day, dear Father (who was so pathetically sorry afterwards) devoted the morning to the amusement of B. G.; had him alone in his study and told him story after story of old days, of his painter-friends—everybody; and was irresistibly witty and entertaining—"One of the most delightful mornings" said B.G.[34]

Here is another from the same source—You know, Herbert Spencer bored Father to extinction—They were talking of Spencer and the trick he had of a wider or narrower space between paragraphs according to the significance of the passage. W. M. "Can you conceive of anything more unimaginative than such a proceeding—but what can you expect of Herbert Spencer", and followed a long and eloquent criticism of him and all his works. B. G. "Have you read any Spencer"? "NO"! shouted W. M. "Do you think I'd read that rubbish"?[35]

I must stop, my dear. I've just heard my Sec. is ill and not coming, so I must turn to and do her work as well as my own, which is frantic. Yours with much love

May

* * *

[Quinn to May Morris, 29 August 1912.]
Dear Miss Morris:

I have been intending to write to you for a long time. All of your letters were received. I read the notice in "The Athenaeum" and in "The Times" of the new book on your father, and the fine notices of your work.

I also received Ker's "Middle Ages," which I haven't had a chance to look at yet, the shilling edition of "News from Nowhere" and the "Great State." I haven't even had a chance to look at the latter yet. I read several very good reviews of Drinkwater's book on your father, and what you say about him makes it more interesting still.[36]

I have just received this morning the introduction to the four new volumes, which I congratulate you on having finished. I haven't had time to look at them yet, but they are just open on my desk before me.

Everything I have read about your introductions and work as

an editor, and one reads of them here and there, is splendid and ought to please you very much and be a source of great satisfaction to you. Although, to tell the truth, I have done very little reading. I have had no time to read. It has been all work and no play; a hard year.

I received your letters, but between being exhausted after the Baltimore Convention, being driven with work and getting rid of my former alleged partner, settling up with him and getting him finally out of the office, slaving and working to correct his mistakes and inexcusable, almost criminal, carelessness, and trying to reorganize the office, I have had one of the most unsatisfactory summers that I ever had. Three or four weeks ago I was ready to quit. I have been on a diet since. I dissolved with Shoemaker July 17th but he didn't leave the office until the middle of August.[37] He wouldn't steal or lie or take what didn't belong to him, but what he did was to neglect the few matters that he had all winter, put them off, go only surface deep into them, and I have been in absolute peril because of his inattention to matters that he was supposed to be attending to. For six weeks I have been slaving in trying to correct matters that he had neglected, or retrieving his blunders. I never knew a more slipshod, incompetent, or lazy man. His self-conceit was colossal, his self-assurance boundless, his laziness equal to both. Yet when it came to dividing he wasn't a bit backward and put down on my matters as earned amounts that I cannot collect or ought not collect for months and claimed that this, that, and the other thing was finished and ready for a bill, and I have been working on them since and I can't collect on some of them for months. So that while he wouldn't steal he really did hold me up on the partnership agreement. I paid him $4,500 cash to get rid of him and he didn't do as much work during the year he was with me as a good $40 a week man could do in two months. I am sorry that I didn't drive him out of the place last March or April. I kept forgiving him and overlooking because I thought he was a sick man. Now that I look back I realize that he made up his mind months ago that he would do as little as possible and go on as long as possible and get as much as possible. He was out of the office in February and March for about three weeks, was back in the office then off and on pretending that he wasn't well, and then in May he went away to Hot Springs, Virginia, where he was for five weeks. When I got back from Baltimore tired and worn out, he said that he would stay here and let me get a rest and we would "dissolve in the autumn." But I said "No, we will dissolve now. I have spent all spring and part of the summer in correcting your winter blunders and I am not going to spend all winter correcting your summer blunders and stupidities and laziness."

I have got in two new men and have been working day and night. I have worked every night this week till twelve and sometimes one. I worked every Sunday last winter from two to six hours except on the Sundays when I was out of town travelling. I haven't had a week-end or Sunday in the country since last summer and haven't had a day off this summer. So that when I think of the partnership business I feel like—Well, I don't want to write just how I do feel, but it may be imagined. No more partners for me until I have lived and worked and had dealings with a man.

I have just had a cable from the other side from Mr. R. on some important matters which cannot be delayed or written or cabled about.[38] He is at Aix. I was to leave tomorrow, Saturday, the 31st, and should have preferred to leave then, because I could have got the "Oceanic," a good boat. But I cannot go tomorrow and will be driven to get away on Tuesday on the "Kaiser Wilhelm der Grosse." I crossed on her once about ten years ago and I remember that she is a six-day boat and there was an almost constant quiver. She is due to land at Cherbourg on Monday, the 9th. I expect to be in Paris by that evening or the next morning and to leave Tuesday night or Wednesday morning for Aix-les-Bains, where Mr. R. now is, unless he changes by the time I get to Paris. I shall be with him three or four days, and then back to Paris.

My address on the other side will be: care The Equitable Trust Company of New York, 23 Rue de la Paix, Paris. I don't feel much like making this trip and wouldn't think of going if it wasn't for having to confer with Mr. R. about these matters, which cannot be put off.

There is a touch of autumn in the air here now, and if I could go away somewhere and sleep for a week or ten days I should feel a little rested.

I could have gone tomorrow on the "Oceanic" but for a lot of irrelevancies and impertinences and selfishness that have pulled this, that, and the other thing down on me, which had to be done, and so I can't get away, and then trying to get things done in a rush this season of the year is almost impossible when people leave town early and are not here regularly.

The Baltimore Convention seems a long time off now. For ten days I got about three hours sleep out of twenty-four and was played out when it was over. It is too long a story to write about.

Wilson will of course be elected. The Republicans are hopelessly divided, each faction more intent on harming the other than on electing its man, and each one ambitious only to get more votes than the other, and neither thinking of fighting the Democrats. Any good Democrat could have been elected this autumn. Wilson is an able man but not a broad man. He once described himself in a letter to George Harvey as "a man with a one track mind."[39] Underwood, the leader of the House, would have been a much better man. He is a very able, experienced statesman, a courageous man who never boasts of it, and a splendid man in every way, and he could have been nominated if his manager, an old man of seventy or seventy-one, hadn't thrown up the sponge at a critical moment in favor of Wilson out of sheer discouragement born of bodily fatigue which prevented his mind from really working for two or three days.

But I am out of politics now and hope to stay out if I am let.

I don't know what my address at Aix will be, but a letter or telegram through the Equitable Trust Company in Paris at the address given will reach me. I don't expect to motor down to Aix but to go by train. If Mr. R. isn't there I will get in touch with him through Morgan Harjes in Paris and go where he is. But I expect that he will be there by the time I get there.

* * *

[Quinn to May Morris: Cable 3 September 1912. Quinn sailing.]

* * *

[May Morris to Quinn, from Kelmscott Manor, Lechlade, 16 October 1912.]

Thank you, my darling, for sending more Meredith letters in The Century: they are fine. I've not read any books scarcely lately—indeed I've been too hard at it, and dead tired when night comes. "Bookseller" Bain tells me he has forwarded a new "Indian" Bain book to you.[40] I'm afraid they bore you, but you really must have the set, now, and when I have time to get the <u>first</u> volume which has to be hunted for, and is really charming, you can glance at it, and then you can make a Christmas or wedding present of them to some friend, and get rid of them. But "quite the best people" were reading these books, so you are not to suppose it was only my flighty choice. Indeed I find the later ones rather over-luscious and monotonous. Do you know, my father, years and years ago, started translating "The Shah-Nameh,"[41] for our benefit. I wish he had done more than a mere scrap; he evidently enjoyed it, and it is full of fine things. If life were longer, I am sure he would have burrowed deep in Eastern material—I mean out of the way things—he knew much of the usual Eastern "classics".

I have roughed in my next four introductions, or rather two are finished, and the others written in the rough; and I am now going ahead, considering the remaining ones, as the material of these latter has to be arranged carefully and the notes also. I expect to be returning to London the first or second week in November.

I had a magnificent holiday a few days back that was also work—a fine combination isn't it? I had to go to the Vale White Horse some fourteen miles south of us, to make some notes and sketches for my books. It was one of our favourite expeditions, and Father loved the place and visited it every year, as I have done ever since—highly interesting and beautiful, too, to people who haven't the personal feeling about the place. I've been there in storm and in sunshine, but never on such a flawless radiant day as the other day. I started early, and stayed on the sunny lonely hillside till near on sun-down, when I had to hurry away to do my fourteen miles before night closed in. The day was as near perfection as anything could be for me that didn't include you in it. I was working hard the whole time, too, and tramping the rough ground over the hills to the ancient encampment, and the "green road"—the ancient way Roman or British—so solitary, so remote, planned heaven knows when, and set with the howls of dead warriors on the edge of the billowy low hills that stretch to the horizon. This is the White Horse and the Dragon Hill opposite a strange flat-topped hill opposite—all like beaten gold the other day, and the Vale and the blue hills away so fairy-like—unpaintable, as poor me found. Father used to say the Horse was a Dragon really; but he loved him dearly, and I'm bringing it all in the well at the World's End, where the young men start from Kelmscott and go Southward into the land of Adventure.[42]

I am full of doubts and difficulties about choice of fragmentary M.S.S. and wish I had you at hand to go through them and help with advice. I have here two groups of advisers, those whose line is "Print nothing your father did not finish, or did not publish himself", and the others (like myself) "Consider well before rejecting, as the inferior stuff has beauties, and points of interest". . . .

Well, I had a hundred things to say, but must stop and write some detestable business letters for the mail. Can you read this scrawl?

What will happen with you on the 5th November? does the pistol-shot raise the Progressive Candidate's chances 50%?

Yours always and always
May[43]

* * *

4

The Letters of 1913

[Quinn to May Morris, 4 March 1913.]
Dear Miss Morris:

I meant to write to you a week ago. This is only a hasty word now before I catch my train for Washington, where I am going at 3:30 today on a business trip.

This letter is principally about those manuscripts.

I have bought of Levesque & Company, 109 Faubourg St. Honore, Paris, two large paintings, eight feet and a half inches long and about four feet wide, by Puvis de Chavannes, both making a pair, and being the paintings from which he made the third pair of his large decorations for the Picardy Museum at Amiens in about 1866. They are called "La Riviére" and "Le Vendage." I made a payment of a third down, and have until May 20th for the next third, and until the end of June for the last payment.[1]

Now, as to the manuscripts: I have twelve or thirteen Morris manuscripts, about the same number of Swinburne manuscripts, seven or eight important Meredith manuscripts, and others of Rossetti.[2] I have over-bought in manuscripts. In fact a large part of my money for the last few years has gone into manuscripts and I have often made myself hard up by payments for manuscripts. If anything should happen to me the large number of them would load the others down. I don't intend to sell all my manuscripts. I want to sell a selection from them sufficient to make the second and third payments on these two pictures. After all, two pictures by Puvis de Chavannes are finer and bigger things even than manuscripts, and more important, and there is more satisfaction out of them.

The two that I have bought are Puvis' scheme for two of the Amiens panels, and they were selected by the French Government for the Paris Exposition of 1900. I had a very short time to conclude the bargain and only concluded it a week ago today (Tuesday), the 25th, and then only because I got a bill paid by a client of mine which enabled me to make the first payment.

I should be obliged therefore if you would send as soon as you conveniently can the manuscripts which I sent to you in the summer of 1911. I want to assemble all my manuscripts and make a selection of those that I want to dispose of, those of course that I care the least for. I don't know the number yet that I will dispose of. Of course this is in confidence, because I am not going to say that I am merely making a selection, but when I have assembled those that I care to dispose of I will offer them as a lot, not publicly of course but through a private dealer.

All this, I daresay, at first blush sounds very mercenary and businesslike. But I assure you it is not. It is merely disposing of more manuscripts than I care to have and putting in their place two fine things that are really bigger and finer than the manuscripts. Besides, the manuscripts have often worried me. For example, a year ago last summer I had to put them in a safe deposit box while I was away. If anything should happen to me, they might be lost or stolen. If I had a large house, or expected to have a large house where I could have safes to keep them in, that would be another thing. I have given careful consideration to it and I believe that I am doing the right thing both for the present and future, to do what I have done.

There has been a big international art exhibition here organized by the Association of American Painters and Sculptors, young friends of mine whom I incorporated last Spring.[3] It is at the Sixty-ninth Regiment Armory and began on February 17th and ends on March 15th. It is away ahead of the two Post-Impressionist exhibitions in London because it has the classic people of the nineteenth century, the Impressionists, Gauguin, Van Gogh, Cezanne, Matisse, Picasso, Picabia[4] and all of the later ones, the Cubists and Futurists, and the tin ladies coming down the stairs, and so on. I lent all of my John things to the exhibition and a few other pictures. It is a great success. They put it up to me to get a speaker for the opening night. But the Governor failed me and the Mayor couldn't come, and so I was forced reluctantly to say a few words.[5]

A month or so before the show opened they urged me to give an interview. I thought the best way to give an interview was to dictate it myself. I did so and sent it to them. They cut it down and published it as an article in "Arts and Decorations" for March.[6] I didn't have a chance to read it in the proof, and so it is a little jerky because they dropped out some things that I had dictated.

I send you under separate cover a copy of it.

I send you also two extracts from the Evening Post containing the first and second notices of the show, and a page from last Wednesday's Post containing a letter by Spingarn, a cultivated former Jew professor at Columbia College, which says some rather fundamental things about certain wealthy American collectors of a certain kind.

As to sending the manuscripts, I shouldn't like to have any trouble about packing them. They can either be sent in one case and insured or sent separately and insured. But I should think the easier way for you would be to have them delivered to Maggs Brothers[7] with the request that they carefully pack them, case them, declare them, express them, and do all that is necessary to get them here promptly.

The best domestic agent here is Pritchard & Company. Their London agent is Stockwell & Company, 18 Finsbury Street, E.C. They might be able to have them carefully packed and crated. But for your own protection you should get a receipt for the manuscripts from the person or firm to whom you deliver them for shipment. I have a recollection of your telling me that they were sent over to you in a zinc-lined box. I don't know that that is a necessary precaution, but perhaps it is a wise one, because the box might be put down in the hold and it might get wet, although zinc-lined cases are not as necessary as they used to be in the days of sailing vessels.

I am off to Washington at 3:30 this afternoon on a business trip.

As I think I wrote you, I am in the Stock Exchange matter and it is taking me to Washington and Albany a great deal, as the Stock Exchange has literally a fight for existence on its hands—one of the many attacks upon everybody in this country that seem to be anybody or have anything.[8]

Professor Wilson is inaugurated today. He is an able man for a professor. But I can't imagine the English making a former Oxford professor prime minister. Just twenty years ago today I witnessed the inauguration of President Cleveland in Washington, standing about six feet behind him. It makes one glance forward twenty years wondering who will be inaugurated then and where one will be.

I was sorry to hear that your mother hadn't been well. I hope that her visit to the seashore has benefitted her.

This is dictated on the jump and between constant interruptions and trying to get ready for the train.

Faithfully yours,

* * *

[Quinn to May Morris, 18 June 1913.]
Dear Miss Morris:

I have been intending for a long time to write. But the old story, pressure of business morning, noon and night, day in and day out, trips to make, often at night, and fatigue and Sunday work and all. During four months of the legislative session I never had a free Saturday or Sunday. I was one of the counsel for the New York Stock Exchange and it was attacked viciously both in Albany and in Washington, in the State Legislature and in Congress. The Legislature adjourned May 3d, and now it has been summoned back in extraordinary session, and I have just heard that the Governor is going to re-submit the Stock Exchange matter to it. So I shall have probably three or four more weeks of that.

Then I am in the middle of the reorganization of a company, which has a thousand and one details and will keep me going until the end of July at least.

I dismissed one man a couple of months ago for incompetence and took a man on from Washington who was in the Attorney General's office for some years. He of course is only familiar with Federal practice and not with the State practice, and at present he is not of very much assistance, but I am hoping that he will improve. If he doesn't, I will change. I have made up my mind to keep on changing until I get the right kind of a man.

I daresay that you are at Kelmscott now. The American exodus for Europe has begun. I imagine that you are deep in the work of Volumes XVII to XX.

I was sorry to hear that you had trouble with the teeth. I had trouble about two months ago, and had to have them looked after. For the last six weeks I have been on a soured milk diet, oftentimes only one meal a day, occasionally a light breakfast, but never lunch. I have two bottles of soured milk, prepared by the boy, brought to my office every morning, and, except when I forget to take it, it does very well throughout the day. I save an hour and a half at the middle of the day and get along much better. I found that as soon as I went on the soured milk diet my teeth improved. There is a close connection between fermentation and auto-intoxication and the nerves of the teeth and the gums, although very few dentists have discovered it.

I received a copy of "The Nation" and of the other papers that you sent to me and was glad to read them. I subscribed for the new paper edited by the Webbs that Shaw is supposed to contribute to, and I found it dull.[9]

The International Exhibition was held here February 15th to

March 15th. I think I wrote you before that I incorporated this body of young artists last May. The show was an exciting and interesting one. I never got tired of dropping in there a few minutes in the evening, generally though just before it closed. Sometimes when I went to the Appellate Division, which is near there, I would drop in in the middle of the day.

I am sending you under separate cover a copy of "The Craftsman" for May, which contains a short account of it.[10] The mention of my name is rather unfair to the artists. I had nothing to do with the collection of the pictures. I did conduct the negotiations for the renting of the armory, but that was lawyer's work. The exhibition was a mighty good thing for American art and has stirred up some of the sleepy old ones here.

Well, I sold the manuscripts, for just what they cost plus interest. It was a wrench to do it, but I had to do it. Two large fees that I expected to come in, one in the Stock Exchange matter and one in the Astor Inheritance Tax matter in which I have been for ten months counsel for the State Comptroller, were not paid when I expected them, and in fact have not been paid yet, and the State Comptroller is ill in Germany and I may not get my money until he returns in the autumn. I had some debts that had accumulated for over a year. I sold the manuscripts to Henry E. Huntington of Los Angeles. He has a great library, and they will form part of the magnificent library that he has donated to Los Angeles, California. I had Mr. Watson compute what I had paid for them from the bills, and add interest, and they went for what I paid for them; for example "Child Christopher" I bought at the Hodson sale for £52, although it is perhaps now worth several times that.

I saved out the following: Your father's "House of the Wolfings"; Swinburne's "Ode to Athens" and his six letters to Stedman; and Meredith's "Ode to Napoleon."[11]

I wanted to keep your father's "Glittering Plain" also but the man knew that that was in the collection and I couldn't keep it out.

I should have acknowledged the receipt of the manuscripts long ago, but I knew that you would know they had been received and you wrote that you had taken a receipt for them.

The two paintings by Puvis are in my apartment.[12]

Of course I like John's paintings. I don't buy "modern American pictures" or "Post-Impressionist sketches." I bought a few pictures out of the International Exhibition here, and don't regret it.

The manuscripts worried me at times, because there was always the possibility of loss or theft out of my apartment, and when I went away I generally had to have them put in a safe deposit vault, and in fact most of them were in a box in the Mercantile Safe Deposit vaults up to within a week of the fire that destroyed the Equitable Building. It was a pure piece of luck that something put it in my mind to have my bookkeeper get them out when he did.

I was paid only on account anyway for them. But what I did get was used at once to pay pressing bills, and as the bills in the two matters that I have referred to have not yet been paid I would have been in a hole if I hadn't sold them. I had intended to keep out "The House of the Wolfings" as the one of your father's that I liked most and should have liked to keep out "The Glittering Plain." I liked that better than the "Aeneids."

At any rate, I didn't make money on the manuscripts, nor did I ever purchase them with that intention. But I always thought that in my will I would dispose of them to some library where they would be safely kept and preserved, and that is where they will be now.

I was glad to know that your address at Leicester on your father was so well received and that you enjoyed the reception at the School of Art.[13]

I think I wrote you that I appeared before the Ways and Means Committee of the House in February in favor of removing the duty on contemporary art, painting and sculpture less than twenty years old. The House had adopted my suggestions in toto, but the draughtsman of the bill made a few errors. The papers gave the statement that the duty had been retained on modern art, and that lulled the dealers to sleep. A week or ten days ago, when I was in Washington on the Stock Exchange matter, I saw several members of the Senate Finance Committee who had the new tariff bill in charge and found that they were still in doubt about some of the art sections of the new bill. So I came back and hacked out a supplemental memorandum in the course of a couple of afternoons and evenings and sent it to Washington. It is badly printed and has two very bad blunders. I send you a copy of it with "The Craftsman." Please say nothing about it to anyone for a month or so. If the dealers knew that I had sent this brief in, they would be hiring lawyers and might try to bring influence on the Committee to restore the duty. You will see from my brief that if the Senate puts in the words "Original art" it will be in the power of the customs inspectors to shut out all forgeries that are not a hundred years old or else require them to pay duty, and that will do more to cripple the importation of frauds and fakes and forgeries than any other one thing. Only I don't want any dealer to be advised of this in advance, and to the few friends to whom I have sent copies I have asked that nothing be said about it for a month or so.[14]

I have been so driven that I haven't written even to either of my sisters for two months. But they are used to that and know that no news is good news. I haven't read much lately, but on one of my trips to Washington I chucked Masefield's "Daffodil Fields" into my bag and read it on the train going down, and it struck me as a rather powerful thing. A year ago I had read his "Everlasting Mercy." I thought the "Daffodil Fields" the better, although, like Thomas Hardy, Masefield tends a little too much for my liking towards sordid, sad and depressing things, like a man who hasn't enough to do or who has too much time to brood over the ironies and tragedies of life.[15] But he can tell a story in verse, just as your father could, but he can't write poetry as your father could and as an artist isn't to be mentioned in the same breath.

Lady Gregory, who was over here this winter with the Irish Players, sent me a copy of Tagore's book of Poems, a la Whitman.[16] As a member of the India Society I had a copy, and I sent you my copy. I suppose there is as much Yeats in those poems as there is Tagore, for Lady Gregory said that Yeats went over them and revised them. They had beauty and pathos in spots, but too much of renunciation, too much of fading out of life, too much about death and vanishing and farewells, as though the writer was a man of low vitality. I am rather sick of all the talk about mysticism anyway. But then I have to think of paying salaries weekly and office rent at the end of each month, and other bills to meet, and of harmonizing differences, advising banks, and so on; and perhaps I am not a good judge of mysticism. The only mystic that I ever knew that amounted to anything as a man was George Russell, and he is now getting fat and living better, and is the able and successful editor of the Irish Homestead, perhaps the best agricultural paper in the world, and is an authority upon farming and agricultural banks and agricultural credits. I imagine he doesn't see as many visions as he used to in the days when he ate less and his blood was thinner.

Lawrence *[sic]* Binyon was here last winter lecturing on old Chinese and Japanese art. I heard him one evening at Montross's Gallery and liked him very much. He read his lecture charmingly.[17]

Well, this <u>is</u> a long letter, but I trust it won't bore you. I hope it will find you well and not working too hard over the collected edition.

With best wishes, I am,

Faithfully yours,

* * *

[May Morris to Quinn, 22 July 1913.][18]

. . . grief at being so cut off from you, and seeing no hope of any change; these things, especially the latter which has to be kept out of sight, I got toothache, and later on, of all idiotic things, an attack of German measles. I was then trying hard to finish my four volumes in hand, and when the Doctor told me, I merely laughed, but was amazed when he told me it meant careful nursing, throwing up engagements and work. I got all right, though slowly, but he kept saying I should have six months' change, which of course made one scoff once more.

I wish you could be here with me.

. . . and should have done so to you, but never hearing, I thought you would be too busy to read as well as to write letters and so have waited—to my loss, as it is the one material link I have with your life.

Much love, my own Dear.

Dear John, it is ungrateful of me to forget to thank you for the Indian book till the last. It is full of charm, but I agree with you about the vagueness. More later.

* * *

[May Morris to Quinn, 29 July 1913]

Goodbye, my own dearest, Good luck to you, and much love.

* * *

[Quinn to May Morris, 5 August 1913.]

Dear Miss Morris:

I have been wondering why I have not heard from you. I wrote you a month or six weeks ago. I hope my letter didn't go astray. I hope that all goes well with you. There is nothing new with me except hard work.

The end of May one of the Judges here who is a friend of mine had serious charges filed against him, although in justice they were unfounded, and as I was one of his counsel it took from two to six hours of my time every day for four or five weeks, including a week at Albany, where there was a hearing before the Joint Committee of the Senate and Assembly. That delayed other work. Since I have got back I have been in Court solid from 10:30 in the morning till five and half-past.[19]

There has been a series of mishaps to friends of mine, serious operations for appendicitis and other serious ailments, and I have had to do this, that, and the other sort of things for them.

The Justice against whom the charges were filed sailed away about two weeks ago for a vacation on the other side. But work which I was just starting when he left, a large reorganization of a typewriter company, must be done and other arrears brought up to date. In addition to that, Beatty, my first assistant, has the entire left side of his face and half of his tongue paralyzed. The doctor says it is only temporary, but his wife is dreadfully worried about it and so am I.

I wonder if you got the copy of the brief that I prepared in the free art matter. I think I wrote you that I made an argument before the House Ways and Means Committee in Washington in February. The brief was a re-shaping of the one that I submitted then. I had been intending to go to Washington to look over the ground, but it has been utterly impossible for me to get away.

New York is dreadfully hot now and the town is empty, and only those who are slaves to work appear to be here. But the financial situation is very precarious and officers of banking and financial institutions are here all the time. I doubt whether I shall be able to get away much at all. I haven't been in the country a single Sunday or even to the Coast at any time this summer. Last week it was almost unbearable here; it is a little more comfortable now.

I hope that all goes well with you and with the collected edition. When do you expect the next four volumes to be published? I wonder if you noticed the quotation from your father in the brief? I came upon it in a magazine.[20]

Faithfully yours.

[Handwritten:]
7:00 PM.
My dear May,
How are you? What are your plans for the summer? People who have come back from abroad complain of the cold and rain. Here it's killingly hot. I wish I could get away. Politics seething—but I am out of it all—nothing but hard work for me. No vacation in sight. Good luck & regards. Faithfully JQ

* * *

[Quinn to May Morris, 17 August, 1913.]
Dear Miss Morris:

Strangely enough, the morning after I wrote you my letter a few weeks ago, I received your two installment letters. I was glad to hear from you. I read the two letters, in sections, and with interest. You seem to have struck a good place for your rest and vacation. It is a good thing also that you went with some pleasant companion. I think it is a mistake to be too much alone. I received on August 14 your long letter of the 29th of July written the day before you were leaving. Your trip seems to have greatly benefited you and I hope the improvement will be permanent. I do not quite understand how long you were there but I gather it was six weeks or so. One can hardly get a rest under six weeks or two months.

I am leaving today for the mountains. Nothing particularly wrong, but the doctor tells me I am under weight and run down and nervous. I have been working for a long time beyond my strength and he recommends a month's rest, wholesome food, moderate exercise, rest before meals, and as much sleep as possible. A friend of mine suggested a trip to Nova Scotia but the doctor is against it and against all ocean traveling. He recommends the woods or the mountains, where he thinks in a month or six weeks I will be all right. It has been terribly upsetting to be ordered away. I had made no plans. One of the men away on vacation I summoned back at the end of his first week and he is coming tomorrow. I shall do no writing while I am away. If I am near a golf links I may play a little golf. I shall do no reading except what I need to read myself to sleep, and no writing, so if you do not hear from me for seven or eight weeks it will be because I am in the woods and writing to no one. And the office won't always know where to forward letters to. I have left instructions to have everything held at the office, books, letters, magazines, and periodicals. I have had to do that in self-defense. The whole fact is that the doctor thinks I should not put off my vacation, as I am under weight and nervous and need complete rest. I thought I did not need to go away, and so let the other men go away. That was a mistake, of course. But I thought I could stand it. Lately I have found myself getting very tired at night and a few times when I left the office at 5 or 6 o'clock I felt so tired that I would go to my apartment and take off my things and sleep. These are signs that I ought to have been awake to. But the doctor says it will be all right if I carry out the above program.[21]

For many reasons I am sorry to go. I have several important

cases going on and a lot of unfinished business, and a big reorganization which I must turn over to one of my assistants in the office to complete. For other reasons I am glad to go away. I will escape the Sulzer hullabaloo—the effort to impeach the Governor. I will also escape the campaign excitements and banalities and the thousand and one unnecessary letters and applications for help. I have done a lot of hard thinking the last three or four days and I have made up my mind to work more for myself and less for others who have no claim on me in the future. If to do that I must be "hard," I shall be hard! If, to do it, I must be brutal, I shall be brutal! And to the devil with the Irish or all the rest and their appeals and their letters!

I am taking a few books along to read and if I want more I can send for them. My servant is going with me for the first ten days or so. Then he will return and do the housecleaning. I am going to do no writing while I am away.

You are probably back in England by this time and I hope you are continuing to improve and that you will be able to pick up the threads of your work satisfactorily.

Good luck and best wishes.

Faithfully yours,

[Handwritten:]
1 PM
My chief stenographer is ill. Hired men: poor and negligent and so I'm annoyedly delayed, but I shall go today. I am tired of New York—tired of people and tired of papers and it all seems foolish to me—all the work and worry about non-essentials! and so many of them do not help one to live but really hinder one. John—

* * *

[May Morris to Quinn, from Kelmscott Manor, Lechlade, 30 September 1913.]
My Dearest

Here are more stray notes from Mallorca: Shall I tell you of a day we took up on the mountain—the three English houses with their three respective maids? It is the custom here for the people to spend a day in their distant gardens—for they all possess land, carefully, admirably cultivated—and we had been invited to the garden of our friend's servant's family, Catalina [Rojo?] (Kathleen the Red i. e. of the 'Red' house, not herself red). The dear little servants simply loved this sort of outing (as much as they loved showing us round to their friends, and especially taking us to church) and were very busy and important with their baskets of provisions, and getting us collected and off in good time. All the cultivation in this mountain valley is of course in terraces, and it is difficult to imagine anything more deliciously fresh, more poetic, than these hanging gardens with their great water tanks, their sparkling aqueducts, their terrace after terrace of fruit laden trees, radiant against the [?] grey mountain-side. It was a graceful spot chosen for our day's encampment, in a well shaded clearing outside the 'casita', with a great flat stone for a table. Every garden has a casita, a little window-less house, with sometimes an inner room, sometimes only a raised partition with rough accommodation for sleeping: a well always, and perhaps a cooking-place for rough weather (the cooking is usually done outside). They are usually built in a line with the terraces—all part of that strange rugged mountain-architecture that so impressed me, cumbrous giant-building which has a certain splendour, and in which the Mallorquins excell: a little house built here on the mountain-side might be part of the mountain itself, so little does it stand out as human work, though the rough huge stones that compose its walls fit in to the rock it stands amongst with a great skill of choice and of adjustment. . . . The men will leave their families in the town and come up to their casita for a week or so at a time, working on their land. Sometime it is a bigger house, and they all live up there during the week, coming down to the joys of the town for week-end.

Well, in our garden, we first fell upon a cherry-tree, being hot and thirsty after an hour's walk into the heights—and I think we cleared that heavily laden tree. Then the servants began to make a fire, deftly and swiftly, and prepared vegetables; and all went about the work of getting the meal ready, singing and chattering like so many dicky-birds. Then a handsome tall woman, a neighbour in the town, came sauntering through the orchard, with her husband, to have a chat with us, and brought a great armful of white virgin lilies. So our feast was every way complete; and we sat and lay about under the fruit-trees, eating our rice with wooden spoons, and drinking red wine out of old double-eared earthen bowls of green, and feeling rather like a scene in Theocrites. Then after dinner the girls sang to us with much more laughter, and then when all was put away and we had rested, we went on and up to visit the not far distant garden of Francisca's garden. Francisca being the servant of the second English family, and a splendid-looking young person, comely and strongly-built, with a sculpturesque head, and two attractive dimples in her otherwise determined face. This garden higher and nearer to the wilderness of the uncultivated mountains was more romantic than the last and looked out over a fine amphitheatre of terrace-cultivation: We pottered about and tried in vain to blow the great conch-shell that is a feature of mountain-life here. Francisca took it, stood up facing the valley, filled her lungs, and blew a great blast that resounded in great waves through the mountain hollow. The conch in the mountain has its signals: 3 times for dinner, 4 times for a fire, and 5 for a doctor and urgent help.

Well, we were taken up and on (being for the day in the hands of our 'girls') and we get to the limit of the live cultivation, and pretty it is to see the struggle between rock, land, and tilled land, but the soil is so rich that in any scrap of a corner a great-luxuriant tree will spread out against the grey rock—huge fig-trees, cherry trees laden with fruit, some so perched that it is hard to come at them. At our feet lie the great circles of pale olives, and above as the burning golden crags, where just now hover two vultures.

Our girls are busy filling their baskets to take down to the valley, clambering the trees like young monkeys, and I sit on a rock and watch them, and just fill myself with a picture of the beautiful wild place with its clustered vines and scattered fruit-trees, with a strong yearning upon me to dream away many hours there. . . .

Here is another note of a Garden on the hillside: Our servant Magdalena's Mama came to call one day on her way up to her garden, and sat awhile giving me a spinning lesson. She is a clever woman with a handsome small head and fine features: she has delicate hands too, but for a thumb—ever so broad, like that of the Spinner in the fairy-tale, and I think it must be past inherited and past acquired, but it really is remarkable. She is a fine story-teller and people willingly draw round as she sits and tells a tale, with the points well-made and with due emphasis and expression. She presently took us along to her garden (that is, my companion Miss Sloane and me) which overlooks the Torrent-path about our houses. It is a delightful sort of camping-ground and here, she tells us, her husband passes a great deal of his time when at home (which is only part of the year, according to the custom of Mallorquin men, who go to France etc. with their produce). There is a fine old rugged casita, a regular rock-building, which he thinks of pulling down to build a new one. We lament and exclaim (and I look up from my distaff with horror) and she agreed that after all the work of one's ancestor was worth keeping. . . . These dear people live in a beautiful old antique house in the town, which the children long to have rebuilt in the modern French taste—I'll never go and visit them again if they do!

The next garden we also visited, which belongs to a dear old 'Witch' who hobbles past our courtyard up and down every day from her home in the town to this place where she passes her whole days, sitting under an immense Nespoli tree, surrounded by her animals; she sits there day after day, facing the romantic stretch of grey [?] and blue mountain—a strange solitary life of it among her 'dumb' friends.

There, my dear, you will have had enough of this, even on a holiday.

I am very busy on "Sundering Flood". I hope you are really resting. I dream of you.

May

* * *

[May Morris to Quinn, from Kelmscott Manor, Lechlade, 6 October 1913.]

My Dear

A few more Mallorca notes: This Fortunate Isle gathers all its mountainous region into the N.W. part where we lived, and the only serious mountain-peak of Puig Major was, wherever we went, a feature among the strange picturesque sierras around us. We were, more or less, at the foot of Puig, and felt bound to explore him. It is not real Alpine climbing, of course, but a long day's tramp of heavy walking, and bits of it exceedingly laborious. But, isn't it strange what satisfaction one feels over accomplishing a difficult climb—for nothing but the mere pleasure of overcoming these slight difficulties, and the other great pleasure of the open-air-life in lovely places.

We had agreed to start as early as we could possibly wake, and of course I merely took 'cat-naps' and looked at my watch all night and about 2 a.m. began to get up and rouse my good Sloane. There was a glimmer of dawn well after three when we really started, though the woods were still dark; and it was pretty indeed, plunging into the fragrant gloom of them and zig-zagging up the stepped track that leads among the olive-terraces to the mountain, the three of us each laden with a portion of the day's food and drink, listening to the quiet music of the water and the chirping of sleepy birds, and watching the myrtle and pomegranate bushes and all the wayside growths gradually take form and colour until the full, glorious day was upon us. Our first halt was by a spring with carefully-planned aqueducts to the cultivated land below. Here were massive stone stools set round a huge stone table in the semi-circular clearing of the wood (the springs usually being charmingly arranged in bygone days for the convenience of travellers), and here we drank from the mountain stream and listened to the wakening nightingales before leaving the track for the higher woodland which gradually thins out to the rockland of the mountain-side. I like the mixture of wood with boulders and clumps of coarse grass, and asphodel, and like to watch the change, the trees slenderer and more sparse, the boulders more massive, till one feels it is become the mountain, with its vegetation a few stone-pines, and the rugged ground decorated with masses of delicious rosemary (so blue now) and endless clumps of the pungent camomile. And the horizon changes, and new peaks show, and the long almost perpendicular line of cliff that we look out on from our little valley is well below us and looks quite different.

We are now, please imagine, at our last watering-place (a little more than half-way to the summit of Puig) the Fuente de la Paloma—the Fountain of the Dove—such an enchanting spot of green in the wilderness, and here our guide and neighbour, Mr Webb,[22] has to fill the flask with water to last the three of us till we come down again in the blazing afternoon. The spring is a thin trickle of water among maiden-hair fern at the base of a strange isolated chimney of rock which shoots up among a desert of loose stone at the bottom of our next steep ascent, something like this: [hand-drawn picture follows]. Whence we began the ascent of the waterless land, working up to the 'col' of Puig by a track half-made, half rock. There we were, at the top, in a land of mountain-peaks, looking down on our 'chimney' of the Fuente—a mere stick below us—and allowed a short halt for rest and a bite before ascending the very mountain-top—our couches were luxurious, fragrant rosemary in full flower, the fresh morning heat (8 a.m.) incomparable, the lines of the rock-land whichever way one looked, interesting and strange and lovely (like all lime-stone formation, I think). The characteristic about Mallorcan hill-country is, it seems to me, that the heights appear to be on a very grand scale, they are very splendid and impressive, while really they are not very extensive or very high.

Now we have about an hour's rough stumbling on the loose hillside, with an eye and a half on our feet, and the other half eye on the dramatic stretch of land below. Then we reach the regular halting-place where we are to rest for three hours or so—a sort of cave among the beetling rocks, which no one could find without a guide. We turn in here with squeaks of joy for the deep shade and for the lovely carpet of fine green and jewel-like flowers, incredibly luxuriant and delicate. This great sort of cave is refuge for animals and humans and I imagine the beasts eat the flowered herbage eagerly, but save for a few sardine-tins, it was all fresh and trim, and a stone fire laid with wood, had we wanted to cook. There are extravagant tossed cliffs right and left, and in front the blue, blue sea, and below, what seems miles away tiny waves breaking almost soundless, which makes one feel very high up. We eat and doze here and everything is perfect but the lack of water; and then we have another hour's scramble to the Peak. Here we stand on the burning rocks and look out on the panorama of the whole Island, fixing the picture of it forever in our minds.

I think these heights are so impressive because you can get at them and pat them, so to speak—some mountains are so huge that you can't see them, or can't take them all in. It is an amazingly dramatic landscape, and the long flat curves of the distant bays all round give extra emphasis to the long gray sierras and the sharp peaks nearer to our eye. The distance is fairy-land for its lovely mysterious colour—a mother-of-pearl dream-country but off from us by the grim barrier of a long, strongly-marked double line of sierras with the most lonesome conceivable valley running between the two ridges. [Hand-drawn picture follows.] Scanning this stretch of rock land up and down we can see one or two meagre farms, and the circle of a threshing floor—oh so desolate is this attempt at cultivation among the bar mountains. And beyond the sierras (the 'saws') are traces of olive terraces and vineyards, deserted now, and all this track of highland to the plain is called El Deserts—perhaps because it has fallen back to desert, but I do not know.

I find in my notes about the plants we saw on the mountain the following items: the 'Evil prickles' (my own name) an awful thing like a wig, that is misery if you put your canvass-shod foot on it. The 'green prickles': looks like bland soft moss and is much worse than the last. Names of these two joys unknown.

So the walking on these burning tracks was not all bliss. But I wish you could have been there; I wish you could have enjoyed the beauty of the descent, as we came down gradually to the cool green of the oak-wood, to the delicate sounds of our upland valleys—the nightingales and the murmuring springs. I shall certainly never forget the splendour of those marble cliffs, nor the perfume of rosemary and camomile as we stumbled down the burning steeps.

You'll be tired of my Mountain, dearest, but let me finish shortly: coming down to the higher gardens, we enter one that we know, and the farmer comes laden with a huge limb of a large cherry tree that he has sawn off for us to eat cherries from, while he stands by, mainly smiling at our pleasure in it and in his large kind hospitality. Then the scamper down by the water-falls, into the twilight, up our own stony path, with Old Malgherita meeting us by the pomegrante-tree, and looking very statuesque in the uncertain light, with her questions of how we fared. And gentle old Magdalena in the door of her cooking-hut, with a tiny oil-lamp flickering in her hand. And the beautiful night comes, and the stars rise behind the cliffs.

Good night, my dearest.

M.M.

* * *

[May Morris to Quinn, from Kelmscott Manor, Lechlade, 14 October 1913.]

My Dearest:

Here is a truce to the Balearic letters—perhaps till I hear whether they amuse you, perhaps only till next week, according to the moment's fancy.

This is to be a 'limited' letter, as I mustn't give myself room to dwell on how much I wish to see you—just at this time too, when there is generally the possibility. Send me another post-card, John, dear, to tell me that you are rested and that the place has been doing you good.

I am still working at Kelmscott, with occasional flying business-visits to London. And the other day to Clutton-Brock (of the Times) in Surrey, where I spent a day or two with his family, and exploited his brains for my work. He has an admirable, sympathetic critical faculty, and had long promised help when wanted. So we went through batches of M. S. poetry of my father's, making selections, and rejections. And to my great satisfaction, I found his opinion entirely coinciding with mine (of course I said nothing about what I wanted) and in one case with <u>yours</u>: He is very strongly of the opinion that 'The Pilgrims of Hope' should be published, and even added that the 'March Wind' and the other published portions gain very much in the setting of the rest . . .

I have to consider three volumes at the same time, for the two volumes of lectures may include some fragments on kindred subjects, to lighten the last volume. Indeed, I don't know how I'll get all the matter in, at all. There are many short things of interest one way and another—magazine articles, letters to the press, etc.—and at present I'm in a fine state of bewilderment, calculating quantities (my own way, for it will be done professionally when I have arranged the material a bit), conning over and comparing lectures, to see what is worth saving, and what is repetition, or how far the repetition even may be of value, in the different way of presenting a subject. (I haven't even begun upon the Socialist lectures yet—only the art ones). Mr. Cockerell[23] has his very excellent rule that my father wrote so much that we should now present nothing hitherto unpublished that is not up to the highest standard. But like many rules, this is quite good until the obvious reason for breaking it comes along and I'm afraid we shall have some discussions before we're agreed—entirely amiable, of course. There are one or two queer, queer early poems Clutton-Brock and I both want to include, for instance, and I expect a protest . . .

I see the Underwood Tariff Bill is signed and becomes law now. I would like to know what happened over the art-part of it, and your Memorandum about Modern Art?

I am reading Lloyd George's long address on Rural Reform. The air has been full of Agricultural Reform lately, and it interests me more than any other side of English politics. There was a charming article of Russell's—"A.E."—in the New Statesman on an aspect of the Irish side of it a few months back.[24]

All my love, dear one.

May Morris.

* * *

[Quinn to May Morris, 16 December 1913.]

Dear Miss Morris:

I received all of your letters, some forwarded to me in the mountains and others received since I returned.

The accounts of your visit to Mallorca contained in several of your letters would make a charming little personal essay. The two little photographs gave one an idea of the simplicity and charm of the little house you occupied. You seemed to be quite at home in the place.

The Mallorca installment in the letter of September 30th was very interesting, and yours of October 6th from Kelmscott continuing your Mallorca notes I carried in my pocket several days before I had really a chance or was in the mood to read it.

First, as to myself, to get it over with: I wrote you just before I went away, about August 21st or 22d. I got to the mountains Thursday and tried to sleep for two days. Sunday morning I started early for Buffalo and reached there Sunday night about eight o'clock. I had a hard time in Buffalo because the man in the office who was supposed to make the brief had botched it, hadn't even started it, and we had a three days' argument of a case that had been on trial for some months. It was before three Commissioners. The chief Commissioner lived in Buffalo and was a former Judge of the Court of Appeals, and so the hearing was held there. I had to send for a stenographer from New York, turn my bedroom into an office, get up early in the morning and dictate enough to carry him until noon, get in a little bit of more dictation at the lunch hour, and for three nights I was up until half-past two, half-past three, and one night until about four o'clock. You can imagine in what condition I left Buffalo Thursday morning. I got back to the mountains Thursday night. I had two friends of mine with me whose stay over-lapped a little. I found I couldn't play tennis, and even trying to climb a small hill set my heart going like a trip-hammer. I did the last two or three weeks take up golf, and enjoyed it very much. I hadn't gained any in weight by the time I came back. I left there the first of October; came back feeling rather hopeful and cheerful, but I ran into a frightful accumulation of worries and cases unprepared, and the worries and the anxieties got hold of me and inside of a week I was almost as badly off as before I went away, nervous, weak, troubled with my throat, night sweats about every other night, and feverish. I had one long case that took five days, which I hadn't prepared and which I had to try "on my nerve," as the phrase is, and then another long eight-day case, which spoiled two weeks and over a week in preparing for it, because its preparation had been utterly neglected by the man to whom I turned it over in the summer time. And then an attack of grippe put me down with a fever and kept me in bed four days and knocked me out for ten days or so, and then a temperature in the afternoons about four o'clock and that is as depressing and annoying a thing as can happen to one. I fired a doctor or two and finally I got a good stomach specialist and a general man to look me over, besides my throat doctor. My throat, I am glad to say, is better, although talking on the telephone is very fatiguing and wearing and exciting. Under doctors' orders I have been piling in food, and although I did not gain a pound while I was away, I have gained twelve pounds since I came back. The doctors have ordered me to stop working at five and not to come to the office on Saturdays. I don't think I have left the office by five o'clock a single day since I got back, but on the contrary have been here till seven, not seldom dining downtown and working later, especially while these cases were on. I have been here every Saturday and have worked most of the Sundays. The chief worry was caused by Mr. Beatty, to whom I had outlined a program of work, not carrying it out but allowing his time to be taken up by minor things and neglecting the bigger things. The result was that when I got back these two big cases had not been prepared. The doctors have ordered me to take exercise, but exercise takes time, and thus far I have had no time. I am hoping that next week or next month will be better. They ordered me to ride, but again I have had no time. And now that the cold weather has come on it will be impossible to ride. It is too late now for golf also, because the ground is frozen, but I hope to be able to get in some sort of exercise for at least half an hour morning or night, some time after the first of the year.

Your last four volumes came, with your autograph, and I was delighted to get them. But I am going to be perfectly honest and say that I have not been in the mood to read them. One does not want to read a book like that unless one has the leisure to read it carefully and enjoy every word of it. That, too, I have been putting off "until tomorrow and tomorrow."

I am glad to know that Clutton-Brock agreed with you as to unpublished matter. It strikes me that there is every reason why "The Pilgrims of Hope" should be published. It is natural, of course, that now that you are on the last four volumes you should be really crowded and embarrassed at what to include and what to exclude. In fact, it is a tremendous task that you have had to go through, to read so much and weigh it and value it and compare it with what has been published.

Yes, we won, or I won, the fight for free art. I broke my vacation to go down to Washington two days to put the finishing touches on the bill when it was "in conference," that is, after the Senate had passed it and when the House and Senate appointed conferees to put it in final shape and to agree or disagree as to the various amendments. The Senate was firmly against it. Wilson had nothing to do with it, although some of his friends are claiming the credit for him. Underwood told me that Wilson never spoke to either the Senate or House Committees on the subject. It was Underwood and the House Committee that did it, and Underwood did it for me, although it was a meritorious thing to do and he has received more praise for it than almost anything else in the bill. I started the fight; I made the only argument before the House; I submitted the only brief to the House; I submitted a brief to the Senate; I interviewed the Senators; and finally, I submitted a final brief after the Senate had acted. I started the propaganda, sent the stuff to all the newspapers, collected the newspaper editorials and cartoons; my office sent out all the circulars. Over 2100 copies of my third brief, the brown one, were distributed. I bore all the expenses of the campaign, and not until after the Senate had not only restored the duty but increased it from fifteen to twenty-five per cent and had taken antiquities off the free list and had moved the exempt period back from twenty to fifty years, did the museums wake up in a halting and inefficient way. But when it was over, I found the President of the Metropolitan Museum quite willing to claim the credit of it, and the editor of an art paper who, I am told, lives principally from advertisements of the dealers, inclined to give credit to everybody and merely referred to "Mr. John Quinn's able work," or some words like that. I made the fight nominally on behalf of the Association of American Painters and Sculptors, but that is really because I wanted a peg to hang my brief on and wanted to represent some art body other than myself. They had no more to do with it than you had. And yet they were quite anxious when the fight was won to claim the credit of it.

In addition to that, I read into the law for the first time the word "original," so that it now provides that only original paintings in oil, water, pastel, and original drawings, and artist proof etchings unbound, and engraving unbound, and original sculpture and not more than two replicas, come in free. All copies are taxed fifteen percent. I did that deliberately to put the importers, largely Jews, I am told, of fake Corots and Raeburns and so on, out of business. And the result has been precisely as I planned. For example, the other day a Sir Joshua Reynolds was sent over valued at $50,000. It was sent as an original. The examiners examined it and pronounced it to be merely a copy and levied a duty of fifteen per cent, or $7500 (£1500). Result: the New York dealer sent it back to the London dealer and America is relieved of that fake. I might add that my legal opinion construing the law has become the official one of the Department. In other words, I drew the law and my interpretation of the law has been adopted by the Department just as I planned. That of course is not known publicly, because I passed on my opinion to the examiners, who passed it on to the Legal Department, and it was adopted in that way. So that I have done that much for the freedom of American art and for the purity of American art. I had got rather tired of people on the other side poking fun at America because of the number of fake Corots here and fake other things.

I sent you last week to Hammersmith Terrace a barrel of Newtown pippins. I think they caught the Oceanic and they ought to reach you before Christmas.

I hope that you will have a pleasant and happy holiday-time. I dare say you will spend it with your mother at Kelmscott.

Business is rather depressing here and the Mexican situation does not look well. But each country has its own troubles. And I gather from a reading of Lloyd George's long speech on the land question that England has her own troubles. So far Mr. Wilson has not been much criticized. There is a sort of tradition with us that a new President should not be attacked or assailed during the first six months or so of his term, on the theory that he should be "given a chance." But it is curious how, whenever one of his policies is discussed with a slight note of disagreement, not rising to criticism, the phrases "purity of motive," "integrity of purpose," "high devotion to public duty," "nobility of ideal" are used. If the papers constantly referred to Mrs. Pankhurst's "purity of motive," "integrity of her life," "nobility of her purpose," one would begin to suspect after a while that there was something wrong with her virtue.[25]

I doubt if I will be able to leave town during the holidays at all, but I am hoping that after the holidays I can get away for a week, maybe by the middle of January. The end of the year for banks and companies is a very hard time, and in the early part of the year there come annual meetings which a lawyer has to prepare for and practically run. But after the middle of January I hope to get at least a week's rest.

I have read scarcely anything since I got back, because I have not had the time or been in the mood. I have made a desperate effort to read Joseph Conrad's latest novel "Chance." I have not been able to make very much progress.

I have not written any personal letters to anyone, and it came upon me with a shock yesterday when I realized that the Mauretania, sailing today, was the last boat that would get a letter to you for Christmas. So this letter will go on the Mauretania, and it takes with it my best wishes for a pleasant Christmas and a satisfactory New Year for you and yours.

Sincerely yours,

P.S. The boy is waiting to get this, and men are waiting outside. I hope this will find you well, and also your Mother. I will cable you on Christmas. This is a long letter, but I did not realize till yesterday evening that today's was the last boat before Christmas.

It's no use talking about work—that's an old story. But even now it is worse almost than ever. But I hope and hope it will be better.

Good luck, kind thoughts and best wishes.

Faithfully
John

* * *

[May Morris to Quinn, from 8 Hammersmith Terrace, 23 December 1913.]

My Dearest John:

The other night I had a pretty and idyllic dream about us: we were in some woodland and I was picking white violets and showing them to you; it was all very fragrant and lovely. Somehow we knew we were only snatching a few moments of you in each other, and yet the knowledge did not spoil the perfect serenity of the moment. It was like a sudden vision of some other life . . . a life in another world, as far as we are concerned, I suppose,—such a sunny calm. I've gone to bed each night since, desiring the same dream—and dreamed sheer idiocies!

I believe I promised a letter of chat, but what has an anchorite got to talk about? Well, for an anchorite I've done more than usual in the way of meeting people just this week or two—dined at the Binyon's one night, where were Ricketts and Shannon[26] and Binyon told pretty stories in a perfectly ravishing quiet manner—perhaps I told you this? Then one night we Fabians had Anatole France to address us, G. B. Shaw in the chair of course.[27] From his looks which tho' I admire greatly I don't altogether take to, I expected to find the great Frenchman rather aloof and inhuman, but he was rather a dear, and we were all very pleased. Hyndman spoke of course, and Keir Hardie, etc;[28] and afterwards we wandered round and hailed old acquaintances. I had a few words with Anatole, and he kissed my hand and said pretty things about my father. Somebody who was here last night, who is very much 'in the swim' in Paris literary and art matters, told me that over there A. F. is quite the 'pontiff' and lays down the law, and you have to agree with him, and so forth. Well, I expect he rather enjoyed his week's fêting in London.

Another night I went to what I must call a "Collectors' dinner" at the house of a lady who has some very choice things and where I was the only person who wasn't either a collector, or a Trustee, or a Head of a Museum. The talk was all about sales and exhibitions and all the latest news—the news of tomorrow—in things artistic. I was taken down by a Trustee of the National Gallery, and last night, telling my guest above mentioned about the dinner, I received some rather racy information about the gentleman's political career, his title etc; simple enough, but it amused me. While the men remained for their after-dinner talk, we wandered about above, looking at Conder fans[29] (I show my Ricketts one, which is rather choice) and Shannon drawings, and Chinese lacquer and the rest: and all the time, my dear, admirable as most of the objects were, I was feeling that my ramshackle home with its bare white walls and casual fittings was on the whole more liveable—though I do sometimes long for just one big room to receive people in, where pretty clothes have a chance of display. Then I had a long talk with a nice woman about the painters who painted with their heads and those who painted with their hearts or souls, or whatever the divine spark manifests through. Then the men came and so it goes . . .

By the bye, my last outing was to hear W. B. Yeats on Synge and the Irish Theatre—I would have liked to hear more about Synge.[30] There wasn't much (have you read his life by a charming young Frenchman, Maurice Bourgeois?).[31] It was very pretty and all that, but not striking, and very unfinished: yet you couldn't call it quite spontaneous, partly because he indulged in a great deal of studied gesture of a very precious and modern description, and the talk though quite nice, wasn't itself either precious and finished enough on the one hand, or strong enough on the other, to bear the weight of this accompaniment. Then, all of a sudden, he passed his hand over his face and said: "Let me see . . . Yes, I think that's all I have to say about it." and retired amid applause. I can scarcely think this is prepared enough to be one of the lectures he told us he was going to give to the American Universities and literary circles before long.

Yesterday I turned in for a few minutes to the Goupil Galleries to look at John's things. They are very charming for colour and effect—one especially, startling but beautiful, of a jade green frock against a bright blue sheet of water, and white cliffs beyond; and another where he slams a bright blue mass against a slate blue, and a sort of malachite-green against the green of the grass. And yet, I want something beyond all this, and paint slammed on in chunks like this begins to look cloying and "jamming" after a time, and one begins to think of the lovely transparencies of people who had studied technique.

I stupidly forgot to look at his big thing at the New English the other night, being taken up with "Anatole" (We met in the Gallery).

Your letter of the 16 December has just come. I am afraid, my Dear, this of mine won't find you in the mood to read a long letter of gossip. It is the old story of work, work, and over-work, and disregarding doctors' orders—it is grievous to people who are fond of you. I'm much interested of course to hear about the fight for free art. It is a splendid piece of work you've done—quite splendid. And as far as you are concerned, it gains in fine-ness from the fact that others are crowding in and claiming the honours of the fight. Another's of life's Little Ironies . . . It makes me angry, though. But that is an absurdly clever stroke about the 'copies' being dutiable.

Goodbye, dear and astute man; don't get shot at by fake-dealers!

Yours always
May

5

The Letters of 1914

[Quinn to May Morris, 10 February 1914.]
Dear Miss Morris:

Yours of January 30th was received at the office last Saturday, February 7th, but as I wasn't in town Saturday was not called to my attention until yesterday (Monday).

I hadn't seen the account of your mother's death, but Mr. Watson of the office told me that he had seen it in a morning paper and I at once cabled to you on the 29th.[1]

I received your cable of the 30th also.

There is nothing that one can say about such things that can give any comfort or lessen the blow or the grief. Time is the only thing that will do it. I am certain however that you have nothing to regret or be sorry for in regard to your mother and that you have always done everything that your mother looked for from you. But however much time one has spent with one's father or mother, however close the relation, when they are gone there is always regret and sometimes remorse that one has not been more to them and more with them. I know that was the regret that I had for years when I lost my mother and before that my father. And time is the only thing that softens it.

I was summoned to Ohio some two weeks ago by the sudden death of a cousin of mine. I was in Washington on a law case on Saturday; I was very tired and intended to spend the night there and come back Sunday. But late in the evening I got a letter from the office about a law matter that rather upset me and meant long-distance telephoning on Sunday, and rather than tear my throat with that I took the midnight train and came back. I got to my place about 7 in the morning, very tired, and went to bed, and was waked at 9:30 by a telegram from my sister announcing my cousin's death on Saturday afternoon. She seemed perfectly well and died in fifteen minutes after she fell. She was thirty-three years old, an only child, and her mother and father are simply heart-broken. The relations between her and her mother were beautiful and always very affectionate and close. She had been for some months at Holyoke, Massachusetts, on the editorial staff of a magazine called "The Nautilus," but had gone home for the holidays and, I was told by a friend of hers, decided that she would never leave her mother again. Her mother is a woman of some sixty-eight or nine. She was a tall, very handsome, striking girl, with wonderful auburn hair, and was one of the best girls I ever knew. I had often been tempted to get her a position in New York with someone of the big magazines. She wrote very well, both in prose and verse. But I never felt justified in interfering between mother and daughter. I knew that if she came here and got caught-up in the grind of hard work in this town, it meant separation from her mother and father, and particularly from the mother, except for a few days or vacation time in the summer. I had often regretted that I hadn't done something of the kind for her, but now I don't regret it. The poor mother didn't go to bed for three nights. It was a pitiful sight. It was a mercy that she was at home when the attack came and that her father and mother were both there. I came back almost unnerved by the experience.[2]

You of course will be reminded every place you turn at Kelmscott of your mother. There is nothing for you to do but to do the work that there is to do, both as executrix and what there is at your home, and to go on with the work on your father's collected edition. It must have been a great joy to your mother as you went on with the work and you must have discussed every phase of it with her. Work is the only thing to do under the circumstances.

I have been meaning to write to acknowledge your other letter, but I have been driven and pressed with work, and I find that I tire easily and am jumpy and full of nerves and sick of going to doctors' offices. I had trouble with my throat for two months and had to go to a doctor's office two and three times a week. And then I found that it was from the stomach, and now I am taking medicine for that.

I enjoyed your letter of December 23d—the long, chatty letter—But you are in no mood now, I imagine, for such things. Besides, one gets sick at times of art talk and talk about exhibitions and collections. Sir Hugh Lane has been here, and Berenson is here, and one night at dinner I had two hours of Berenson versus Bode and Bode versus Berenson and Lane versus Berenson, and so on, until I was surfeited with it.[3]

W. B. Yeats is over here now; came a few days ago, and has, I believe, just started in to lecture. I haven't seen him and I daresay I shall not run across him.[4]

Confidentially, my relations with Mr. R., for some reason, seem to be different. I haven't seen him for a long time and he is having his personal affairs attended to by another lawyer, of which he told me on the telephone sometime ago. I am going along and saying nothing. What the cause is, I don't know. I imagine that it is due to "knockers," a slang word in use here to denote unfair or under-handed criticism or harmful statements.[5]

Mr. Beatty, the man whom I took in last summer when I was ordered away by the doctor, has turned out a big disappointment. He is a good lawyer but he has no judgment or discretion, talks too much and to the wrong people, and has no idea of getting on with people. I am trying to land him in the Corporation Counsel's office or in the District Attorney's office, as I don't want to hurt him with the Bar by bluntly announcing that he has been dropped. If I get him a position in any one of those two places it won't be a reflection on him. Although he has been associated with me on a profit-sharing basis for only some six months, that involves accounts and adjustments, and so on. If I lose Mr. R's business, it will mean a serious hole in my income and a readjustment of office charges. But I propose to say nothing about it; in fact, there is nothing for me to say. It is all in his hands.

There will perhaps be many things for you to consider and determine in regard to your mother's estate, and I am sorry I cannot be of some personal assistance. But you will no doubt have good friends and friends of your father and mother to counsel and advise you.

Faithfully yours,

P.S. It is of course out of the question for me to attempt to make any plans thus far in advance about next summer. Something depends upon how I feel or the condition of my health and what the doctors say and how things are in the courts and in the office. I couldn't have gone abroad last summer, and I did the wise thing in getting away, but even then I was on the long-distance telephone two and three times a week, sometimes for long talks, and there wasn't a single day passed that I didn't get things from the office requiring attention, sometimes for three and four hours.

I mention this now only because you refer to next summer.

If there is anything you care to write about or submit to me for advice, I shall be only too glad to advise and to be of any help I can. But I daresay you and your mother's friends who know the facts will help you.

Good bye. Kindest regards.
J. Q.

* * *

[May Morris to Quinn, from 8 Hammersmith Terrace, 15 April 1914.]
My Dearest
I send much love for your birthday. You are always in my thoughts.

Your May

* * *

[Quinn to May Morris, 4 June 1914.]
Dear Miss Morris:
I received your note of April 15th sending greetings for my birthday. Not till I was reminded of it by your two lines did I think of it. Thanks for your good wishes.

I hope all goes well with you. I imagine from your long silence that you have been busy on your Mother's affairs and other things and also on your editorial work. I hope that no troublesome complications have arisen.

Thanks also for sending me the copy of Arts and Decoration for March[6] containing the Pre-Raphaelite illustrations and the article on that exhibition. Much of Burne-Jones' and Crane's work (though I don't think Crane in the same class with B-J.) strikes me as over-sentimental. It has beauty but the beauty is spoiled for me by the sentimentality. I like things like Greco and Goya and Manet used to do—things with "grip" in them—with what I call "the radium of painting." Van Gogh put radium into his best things also.

Real art is the expression of its time; it ought to appeal to its own time and to respond to the emotions of its own time. When time passes and the emotions change, the appeal that the work of art made to its own generation is less to another generation. I feel that my generation is that of Van Gogh and Gauguin and Augustus John, though I don't deny great beauty to the Pre-Raphaelites, but I can't stand the sentiment. In your Father's work I find no sentimentality—no mush—no morbidity. That's because he knew life and was a great normal healthy man.

But I was delighted to get that little life of your Father by

Clutton-Brock that you sent me.[7] I took it on a railway journey and read it all with great pleasure. It is on the whole a good piece of work. I was amused at his "once-born" and "twice-born" and his "conviction of sin" and the "rebirth" that he "calls conversion." Mr. Clutton-Brock must be or must have been a preacher of some sort. He strikes a true note when he speaks of your Father's "purchase of his freedom" and "his desire for his own freedom" leading him to wish it for others. I have long felt that a man who has not a competence but must depend on the will of others is not a free man, in the wide sense of the term.

By the way, W. B. Yeats, who was here last winter, told me, apropos of something I forget what, that your introductions together were the best things yet done on your Father and his work—even better, he added, than Mackail. I imagine Yeats was only repeating the current London talk among his friends or some of them.

I have been to just three dinners all Winter—ones that I couldn't very well refuse to accept. The last was a dinner of Miss Belle Greene[8] (Morgan's librarian), and Fairfax Murray, Sir somebody Reid, and a young Englishman who had come over with them were there. I liked little Murray, but the talk was rather too much about dealers and prices and collections, and so on. Reid I liked very well. One gets awfully tired of "dealers' talk"; it almost gives one a distaste for art.

I have nothing new to say of myself. The Winter has been a hard one, full of anxiety, and at times going constantly to doctors. For two months I worried constantly, but gradually threw it off. Latterly I've had hard railway journeys—ten or twelve nights in three weeks on the trains, till I was nearly exhausted. I have and can make no plans for the Summer, till Congress adjourns, and no one knows, not even Wilson, when that will be. Wilson has gone down fast in the last two months. His last "break" was when he said that the business depression was only "psychological"—a condition of the mind! Even the man who sells milk or sweeps the street who reads that knows that it is an absurdity. No one in W's[9] cabinet has any horse sense, and the problems of a great country like this require knowledge of life and men and cannot be solved only in a library or among books or <u>a priori</u>. The reform of the tariff has not done it, but that is likely to be blamed for it. W. has simply tired the country out by driving at one thing after another and by trying to change conditions that have grown up in the last fifty years in six months or a year.

Well, I must stop. I am in Court tomorrow in Brooklyn and the next day must go to Washington again. I hope that this will find you well and not worrying about anything. Some one sent me Shaw's last book of plays, but I gave it away and so have not read it yet. George Moore's last book "Vale" has caused talk, but I daresay you have not read it.[10]

Good-bye and my kindest regards.

Sincerely yours,

[Handwritten:]
7 P.M.
P. S. Just came back after a heart-breaking day in Court—Jolted and damaged by surprises and inadequate preparation, and so I'm in a depressed and angry mood and might work now perhaps late to attempt to reform our broken lines and try to amend or save the situation: and all because my men were too "cocky" and confident and asleep but the responsibility is mine and the worry.

But pardon this note. Please forget this P. S. I hope this finds you well and happy and no troubles or anxieties. Good luck.

Faithfully yours
John Quinn [signed]

* * *

[May Morris to Quinn, from 8 Hammersmith Terrace, 7 October 1914.]
My dearest John:

We have been at war for over two months, and the life the other side of it seems as tho' seen through a dream, a ghastly dream, so unreal and impossible all these happenings seem, all this suffering and blotting out of splendid young life.

When will any of our poor countries recover from it? Not in our time, perhaps.

In my humble way I've been luckier than very many in having a definite 'job' to go plodding—a job that must be got on with, or the printers suffer—and so forth. People whose work is stopped just take up what public helping-work they can, shelter homeless refugees etc, and I admire them for it—before the tale is done we shall possibly all have our work to do—And with all that there is the vexing side of the situation: amateurs eager to help, tumbling over each other, touchingly incompetent! Committees dealing out the wrong guests—artisans to distinguished University professors' families, Louvian Professors to those who can't amuse them, and so forth. And people offer lovely houses and free food to whole families and get snubbed—there are all sorts of absurd tales of the sort. Yet we've never been so earnest over war in our lives, and few of us until now have known what it means. I was at Cambridge on business last week, and to see the spacious quads of a great college given over to beds and nurses was like life upside down . . . The Universities are half-empty, and a great many of the boys who joined at once will never come back . . . The waste of it, the pity of it!

Reaching the station and waiting for my train to London, there were crowds waiting, and the opposite platform lined with nurses and white-clad men—with stretchers and beds and the hateful smell of disinfectants—people eagerly waiting for a hospital train from Southampton. It drove it all home and I was thankful to get off before the train got in.

London is strange—quiet in the day, dark at night: at Charing Cross a great search-light sweeps over the dark city after dark, and a little while back in the day one might watch the great Admiralty air-ships in the flawless mid-day sky. I stood on a refuge near Piccadilly and gaped at one quite a while; it seemed so near one might have patted it in the brilliant air, sleek and glistening as the skin of an onion (like the old Greeks' comparison for exquisite pale silk, you know!)

I've been much interrupted over work, with business matters and paying visits I dared not neglect longer, lest death should come to the old friends, and I regret in vain that I had put it off.

I've been poorly too—over-worked and worried, and there it is—three volumes all but off my hands, and Introduction to Vol. 24 half written—the last half, which haunted me and had to be disposed of.

The last I received from you is dated June 4th: letters may be strayed for I don't suppose at this year of my life of all others you'd leave me without the help of an occasional message. I hate to think of the chance of letters being strayed and wasted. I am also most anxious to hear of your welfare; very anxious too to know how you view our position. I can't talk politics, for my head is aching; but this isn't politics. It is a struggle for life; and everything that matters.

Yours always
May Morris

All my most precious relics of past days are lying, hurriedly packed, in the vaults of the Louvre Museum—the illuminated

Horace, the painted wardrobe, Mother's embroideries—everything.[11]

* * *

[May Morris to Quinn, from 8 Hammersmith Terrace, 5 December 1914.]

My dearest John:

I sent you the other day a copy of Clutton-Brock's 'Thoughts on the War'—papers from the Times, which I think well-written, and the thought in them often beautiful.[12] At any rate, they always cheered and comforted me when they came out, and we want all the cheering and comforting we can get these heavy times.

We have lately had a pronouncement on the War of a very different calibre which doubtless you have seen, though you are always too busy for reading such things—i.e. G. B. Shaw's New Statesman Supplement, 'Commonsense about the War'.[13] I hate to be always criticizing and condemning the work of an old friend, but this thing puzzled and angered me, and in spite of the one or two matters in it that one agreed with—obvious things—I felt vaguely and uncomfortably that every situation, besides being turned inside-out (which is permissible), was turned upside down also, and distorted; and the subtleties in it were not convincing. Public writing at this juncture should be large and humane and very simple. If I can find them, I'll send in this one or two cuttings by well-known writers about it—tho' perhaps these have been quoted over there by now. An official friend of mine (in the India Office) was here soon after it came out, and was almost gnashing his teeth over it, so much so that by a sheer instinct of fight, etc., I had to take up the cudgels on the other side for the time.

Life is all upside down and all one's friends wonderfully transformed; my good friend Sir Herbert Thompson, whom I've mentioned often, who is a distinguished Egyptologist besides many other learned things, goes out special constabling day by day: God knows, doubtless, what other service he does, in private helping and private giving, but he is not the person to tell of it; my beautiful Mrs. Stillman, Mother's beloved friend, fragile and worn and old as she is, goes out every morning and teaches and helps all day in some work-scheme, and when she comes home teaches English to French-speaking Belgians.[14] Another scientific friend is doing important work I am not allowed to speak of, in London. His beautiful old country home is being fitted up as a hospital, and before coming to London, he found time to drill the whole country-side into useful public service. It is he who said to me the other day, "I am thankful to have lived in such interesting times". I, on the other hand, am thankful that my Mother passed away before this nightmare settled upon us: it would certainly have killed her in misery—thankful too that my Father never had that mental vision of lovely North France and Belgium in flames and ruin, that vision of the long peaceful roads blackened by the crowds of flying homeless people. Some foresight of it he had, though, some foreboding of a general European war coming on the heels of the ferocious economic struggles of those times . . .

Your country too is hit by it all—please tell me what you are doing: it is so hard to have no news.

I have been much luckier than many people, because I had to go on finishing my job, if it were only for the sake of the printers and so forth, "to keep things going": so I have been just pounding along, and the printers keeping me waiting which has long delayed publication of these four volumes. A wretched time for publishing, isn't it? Two will be out directly, and two more in January, and I am free for the present: but it was impossible to get all my unpublished material into the last (24th) volume, and Longmans have consented to three extra volumes, the last including Indexes etc.; only we shall wait a little before starting on them, I think. Only there is a slight hitch, as Longmans says the bargain was 24 vols. and I must make no announcement of the extra ones, as it will spoil the sale, and I say that the bargain was to collect all material & I can't help it if it takes more room, and that we are in a false position if we don't announce them—I specially so, as people will be surprised not to find in this 24th, no acknowledgements, or Indexes, or general winding up, and people who know what to look for will wonder where is the material promised. Altogether we are "in a cleft stick", and of course I have had to give way, but have told Longmans I wish them to send out a prospectus for the extra volumes within a few weeks of the publication of these four, and have had no answer yet. I hope I'm not going to have a bother over it. They have been very nice and generous all through about the get up, and I do hope the edition will sell out, in spite of the War.[15]

London is wonderful at night: the lights are low, and the light-wheeled cars go stealing about the streets almost in darkness. The city has never looked so fine, and on the glorious moon-lit nights we have had through the autumn, all the colour and tone of the night was a thing to remember long. By day, it is curious to see the emptiness of the central streets, and every now and then, there comes the sound of gay singing and the tramp of feet, and then come marching quickly a little squad of men in khaki—so many and bright-eyed, one and all, John—oh my heart is heavy over all the destruction of this fine courageous life, and I simply can't write of that side of it—it makes one mad.

The immensity and many-sidedness of the distress is overwhelming, and of course public help has to be supplemented by private local help all the time. For instance, here in Hammersmith a small organization of people (mostly 'Terrace' folk, artists, and others) who have a pleasant and successful Club for the workers (the windows of which look on our old Kelmscott House garden), have formed a Hostel for Belgians and have fitted up workshops for them (cabinet-making for the men, embroidery and dressmaking for the women) and so are helping a little knot of the Refugees and keeping them active and cheerful. This is a small thing, but typical of other activities.

When I go down to Kelmscott next week I shall collect all the apples available from my garden, and go round begging for apples and pears about the country, to send up to hospital-ships up in Orkney. The poor fellows are craving for fresh fruit, and they have none there. I am also going to start people making warm clothes. The men want all we can do. I have no money to spare unfortunately, as everything goes on some expensive and beautiful cottage-building I am doing in memory of Mother. It was begun just before the War. The men are only too glad of the work now, and I have to consider that my present contribution,—but it is hard not to be able to send generous parcels to men at the front; or to the hospitals.

We all live so simply and frugally now—at least my friends do, for I always have done—Do you suppose that we in this country have ever felt so intimately the seriousness and responsibility of life?

John dear, if you had the intention of sending me delicious apples this xmas, (please don't, but send me just the mere "dollars", that bought them:) it would give me real pleasure to use something from you in my small parcels for wounded men up North.

This is written as often before in wakeful hours before the house is awake.

I think of you constantly.

Yours
May

On second thoughts, if you <u>had</u> very kindly thought of sending me apples, let them come just the same, and I'll send them up North just as they are. This is a broad reminder, isn't it? but it is not for myself.[16]

* * *

6
The Letters of 1915

[Quinn to May Morris, 10 February 1915.]
Dear Miss Morris:

I received yours of January 13th. I meant to write you a long time ago.

I cabled you at the holiday time and am glad to know from yours written from Kelmscott that you received my cable.

I hope the apples have arrived in good shape by this time. They hadn't arrived when you wrote your letter on the lst, but they have doubtless got there by this time.

I should have thanked you long ago for Bain's "Syrup of Bees."[1] I can't say that I read it or that I ever will read it. The truth is I can't stand very much of that sort of writing. It is too sweet and romantic for me. Lord Dunsany writes somewhat in the same way, but I can read him.

I did read very fully and carefully Clutton-Brock's life of your father in the Home University Library series. I sent for five or six copies of it and presented them to different friends of mine. It is a well done book.

I also have to thank you for volumes 21 and 22 of your edition with your autograph as usual. I read the introductions with great pleasure, read them in bed at night when I came in, and I congratulate you on them. I just received today the Athenaeum sent by you and containing a short but good review.

I also want to thank you for sending me Lawrence Binyon's little volume of poems. I glanced through them the other night but none of them struck me as particularly fine.[2]

I haven't read Clutton-Brock's "Thoughts on the War" which you also kindly sent me, although I have taken it with me in my bag on two or three trips expecting each time to have the leisure.

I have been dreadfully driven for the last two months. I have had a very large and annoying matter in Washington, a suit against the Bank that I am counsel for going back nearly ten years and involving $1,200,000 (in English money £240,000). After weeks of negotiation and consultation and visits to Washington and Philadelphia, digging up facts, conferences, offers and rejections of offers, the matter was finally compromised by the directors paying in $750,000 (£150,000) and buying the asset which the Comptroller of the Currency claimed the original board had no right to buy. There was no element of bad faith involved in the transaction and no other Comptroller had ever objected to it. But this was part of the campaign of the present administration to get at what they call "Wall Street."[3]

The matter was closed the latter part of last week and left me about exhausted. I have taken a cold since and I am so hoarse that I can hardly talk in a whisper.

As I promised you, I enclose herewith London draft to your order for £20 to do just as you please with.

Times have been rather hard here and collections never worse. But people in this country ought to be thankful that they have peace. I too have often thought of the poor devils practically condemned to death out there in the trenches at night with death from a bullet or cold or pneumonia almost certain for many of them. It makes one hate the whole nation that is responsible for this slaughter, not the people of the nation but the leaders of the nation. How long it will last no one knows. My sympathies of course are with the Allies. I think fifty per cent even of those of German blood do not sympathize with the Germans. My friends among the Allies think that the good weather will help the Allies more than the Germans. On the other hand I had a long twenty-page typewritten letter from a business man in Petrograd recently, and I met at lunch yesterday a man who had just come from there, and both the writer of the letter and the man I saw yesterday were very much discouraged regarding Russia's ability to whip Germany in the east. If Italy were to come into the thing and remain in, it would clean the business up. But Germany is prepared, and preparation is two-thirds of the battle.

Nothing that England can do in the way of searches or seizures or enforcement of new contraband rules will change the opinion of people in this country. If I were in power in England and it were necessary to keep copper or rubber or other things that are used in powder or explosives or guns or other war material out of Germany, or to even keep out food in order to starve them into submission—if it were necessary to accomplish this to make new rules of contraband, I would break all the old rules in order to break Germany. The American Civil War was begun to save the union, to prevent secession. The slaves were not liberated by Lincoln until the war was on for some two or three years. There were people then who told Lincoln that it was unconstitutional for him to issue the emancipation proclamation. Lincoln said that it might be but that if it were necessary in order to save the country to break the constitution, he would break the constitution. That is a dangerous doctrine, but there are times when such a decision is the only right one.

It must seem queer to be in London now with its darkness at night.

The raids of course are terrible but in a military sense they are good for England because they will brace up the enlisting.

I knew of course that you would do all you could in the ways that you have described. But it is fortunate that you have had your regular work to do in connection with your father's edition. These are times of course that try people to their very souls. They are desperate times for England, but not so desperate or so awful as for Belgium. England has not suffered anything in comparison with France. Poor Poland has perhaps suffered even worse than Belgium. And in Serbia perhaps the slaughter has been the greatest of all. It is a horrible war for all of the countries concerned. England will perhaps suffer the least and perhaps when peace comes gain most. With her it is a life and death struggle. She has either got to win now or lose her control of the sea, and if she loses her control of the sea she loses her primacy in the world.

I have always felt that in personal relations as well as toward public questions you were a woman with a big heart and a broad mind and incapable of selfish thoughts and what you write you have been doing is exactly what I should expect you to do. But it is all a sad business, and it is a mad, bad, horrible war. It is bad for everybody, and particularly bad for artists. It will, except in the supremely great artist, kill art except art connected with war. The events of the war are so thrilling and absorbing that no fiction or poem can rival them in interest, and even if I were a writer, a poet, or an artist I would feel that every inspiration inside of me was dried up and that I only reacted to some excitement or news from without.

Kuno Meyer has been out here lecturing. I knew him in Dublin and I met him here. He dined at my apartment one night. He is a charming, witty, delightful man of the world. But it is a pity to see a scholar like that turned to propagandist and politician and fraternizing with a group of hot-headed Irish who sympathize with Germany. Ninety per cent. of the Irishmen in this country are back of Redmond and feel that he is right and do not sympathize with the small group of hot-heads who are on the side of the Germans.[4]

Sir Roger Casement stopped with me a couple of weeks during the summer time before the war began. He was with me when the war started. He got so excited that I really had to resort to a strategy to get rid of him. I couldn't stand the war morning, noon, and night. He is a charming, delightful, chivalrous man. But he kept wringing his hands and talking about "the poor Kaiser—Oh, the poor Kaiser and all the Kaiser's advisers."[5]

I didn't get away a day this summer. I have had to stick to business to get in money to go along with. I owed considerable money before the war started. Collections were bad. Bills that I had rendered before and since the war started have not yet been paid, although in a couple of cases I have had to reduce them in considerable amounts. This is not complaining.

I rented a little place down at Babylon, Long Island, for September and until the 20th of October. That is about forty miles from here on a bay known as the Great South Bay. I had a power boat, and thought at least I might have a week down there. But I never got the week and had only week-ends, Saturdays and Sundays.

Miss Belle Greene, Morgan's librarian, asked me to dinner a month or two ago to meet Fairfax Murray. But I was unable to get away. I have had to give up making engagements. As sure as fate if I make any engagement, even a week or two ahead, that night I am detained at the office or kept working or something comes up that I must attend to, and the only way I can keep free and from fretting and nervousness is not to make engagements in advance. There are a certain number of social and business dinners, however, that it is mere "business" to attend, and those ones I must go to.

Granville Barker and his wife are out here and seem to be doing very well. They have put on Shaw's "Androcles" and are to follow it up with "A Midsummer Night's Dream." There was some talk of Shaw's coming out, but I daresay he won't come.[6]

Aleister Crowley, an English poet, has been out here. You perhaps have never heard of him. He is not a great poet, but I believe he practices magic or teaches the "higher thought."[7]

Young Colum, the young Irish poet and dramatist, and his wife have been out here. He came out to lecture, but I believe it was a fizzle. He is doing some writing for magazines and some journalism.[8]

Cecil Chesterton is out here lecturing, but I haven't seen or heard him.[9]

Jim Larkin, the Dublin strike leader, has been out here too, but I have not heard him, although I met him for a moment one evening.[10]

The English ought not to be too sensitive about Mr. Wilson's note or anyone of his notes or protests. At heart I think the government is on the side of the Allies. But Wilson and Bryan[11] are the kind of men that would lean backwards against or spank those that they were fondest of, just to show how neutral they were. The thing to do is for the English to keep on being quite polite to Uncle Sam but doing just what they please. I know this country and I know that the people of this country wouldn't back up the administration in any forcible measures against England because of searches or seizures or contraband or use of the American flag or anything of that kind.

I was awfully interested in what you said about getting up the supplemental volumes. I don't think that they will hurt the sale of the others at all, but on the contrary they will help them. By the way, I bought three complete sets from Longmans, one for a friend of mine, one to send to my sister, and an extra set for myself. They are a lovely set of books.

Please remember that the £20 enclosed is for you to do with just as you please.

I hope that this finds you in a cheerful mood and not working too hard or overdoing things.

With best wishes for the New Year and with hopes that before this year is out peace may come and a new and better order be ushered in, I am,

Ever sincerely yours,

[15 February 1915.]
P.S.—In glancing over this letter I find on page 2 that in the very next sentence to where I enclose £20, I speak of times being hard and collections bad. I won't stop to rewrite the letter, but for heaven's sake don't think that enclosing the draft had anything to do [end of letter]

* * *

[May Morris to Quinn, from Kelmscott Manor, 4 June 1915.]
My dearest John:

I was indeed glad to hear from you, though only able to send a hurried acknowledgement of your letter received and answered more than a month ago! Little as I seem to do of useful work, I allow myself no leisure for long letters as a rule: but I know you must know and feel that you are constantly in my thoughts.

I believe I just mentioned that having come up to town to do various odd jobs connected with war things, I had to go back to Kelmscott next day to receive my sister Jenny and her household who were literally flying from a raid on the East side of England—Faversham—too near Chatham to be quite healthy. And so here I am, housekeeping and helping, and only able to go up now and then for committees etc. Meantime our beloved friend Philip Webb died, and I went down to his beautiful cottage-home to have the last look at his peaceful face.[12] An old cottage in the forest, John, and in the serenity and simplicity of the study his spirit seemed to linger, outside the dead form upstairs. It was hard to leave the place for always. He was the last of that group of men, and his attainments and fine ideals will perhaps be known about someday. If they are not, it does not matter, because his work has had its effect. Well, I mustn't write more about him, and only so much to you.

Kelmscott, these first days of June, is more of a Paradise than ever before, the blossoms more abundant, the perfumes more penetrating; and one has naturally never felt the beauty of the English country so keenly as at this time of horror and destruction. After our friend's funeral I was kept in town a week or so ill in bed—overdone one way and another—and coming back found my orchard a mere cloud of white and pink blossom, the feet of the fruit-trees wreathed in brilliant forget-me-nots—masses of them; the effect was almost startling; it was the sort of fresh gaiety that seemed to me, in contrast, like a cri out of the eager beautiful life of that close-knit circle, of whom I come more and more to think as young and expectant rather than tired and worn with years. Just so their orchard-garden blossomed, radiant and abundant and full of bird-music: otherwise the difference is great.

I get up at six most mornings to sew wonderful garments for Belgians, and we all knit, at odd moments, at means etc. I've written a war-lecture, but have had no engagements for it yet. There is an extraordinary amount of indifference in the country, and we want to wake people up, women and girls especially. I think it is more the well-to-do petite bourgeoisie (in the towns) and farmer class in the country, who don't realize what a hideous situation the whole world is in. Of course thousands of men and women are working splendidly, but one can't bear to see a Dozen indifferent faces now, and I am perhaps unreasonably impatient at seeing in London smart-young-women peering into shop-windows and the like. I confess, if I did not know certainly that my post is right here for the moment I should long to be in London, sharing the discomfort and anxieties, and doing the 'jobs' that were beginning to form themselves for me. But patience—organising food-supplies locally, and sending out clothes etc., eggs, to hospitals, all needs doing, though it is deliberate work, and not exciting.

I am keenly interested in the situation between the United States and Germany; I wish I knew more of the ins and outs of the matter and could forecast in the least what is likely to happen; but I cannot, and can only wait to see the next move.

I hear such stories of the French non-fighters—those who are left to work the land for instance: their courage, frugality, industry; how they will throw down their implements a moment while a bomb bursts, then go back to labour with fresh industry. If the enemy were here, how every one of us would be awakened to life!

I think the Northcliffe clique of newspapers have deliberately done much harm: the hysteric frenzy with which they write gets re-echoed in the streets, among one's friends—God knows where, and then comes the inevitable depression.[13] Excitement is not steady patriotic work; their influence is unfortunately terribly far-spread, and if it didn't make one sick at heart one could smile to hear people parroting phrases they think their own that they have absorbed from their 'yellow' papers.

I wish the government would not make any concessions to this clique; though I am sure they do it to prevent further quarreling. I wish they would draw their claws.

When I heard of the Lusitania tragedy life suddenly seemed to become unreal, and one went about in a dream for awhile.[14] I have been trying to understand the Prussian mind lately, for everything is such a puzzle, and after all they are fellow-beings though apparently crazy. . . . Human life has always seemed to me so sacred, and now humans are of no more account than swarms of flies . . . It is horrible, and life can never be free of sorrow for this generation.

Yet amidst all the anguish one feels at the sweeping away of the picked men of many nations, I've never once felt anxiety about Germany overcoming the Allies: anxiety, if one had time to look ahead, would be about the sort of peace to ensue, and how we could guarantee it lasting. The entrance of Italy into the fray has moved me very much; it stirs up all sorts of thoughts of the great past, and what Italy means to the world: and now perhaps her noble cities will be laid waste like those of East France. Well, I suppose we shall forget all art now for a time.

Though, I'm on a Committee for trying to organise work for craftsmen and women hit by the war, among other things! People are full of fine courage, really, and hope.

Your XXIII and XXIV volumes are long since sent off. I have the extra Introductions to send you, all waiting.

I haven't had the heart to start arranging my three extra volumes yet—and I fear Longmans wouldn't publish them yet if I were to. People are much taken with "The Pilgrims of Hope" by the bye, and we are going to issue it in a Pocket volume shortly.[15]

Dear John, I am glad to see you write with sympathy and understanding of the French. As I said before, all I hear about them is fine—and when one remembers what they have been through before, and how since then they have made themselves, one can but say "This is a nation gold to the heart's core." They are going thro' the fire once more, and all that is not gold burnt away. They understand the finer arts of life, and they can fight!

It was quaint that you should for a moment think that I could misunderstand your phrase about 'times being hard'. I know you would give your skin away, if it were possible. You spoke of trying times and great personal fatigue: I much hope you are better of that.

You let your amanuensis write you "hope I am" in a cheerful mood" : that is not possible: my Mother is gone; I never see you, I rarely hear from you (tho' the last letter with the kind and dear finish in your own hand, and the kind things said earlier, was very comforting); I think my heart is broken, as people call it, which is a pity; but in the great national trouble, personality counts for nothing, and one's principal sensation is content at usefulness, or discontent at time lost.

It is a great comfort to hear how very much American sympathies go with the Allies. Your letter was full of interest and I have read it through several times: the last page many times.

Yours always
May Morris

* * *

[May Morris to Quinn, from 8 Hammersmith Terrace, 31 December 1915.]

Dearest John:

I received your cable greeting on Christmas Day in the evening, and wanted much to cable back, but you can understand that over here we think twice before spending extra money on our own personal matters at present. Thank you for the Apples. Again, I thought them too much of a luxury for a private person, and am sending them to the Fleet—through a friend of mine at Cromarty.[16]

I received no letter of "six weeks ago" mentioned in the cable. Your last letter received was the only one—written in February last. Think of it, realize something of what that means in ordinary times: in days like these a special grief and wondering. The recent letter has gone to the bottom of the sea somewhere, I suppose. I'm sorry.

It has not been easy to keep the resolution I had made not to write until I heard—the shortest letter, that might waste five minutes of your time; but the days and months pass somehow; and really, we are all so busy trying to help, that personal letter-writing becomes a luxury, too. I work at odd jobs, humble jobs—inclined to envy people who are in a position to get a regular billet: I do a little collecting of useful things, clothing for Belgians etc., cutting and organising making of clothes, arranging village-work at Kelmscott for things for our own men, spending every available penny on Wool—our great need and stand-by. And so on. We have been arranging some small Arts and Crafts shows, too, partly to help artists badly hit, partly to keep those sort of things in view—as art and what it keeps alive in us mustn't go down the wind at this juncture.[17] Goodness knows where we shall all be before we are through with this—and after. Most of our incomes are already much less this year . . . I sometimes wonder if middle-class women, faced with the grave things of life, will learn a lesson and afterwards refrain from frittering their lives and 'spending-money' as they have done these later days before the War? If it will give them an idea of the futility of luxury and the value of art? Some of course can't learn; others I am sure only need a sharp awakening, and God knows we are getting it.

The Zeppelin raid on London in October (by far the worst) was a wonderful experience. It came on a still night of the most majestic starlight I've ever seen, after a lovely sunset with delicate crescent moon. Across the water opposite, a huge booming (of the biggest gun round the city) travelled up the great path of light that was searching the N.E. sky, and there, among the stars were little sparks and moving stars—the anti-air-craft aeroplane guns (what do they call them?) worrying the big monster. I was not in the least alarmed, it was all too strange, but spent the night in a state of intense excitement—waiting (foolishly enough) for more—the murder of quiet folk being all over in 7 minutes and the "gallant crusaders" off again to their country.[18]

Just now I'm doing a little canteen work at a munition-place in Chiswick, and spent this morning in sweeping, cleaning knives, etc. We take pride in doing our work perfectly, and my colleague, stove-cleaning, grew blacker and hotter and more and more beaming as the morning passed! Now I must go to bed to be ready for an early start. This last letter of the year is yours.

I hope you will receive safely "The Pilgrims of Hope" specially bound by Miss Adams who as you know is the finest binder we have.[19] Owing to the War she has to give up, unfortunately. I have also sent the eight last Introduction-proofs. There is still a Jason Introduction, overlooked, which I will send, as in the first instance you seemed to like to have them all.

I hope you are well: it is idle to hope not overworking.

Best wishes from Yours
May Morris

7

The Letters of 1916–1917

[Quinn to May Morris, 20 January 1916.]
My dear Friend:

I wonder if you got my letter written in the beginning of November. The reason that I ask is that letters are going astray more lately than ever before. Our local mail service is about as perfect as anything can be but letters from abroad are often unaccountably delayed or not delivered at all, so much so that with business letters, particularly to France and Russia, I always send two copies in different envelopes and by different boats.

I cabled you on December 24th as follows:

> "Hope you received my letter of six weeks ago. Sent apples three weeks ago. Hope you are well and standing strain of trying times. Christmas greetings and best wishes."

Your barrel of apples went forward on December 4th on the New York. I sent a barrel of apples also to Augustus John for his Missus and the kids and one to Joseph Conrad. I have not heard from Conrad for a long time. He seems to have made a popular success in this country at last with Chance and Victory.

I got about two weeks ago the two parcels containing your wonderful introductions to volumes 17, 18, 19, 20, 21, 22, 23, and 24 of your Father's Collected Edition. I notice that in the introduction to volume 21, the pages containing the two facsimiles of the initial words "Empty" and "Whilom" are missing but there is a note in your handwriting that "they are to be supplied." The introduction to the previous volume I had carefully kept together but to my horror when I looked them over a year or two ago I found one missing. I feel sure that I have it. The first time that I have an hour or two of a Sunday in my apartment, I will make a thorough search, but things have got so crowded with me that once I put things away, carefully as I think, they are often overlaid or hid away by other things. I used to keep up with the magazines and weekly papers and used to have the Nation and the New Statesman and the New Age and the eye witness and the Times Literary Supplement bound, but they have got away beyond me now. I must have a house cleaning soon and bring them all up to date and supply the missing numbers. I started to print about two or three years ago, a corrected edition of Synge's posthumous play "Deirdre of the Sorrows." It was printed from the Cuala edition printed by the Yeats girls. Their edition bristled with errors. Later I got the MS and detected so many things in the edition that I was sure Synge had not written, that I read the MS and then started to make a corrected edition. The proofs have gone to my apartment from my office and back again perhaps a hundred times. Then every six months or so, I have to pay a bill of eight or ten pounds to keep the type standing. Last Summer I swore I would clean it up but I seem to be driven and pulled into doing things for other people that I have no time to do anything for myself.[1]

As I wrote you [,] I was not away a day this last summer. Sheffield was away but I have been driven to the conclusion that he takes drugs. He is a brilliant man, about 48 or 50, and a good lawyer, but he comes to the office sometimes looking like a ghost and does not get there till eleven or twelve or later. Since I wrote you he has been mixed up in a divorce case with his wife. The papers were full of it. He won the case. But it kept him solidly out of the office for six weeks. He suffers from an excess of self pity or rather I suffer from it. For the last six weeks he literally has not done two hours work in the office and yet he has been drawing a hundred dollars every week. I have worked harder during the last three months than any white man should be compelled to work, mornings, evenings, holidays, and Sundays. I told Sheffield a week ago, when we had a flare up, that after he finished his case, I would give him six weeks more trial. But it is hopeless. I shall have to look around for another man but that will be a difficult job at this time of the year. But I don't want to bore you further with my office matters.

I got a few days ago the beautifully bound "Pilgrims of Hope" and it will take an honored place with my edition of your Father's works. I do not know who the binder is, but the design and the lettering are in excellent taste. Who is the binder, or did you make the design?

Somebody sent me the posthumous volume of Watts-Dunton the other day. I enjoyed the article on your Father's work and the wonderful praise that was given to your Mother in the introduction.[2] The writer of the introduction must have been wrong when he quoted Watts-Dunton to the effect that your Father's range of interests were limited and so on. If there was ever a man of his time of whom that statement was not true, that man was your Father.

Do you really expect to get out the three supplementary volumes soon? Perhaps you are working on them now.

There was a review of your Collected Edition in the New York Times book review in June.[3] The book review is sandwiched in as part of the magazine section of the Sunday issue of the Times. I had five copies of the book review taken from the magazine section and mailed to you towards the middle or end of June. I wonder whether you got them.

I wonder where you have been spending the winter—whether at Kelmscott or in London and whether you were in London during the Zeppelin raids.

Philip Webb's death must have been a wrench and a real grief.

What are you doing about the war? Still working for the Belgians?

I will send you three editorials from the Tribune of last week by Simmonds the editor, which put the case strongly but not too strongly. This country is being misrepresented by Wilson. The Germans and Austrians surrendered abjectly on the submarine issue, in order to focus the attention of Wilson on England's blockade. Wilson is afraid of the German vote. He thinks he can get it by girding at England. The Germans have taken Wilson's measure. I hate to say it but I think he is a coward. Cowardice is perhaps not the right word. Treason I think is the right word to describe the act of a man who is willing to sacrifice his country's honor and its place of supremacy in his desire to cater to the German vote and to be re-elected. I hope to God that England will not budge one inch. I hope much from Russia. She seems to be coming back pretty well. England has had plenty of time to prepare the Suez position and she ought to be able to prevent the Turks or the Germans and the Turks from completing the 120 miles of railroad across the Sinai desert. The papers say that the Germans are spanning the 300 miles of desert from Mami to Suez with a double track railway and with water pipes and that half the distance has already been covered. Surely England must have known of that. She ought to have had spies among the Arabs. If Germany ever gets within striking distance of the Canal, it is good-bye to Egypt for this war. And that would mean also the retreat of the English from Mesopotamia. Nothing can withstand the big German and Austrian guns. It was them that cleaned up Serbia so quickly, guns fired from miles off, so that the poor Serbians never got to grips with the enemy. These guns require railroads for transportation. England therefore ought to block the building of the railroad to Suez. A couple of hundred railway engineers and subway builders would seem to be what the English army needs. They are brave and humane but indifferent. Soldiering now is a matter of transport and material and engineering. It reminds one of the alleged remark of a German naval captain who was captured in one of the North Sea fights and who said: "You are brave and humane soldiers and sailors, but you as a nation will never be scientific as we Germans as a nation will never be gentlemen." Which was a most un-German remark and a most un-German admission.

Well, this takes with it my best wishes for the New year. I hope it may be one of peace and contentment for you and that it may bring victory to England and her Allies.

[Handwritten, January 21:]

I got your letter on Tuesday the 18th and can't understand why my letter was not delivered, but many letters are lost these days. Your New Years' card is very charming. I am sorry you gave all the apples away. A friend sent me a barrel and the boy bakes them for breakfast and they are very good. But I am sure the barrel was appreciated in the fleet. This war is [?] everything. I think the Allies will win. Do you remember what I wrote you when you sent me that damnably asinine Norman Angell's book "Lost Illusions"?[4] He and his kind should be sent to the trenches. Your Zeppelin experience is thrilling even to read but I hope it may not be repeated. Your stove-cleaning experience must have been amusing.

I have been in Court to-day. I am practically alone. Sheffield is no good. The number of appeals that come to me is appalling. I have had to stop them. I had to lend money to a former employee whose wife died 3 days ago, and she had none. I will write again soon. I have had no vacation for two years. It tells on the health and nerves, and I have been cranky.

Well, this takes all good wishes for the next year and for your peace and safety during these days [?].

Faithfully yours.

* * *

[May Morris to Quinn, from Kelmscott Manor, 23 April 1916.]
My dearest John:

Your letter dated January 20th reached me in due course—that is after considerable delay. I had a considerable American mail that day, by chance, and of them all, yours only was opened by the Censor. It was my first experience of censoring from the U.S. and I was exceedingly and unreasonably angry. I should have thought your name printed on the envelope was sufficient guarantee of good faith.

I can't tell you how vexed I am never to have received that other letter. But it is not surprising, nowadays.

I have to thank you for (a) a batch of New York Times's which reached me so long ago, and which I never acknowledged, as I was waiting so many months hoping to hear from you: (b) a copy of Huneker's Ivory, Apes and Peacocks (c) Amy Levy's essay on six French poets, (d) the war-book mechanistic view of War and Peace and (e) A. E.'s last volume.[5]

LeGallienne's review of the last volumes of the Collected Works is very handsome; it interests me because he has hit upon some of the good points that others have passed over, and yet he has no sympathy with the Troy poem which to most of us is the finest thing of the lot.[6] R. G. in early days used to wear long hair and an 'intense' tie and bored me excessively. I expect he is much changed.[7]

Mr. Huneker's Essays are very able, and interesting; tho' when I read them I was hurried and tired and did not read them critically. But shortly after reading the "Dostoievsky and Tolstoy', I read a study on Dostoievsky, Tolstoy, and Ibsen, by the Frenchman—what is his name? (I'm idiotic over names just now, being tired). What a difference! It made poor Huneker's seem so slight and superficial; the handling of words was so distinguished, the insight so remarkable, the touch altogether so masterly . . . do you remember our talking of old Ibsen one day? You would have enjoyed the way he is handled, with delicate irony and charmingly veiled distaste. I hope to get the name right before I close. If not, never mind.

Suarez *[sic]* is the name.[8]

I am rather surprised at your opinion on the book on War. For a hospital student well and good; they must face any study of the horrors involved in the destruction and mutilation of humanity—but to a layman who feels the whole thing with the bottom of his soul without seeing photographs of the horrors, what earthly good does it do? George Crile makes his statements,[9] and we all agree (as far as we may in our unprofessional judgement)—but after? At the end of the Chapter on Belgian Vivisection (which

I know something about, alas) he says "a mechanistic view-point would suggest the mediation of the further progress of physical and moral destruction by repairing the homes and fortunes of these exiles" etc . . . Well, so does an ordinary commonsense humanitarian viewpoint, surely. Nothing new or startling here. I read (in deference to your emphatic praise) the chapter on Evolution toward Peace carefully, and of course agreed, and some of it is well put ("civilized man in a death struggle with the Frankenstein of his own creation", etc), and any one would agree that if we are to evolve towards Peace at the long last, it must be through the education of the next generation.

I can't say I read books on the War much; I just set my teeth and do what I can, and go on, trying never to lose courage, and to look beyond all this.

I read Miss Levy's with great interest, and was pleased to get so many [?] quoted, for I knew nothing of some of these men. At the same time, I rather wonder over Miss Levy herself; she seems to me ill-equipped to write an important essay of the sort. She strikes me as I read like one hopelessly outside the atmosphere of French litterateurs. Her phrases are sometimes clumsy and want editing. This does not mean I am ungrateful for the book, as I am so glad to have the poems and the notes on the men which no doubt are accurate and careful. I have been reading a good deal of French stuff lately, and find it soothing.

Wonderful French nation—men and women, how they touch me at the present, in their heroism and cheerful hard work! The women of France will live in history, beside their men, surely.

I think that the proofs of Introduction you found missing must have been the 'Jason' which was sent to you a little while ago (with illustrations); so I hope it will have reached safely.

About the binder of 'The Pilgrims of Hope'; it is Miss Katherine Adams, of Broadway, Worcestershire.[10] She is a very old friend of mine, but prejudice apart, I look upon her, not only as the best woman binder in England, but as the best we have, regardless of sex. And others agree with me. I regret to say that in spite of this excelling in the art, she is closing her bindery, not being able to get enough work. Such is art! I forgot! The most surely welcome book was the dear A. E.'s[11]

Yes, I was very sorry not to keep your apples at Christmas, but, you see, some of us feel the matter of personal luxury in war-time very strongly, and I knew if I took some out of the firmly-packed barrel, I should never get them up to the Fleet in good condition. I enclose my young friend's letter of thanks, as it rather drives it home to one, the Spartan life these fine men are living up there on the North Sea.[12] He is an Oxford man who volunteered at once—the last person in the world to take kindly to such an existence. The way all these young men of the Universities went off without a moment's hesitation, leaving their work and all it meant for them, cheerfully and eagerly, hating the new soldier-life—many of them that I know, at least——Well, there it is.

I have a lovely photograph of Rupert Brooke, by the bye. I wonder if you met him?

I am not sure if I answered in my letter of January 1st the questions you asked before it reached you. I have had to live a great deal at Kelmscott—tho' much torn in two between country and city—partly because the house has needed careful repairs that have been done with exasperating slowness, and needed my constant supervision. Also the building of two cottages in memory of my Mother, which now they are finished seem quite part of the lovely old village. No higher praise could be given. I live here with the utmost frugality personally, spending all possible pennies on 'War-things' on the one hand, and the necessary repairs aforesaid, on the other. I haven't had the heart to begin the extra volumes yet, tho' all the matter is there, and the scheme pretty well planned out. I have before me a lecture on my Father to be given in the autumn before the two Guilds, mine and the men's Art Worker's Guild. I'm rather nervous thinking about it. We shall all be very busy this summer over a big Exhibition of our Arts & Crafts [?] Society at Burlington House in the Autumn. We hope the Exhibition may lead on to great things, for as you know it is not mere exhibition-work we think of, but the national art of the future, and the welfare of the young, whose talent now is not wanted or recognized. I am also busy organizing a modest meeting or Conference of Art-workers and Art Critics. I shall tell you if it is successful. I haven't time to write at length on all these things, but you divine the sort of thing, and know one's aims and ideals.

I have to speak at Bradford to rich manufacturers next month. I hate these talks, longing to work quietly, between writing and designing, and the inevitable war-work. No, I am "off" Belgians at any rate for a time, having undertaken some modest voluntary work down here, and have plenty of casual jobs that take time, though they don't sound picturesque or effective. The movement of Women on the Land is beginning here: it ought to have been organized from the first as some of us said or wrote. It is now being started I hope systematically and wholesale.[13]

I read President Wilson's address and his note to Germany the other day with great interest. What will come next? The same as before, or is this 'business'?

I've been ill (doctor every day, etc.—a silly chill 'suppressed') and had an enforced fortnight idle, to my great inconvenience.

I'm much concerned to hear of your business worries. I'd have thought some intelligent younger man would have been only too happy to join in with you. Why do the wrong people always seem to turn up! You must know of course that I'm always most interested to hear of your doings.

By the bye the Tribune editorials you speak of are not yet to hand.

I don't believe you can have read my letter through, though. You are a strange being.

Yours ever
May

By the bye never again inscribe any books you're kind enough to send, to "Miss" M. M. or put "with kind regards". I won't be treated so formally. The bare name if you're not moved to write any thing nicer!

* * *

[May Morris to Quinn, from 8 Hammersmith Terrace, New Year's Eve, 1916.]

Dearest John:

I was glad to get your cable on Christmas morning; but if one hadn't been so heavy hearted one could have smiled at the promise 'writing soon'. When? Six months hence? Cables don't take the place of letters, my dear. But I am thankful to know that you are there, at least. I received one letter this year—on February 7th. I wonder if I am to conclude that letters have gone to the bottom. Cela se peut [That is possible]; I've sent you various "printed matter" things which I fear may not have arrived—including one I should be sorry about, i.e. the Jason Introduction (with illustrations) which for some reason was not sent in its due place. Well it can't be helped. Let me know some time about this Introduction, if you still care about having the set complete. I would do my best to replace it.

I have been so busy, partly over humble little war-activities, and partly over our big and important Arts and Crafts show at the Royal Academy this autumn, that there has been no possibility of getting on with those poor three "extra volumes". I am now busy finishing a lantern-lecture on my Father and his art-work—the date is getting terribly near—and when that is over, I shall try to concentrate myself, if only for a few hours a week, on putting in order the material for these volumes. Longmans won't certainly take them in hand during the war, but I do so hate leaving my work so long unfinished, and it would be some satisfaction to get it that much forward. We want some more purchasers for the Edition. I only begin to get any profit out of it after a certain number is sold!

My income is of course seriously cut down, like that of so many of us, and more and more claims for help come that one dares not listen to. All decent people live more and more penuringly and we go about in positive rags. Some of the small day to day difficulties of housekeeping we shall smile at in days to come: such as my experience of waiting an hour at my stores and ordering a great many things for the sake of getting sugar, of which commodity I was only allowed a pound, after all that effort.

At Kelmscott, I have turned the strawberry beds into onion-beds, and cultivate all the ground to the utmost, breaking up grass for new crops and so forth; and I much hope that my retaining the gardener, whom I could ill spare in that lonely corner, will be justified if they go round clearing off more men. Indeed we need more labour on the land than we have got now if we are to keep up to the average, to say nothing of speeding up production. Our agricultural question is enormously interesting—and enormously serious. I see no way out of it but a genuine universal cooperation. Well I must not start talking politics or War; or saying all I want to on immediate questions.

This is the last letter I write to anyone this year, and a great deal unsaid goes with it.

Yours always
May Morris

* * *

[May Morris to Quinn, from Kelmscott Manor, Lechlade, New Year's Eve 1917.]

Thank you for your cable, dear John: I was glad to have the message and have news of you.

I came down here to spend Christmas quietly with a farmworking friend, after a very long and over-worked time this autumn and winter; but I promptly got Influenza and had to go to bed. I had sent the servants on a holiday, as we meant to cook and do our own chores, so it was rather a sell for my friend, Miss Lobb, who had to nurse me into the bargain. However, we are through it now, and are sitting in the kitchen for the last time, writing our New Year's Eve's few letters, and expecting the girls back. I've just been ironing some dozen of soldiers' socks—rather proud of them, as they are done by my own 'group' of village-girls, whose work is my entire charge.

This has been a specially anxious year for me, as I have had the responsibility of my sister who is an invalid. The responsibility is a thing sacred and precious to me, but coming on the top of other work, it has all been very difficult and harassing, especially as she has been living here with me, and the place—or the memories of it—always make her far worse. Now, by dint of much anxious enquiry and travelling hither and thither (but partly by a miracle, I think), I have managed to find a delightful home for her in a lovely and beautiful bit of country, and she is picking up strength and spirits wonderfully. The house seems very empty without her, but I must be very busy and try and not think of that.

I think you ought to know that I have received no letter since last February twelve-month—nearly two years ago. A few months back came a long envelope which I welcomed, but found to be a reprint of a public letter of yours. I imagine your letters are gone down with lost mails, for I can't believe that none have been written in all that time. This may not reach you, but indeed, I hope it will. I'd have liked to cable a greeting, which is more certain but as the years of war go on, things get difficult, and one isn't able to do these things.

With love and all possible good wishes for the new year

Yours always
May Morris

Appendix: *Lady Griselda's Dream* by May Morris

Scene—*A London Drawing Room, with the usual blue china, white paint, and Eastern portières. Everything wears a look of fastidious freshness, and a vague perfume of dried roses and orange blossom hangs about the draperies. It is a dark winter afternoon.* Lady Griselda Fairweather *sits in a low chair, facing the fire, with a letter in her hand. Her face is distinguished, though pale and thin; she has the good looks that ripen into beauty in a happy entourage. As it is, she is faded, and the hand that holds the paper between her face and the glow of the hearth looks unwholesomely fragile beneath its load of rings.*

Lady Griselda (aloud to herself). One more look at it! . . . The handwriting says nothing.

A Voice at the door. May one come in to stroke one's Auntie Grissel and run home again?

Lady G. (rousing herself). Oh, come in, Sissie. Have you brought Baby?

Enter Lady Lucy Cohen, *her sister, fair and plump and bubbling with health and spirits. She is followed by a smart nurse carrying the First-born. Picture: the two women bend over the bundle of white satin and cashmere,* Lucy *absorbed and for the moment forgetful of her pretty and exquisitely tailored person;* Griselda, *at once absent and wistful, delicately passing her fingers over the baby's dimples, and smiling vaguely at her sister's maternal babble.*

Lady Lucy. Now, Nurse, you can take Baby home in the carriage. I shall take a hansom after a few minutes' gossip with you, Grissy. Ta, my angelest angel! (*Exit* Infant *and* Nurse.) Now, old lady, one can see you want a little smartening up. Been thinking again?

Lady G. (glancing at the clock). No, darling, only rather tired. I was playing all the afternoon, and, you know, when I forget myself at the piano, I always get done up.

[*Looks at the clock again.*]

Lady G. (nervously). I thought it was going to strike.

Lady L. Well, it wont *bite* you. And, Grissy, *who* made that gown?

Is your idiot of a maid suddenly inspired, or have you taken my advice and gone to Jones, at last? I always said you were splendid material. *Is* it Jones?

Lady G. (blushing). This gown? Why, it's nothing; I and my woman arranged it between us.

Lady L. Then *you* are inspired; or—*(She laughs again, and, suddenly getting up, stands in front of her sister.)* Grissy, I do believe you have an appointment—someone coming to tea and confidences; someone very, very—That Clock really is all right! *Bon, je file!* I'm not going to spoil sport. Ta-ta, sweet one! Oh how delicious your tea-table looks—coquettishly dainty—and your January roses, like June itself! Grissy! *(She raises her long eye-glasses and looks steadfastly and seriously at her sister.)* I do hope he—whoever he is—will appreciate the set of your sleeve! No, he can't: it takes a woman *(with a sigh).* Well, you shan't be teased.

Lady G. (twisting her rings nervously). You don't tease, and I should have liked to tell you, and—and ask your advice. But Baby takes all your attention, doesn't he? *(With a suddenly tremulous voice.)* I feel as if I must speak to some one at last. Lucy! . . . Eugene has come back. I mean, is coming to see me.

Lady L. Eugene? After all those years, Grissel?—and you *let* him, the heartless jilt!

Lady G. Lucy!

Lady L. (angrily). Haven't you allowed him to wreck your life enough?

Lady G. (weakly). He may have misunderstood something. I always think if one doesn't meet face to face . . . And you know, Lucy, men are so different from us. They want change, they want laughter and brilliance and a ready smile, and God knows I hadn't—

Lady L. (impetuously). Who took all that from you? What a splendid bright girl you were before he threw you over without a word to explain . . . Oh if it had been me!

[*Clenches her little hands.*]

Lady G. (with her eyes on the fire). One can't 'explain' a change of that sort. I think he did right to say nothing; perhaps an explanation would have been an insult. Yes, . . they change, and I . . . Oh Lucy! Lucy! Lucy! *(throws herself into the younger woman's arms),* how I loved that man!

Lady L. (gives her a good-natured pat). I know! And a fine halo you set round your love. Fancy a woman of your brains putting up with the crack-brained idiot for an hour. *I* could never understand it.

Lady G. (without listening to her). How happy I was laying at his feet my whole heart's treasure. *(Sobbing.)* Desolate as I've been ever since, I don't think I would change my short dream for all the years of untroubled life I might have had but for that. My beautiful love!

[*Her head drops on her sister's shoulder.*]

Lady L. There, there! *(Strokes her hair, while making, for her own satisfaction, a little grimace of impatience and bewilderment.)* You poor old thing! You unpractical, mooning, dear thing! If all women demanded as much as you—*(Gives a little gurgling laugh of amusement.)* If I clamoured for poetry and love and all the rest of it from my very unpoetic old man! . . . He finds it easier to give one diamonds, and then *(naïvely)* there's Baby. Consider, too, what would the future generation be if we *all* went in for the superior sentiments you indulge in.

Lady G. (raises her head and dries her eyes). Is it my fault that I'm still a lonely woman?

Lady L. (brightly). Well, I think it is. A young man strikes your fancy: while he is tiring of you you are building up that fancy into a passion—I wonder if it is nice to be in love?—and when he goes the way of all flesh and leaves you, in search of new worlds to conquer, instead of bravely shaking the dream off, you sit brooding over your wrong; a wrong that—Goodness me!—nine women out of ten have to experience in the course of their lives, most likely, if they made a fuss and let the world know about it.

Lady G. (murmurs). I loved my dream!

Lady L. (sharply). Yes! for something like ten years you have given yourself up to the luxury of nursing a grievance, and in the meanwhile, scrubby, uninteresting little women like me manage to have a fairly good time, hurting nobody, not even themselves.

Lady G. (faintly contemptuous). What a negative good! I wanted to be . . . oh! . . . so much . . .

[*She stops and broods.*]

Lady L. You wanted to be the artist's inspiration, of course. *Entendu!* But when the divine fire left your painter-man, where were you then? And everyone but you saw that he was bored by you and the Aims and everything grandiose, and was longing to live a jolly, vulgar, commonplace life.

Lady G. (coldly). How could *you* understand!

Lady L. (with good humour). My dear girl, I'm out of patience with you over this visitor of yours. *(She stops and laughs.)* Is it providential, though? The dream may vanish before the man. You are waiting, you are dressed for, the Eugene of ten years ago, spiritualised by the world-fight and by the self-enforced renunciation of his ideal love—is that the expression, eh? Now, I would bet, this afternoon's Eugene Sinclair is a portly and impressive person, not ill-provided with adipose deposit.

[*Walks across the room humming a waltz.*]

Lady G. (smiles faintly and loftily). You say rather vulgar things sometimes, darling, without meaning them.

Lady L. (with incorrigible, good-natured flippancy). Lamentable results of home-life on the lower plane, my angel in white cashmere. Oh, Grissy, promise me one thing!

[*She rests her little plump hands on her sister's slender shoulders and looks into her eyes with genuine seriousness as they stand face to face.*]

Lady G. (nervously). What, darling?

Lady L. Never wear anything but white Indian cashmere, and don't let anyone persuade you to give up those long sweeping lines. You never could be smart, dearest; but you're better than smart, like that. I'm glad I insisted on your keeping grandpapa's sapphires; they're so barbaric, they make me feel two inches high; on you they're romantic. And now good-bye, naughty girl. I can't advise you, for you're not in an advisable mood. Have a good flirt, and—By-the-bye, didn't he marry?

Lady G. Yes. *(Turns away with agitation.)* I suppose his wife's dead.

Lady L. (slowly). H'm—well. All I beg is, don't make a fool of yourself. The world's overstocked, and a woman who can show off the Fairweather sapphires as you do, Grissel, can't afford to make a scandal. It's—wasteful! Really good-bye, my own.

[*Whisks out of the room with a little laugh.*]

Lady G. (sinks on the sofa with a sigh of relief). I am tired and excited when I want to be fresh and cool.

[*The glow of the fire is intensified in the cold failing light outside the windows. She stretches a languid hand towards the bell, but lets it fall, and with a pleased smile on her mouth, her head sinks gently into the cushions and her eyes close. She seems to hear a slight noise above the rumbling of the street, which has grown far-off and dim. The portière has been raised, and a tall man stands in the doorway. As her eyes open he walks slowly down the length of the room, coming gradually into the spreading circle of light that the high-piled coals and blue flame of the logs give out. She raises her pale hands feebly and lets them drop, lying power-

less with her eyes riveted on the newcomer. He walks round the little tea-table and kneels beside her, bends his face and lets his lips rest on hers in a long kiss. Releasing her he remains kneeling, and they look into each other's face with rapture.]

Lady G. Eugene! At last!—at last!

Eugene. Griselda, beautiful love! Not changed, only a richer, nobler beauty.

Lady G. Your face is thinner and your eyes hollow, but it is my Eugene, his smile and his kiss. The smile like the sun itself, the kiss—I've dreamt of it!

Eugene (still murmuring). Beautiful love, beautiful angel! *(He strokes her hand. There is a pause.* Griselda, *who has lain with her eyes half closed, stirs, and makes a movement to leave her sofa.* Eugene *gently presses her back in her place.)* No, don't get up. I love to see you stretched there among the delicate white draperies which lie about your feet vaguely in the shadow where the firelight doesn't reach. That sudden sparkle of the falling log has set a red light upon your gown and touched the little curls on your forehead with bronze. It is a Florentine portrait. Oh, the dear delicate meek throat!—the sweet wrists!

[*Kisses them.*]

Lady G. (murmurs). I must be dreaming.

Eugene. That's what women always say. You admit so little indulgence into your scheme of life that a touch of joy overcomes you. 'It must be a dream,' you say, and only pain is real to you.

Lady G. (after a pause). That seems true to me.

Eugene (absently, playing with her fingers). We must live, from day to day. *(Bends and kisses them passionately, then looks up and smiles brilliantly.)* Are they dream-kisses?

Lady G. Let me have a long look at the dear face. *(He raises his head slowly until the flickering firelight falls vaguely on cheek and hair and eyes.)* You will never grow old, Eugene. You are graver and quieter. (Have you thought much of me out in the world? Have you been sorry for going away those years ago?) Ah, but it is still my Eugene. Eugene! Eugene! *(She closes her eyes, and releasing her fingers passes them over his face.)* That is what I used to do. I should know your face if I were blind. Your eyes shine out of the dark at me, full of youth and hope and confidence.

Eugene (smiles). Adorable folly! My Grissel, we old people can well say that Love never grows grey. But now we must talk. I've done wrong to come to you, as I did wrong to go away when the foolish, aimless restlessness came upon me. But I've come to you as a man always comes at last to a good woman—for strength, for confidence to carry out my resolves. My wife—

[Lady G. *starts.*]

Eugene (slowly). Yes, Grissel; I married some years later. Playing the fool first, till I got tired and had spent all my money, I turned to the simple pleasures of a pastoral life in a country vicarage—*(he shrugs his shoulders)*—painting apple-blossom and studying the vicar's niece. *(A pause.)* She had delicious hands, and played the piano divinely. So I, as an artist, fell in love with the hands as they danced over the ivory and ebony, and—*(Breaks off with a laugh.)* I seem to be telling you the plot of a young ladies' novel! Well, men are all fools in the same way, I fancy. The beautiful hands are faded, and the piano is replaced by the babies' crying. I married her, as many men marry a passing fancy, from a luckless sense of honour. Honourable, was it, to drag a poor little innocent girl, whose life should have been an idyll among the roses, into the squalor of real life?

[*While* Eugene *speaks,* Lady G. *has been making an effort to rise. She finds herself curiously powerless. She lies still, but her breast rises and falls in quick, short breaths.*]

Lady G. So it was true, then; you are married. Well, what do you want me to do?

Eugene. Nothing. But let me come sometimes, and be kind to me, that I may go away heartened up, and soothed by the perfume of harmonious graciousness that hangs about you.

Lady G. The passive rôle again! To live beautifully and be admired. Why should some women be doomed to this? Eugene, I could almost envy my little sister, with her intolerable husband and her young baby. She at least is not told she must be content to live on dreams.

Eugene (tenderly). Such beautiful dreams, love! Are you not proud to be the artist's inspiration, his friend and *consolatrice*? The first and foremost woman in the world for him?

[Lady G. *is silent.*]

[*Another log falls apart and a thin blue flame starts up.* Lady G.'s *cheeks glisten with the tears that fall fast.* Eugene, *still on the floor at her feet, caresses one of her hands; with the other she wipes her tears. She looks attentively at him. The room grows dimmer and circle of light round them increases in intensity. A strange stillness fills the air.*]

Lady G. Not thinner; not a day older. As I look at you, those years fall away; and you grow younger.

Eugene (absently twisting a ring on her finger). How, 'thinner and older'? It is only yesterday I saw you.

Lady G. It seems yesterday now. But they have been long years to me. Oh, it's long since forgiven.

Eugene (smiles radiantly). Why, you have been dreaming, my darling. See, here are my roses that I brought you as my New Year's gift.

Lady G. (startled). What do you mean? What you told me—your wife—

Eugene (with the same unearthly smile). You were dreaming, my sweetheart. All misery is not real, nor all happiness a dream.

Lady G. (breaks into a wild cry of rapture and beats the air with her hands). No, I can't bear this; my heart will burst! A dream? . . . Eugene, where are you? The room is dark, and only your face shows in a pale light. . . . I can't hear your voice. . . . Which is true, your love or my loneliness?

Eugene (leans over her. He has taken up the roses and lays them about her face on the pillow). We shall learn perhaps yonder. You and I are dead, and the June roses blossom on the grave.

[*He kisses her.* Lady G. *screams and falls back on the pillow. A loud knocking sounds at the street door below.* Lady G. *wakes up panting and looks about. The fire has burnt hollow, and the rumbling of carriages in the street increases. The knocking at the door is just ending.*]

Lady G. (whispers). Eugene! *(A pause.)* Eugene! . . . My God! I dreamt it.

[*Goes hurriedly to the bell. As she does so, and stands trembling and haggard, the door opens and a footman comes in, turns on the clusters of electric light and announces:*]

Footman. Mr. Eugene Sinclair.

Lady G. Bring tea at once.

[Mr. Eugene Sinclair *walks down the room with a firm, heavy tread, the least bit hurried. Taking her hand, he presses it gently and long.*]

Eugene. Griselda! I may call you by the old name? You have given me so much pleasure in allowing me to come.

Lady G. (tries to smile). You exercise the right of many years of friendship.

Eugene (eagerly). I am so glad you speak at once and frankly. It shows me that we are friends, and that I and my young misdeeds are forgiven.

Lady G. (with forced lightness). The past buries itself, Eugene. I—

[*The footman coming in with a tray stumbles against the*

jamb of the door and all the tea-things rattle. Lady G. *looks gratefully in his direction. Whilst tea is being set,* Eugene *sits down, puts his smart tan-coloured gloves inside his hat and places that with deliberation on a table at his elbow.* Lady G., *in a low chair by the fire, glances up at him from the tea-table. He is a tall, portly man, with a handsome, solid face, and hair thinning on the forehead; well groomed, but almost too carefully dressed.*]

Lady G. (makes a bewildered attempt to smile at him). I suppose I may ask all sorts of questions about your doings—*(gradually recovering her aplomb)*— since you have been so sweet and so amiable as to remember us. Do you paint still? Of course not, or we should hear of your work, certainly.

Eugene (with a gratified smile). No; I've rather given up the arts—except when we take a holiday in Italy or the East; then one becomes inspired, you know. I've been in New York City for many years, in business, and have always been particularly fortunate. In fact, my home is in the States now.

Lady G. (becomes aware that her visitor has a slight American accent, and turns a shudder into a movement of settling back in her chair). Yes?

Eugene. I married out there, you know. *(Looks down meditating at his boots, which are beautifully polished)* I should like you to know my wife. She's a magnificent woman *(looks up with an arch smile)*; so little in your style that one may safely say that, you know.

Lady G. (repressing another tendency to shudder). Yes?

Eugene (leans forward confidentially with his elbows on his knees). She is what you would call an eminently successful woman—a woman of business. Everything she undertakes succeeds, and she won't accept failure. Went into business before I married her and made a pile; but she had got tired of money when I met her and was studying Art, and *(with a 'young' smile and turn of the head)* that's how it happened, you see.

Lady G. (seeking for an inspiration). Yes? So interesting; do go on! Does your wife exhibit in New York?

Eugene (volubly). Oh, no; she only paints for her friends. And really, considering the want of training, her work is wonderful. All the doors of our house over there are decorated—very handsome. But this winter she is very much taken up by the new house. We are settling in England for a year or two, for Emily says she's tired of money-grubbing over the other side, and wants me to look up all old friends. But I'm boring you?

Lady G. (with a mechanically brilliant smile). No! And you thought of me among the others. My dear Eugene, that was friendly of you!

Eugene (leans forward and taking the cup that Lady G. *offers him).* It's all Emily's doing. That woman's observation is colossal! She insisted that I should come and see you among the first. I was doubtful, for I remember I treated you very, very shabbily in the young foolish days.

Lady G. Please, Eugene. It's all buried and done with.

Eugene (heartily). Of course! That's just what Emily said. 'It's all buried, that old fad of yours,' she said, 'and you may be sure the Lady Griselda will like to *have* you call.'

Lady G. (with some hauteur). Mrs. Sinclair knows her sex.

Eugene. Down to the ground! Thanks, a little cream. May I say how I admire your frock? From Paris, I suppose?

Lady G. (flushing). It is my own design.

Eugene. Is it possible?

Lady G. I used to make your models' dresses again and again, when you were in difficulty over them.

Eugene. Those, yes; but that was another thing.

Lady G. (with some irritation). Do you mean that an idle woman's dress is more important than the costumes used by an artist in his work? You *are* changed!

Eugene (smiling stolidly). Well, I've got into a different groove, that's all. You don't owe me a grudge for it?

Lady G. (upsets a teacup with her nervous fingers, and gives a short laugh as she looks up at him). Perhaps I owe you a slight grudge for—*(she stops)*— for giving up working, shall we say?

Eugene (vaguely). Oh, I work, of course. A man would be bored if he did nothing all the time. But, frankly, Emily is such a splendid woman of business that she quite spoils one—leaves one nothing to do. Fact! *(Puts down his cup.)* I have so much to say that you positively must not let me stay and bore you . . . You can't think what a treat it is to a man like me to come out of the crowd into this haven of rest. *(Looks round the room with sentiment.)* One goes out strengthened, refreshed, and ready for the world's work again.

[*He rises and walks about the room with an air finely suggestive of shipwreck.*]

Lady G. (with her eyes fixed on the sofa, repeats mechanically). Strengthened . . . refreshed . . . *(To him.)* Ah, well, Eugene, I don't think the world has worn you much, or used you ill. You look splendidly—confident and prosperous.

Eugene (rising and taking her hand). And you look—wonderful!

And now I have a parting favour to ask—not too much between old friends, I hope. Emily longs to make your acquaintance; she has a little gathering on Friday, and as the time is too short for preliminaries, she begs that you will kindly waive ceremony and come to us.

Lady G. (meekly). Mrs. Sinclair is too kind. Will you let me look in my engagement book?

[*Goes to her writing-table and turns the leaves of a purple-bound book without reading.*]

Eugene (standing at the fire, goes on talking to her over his shoulder). It's really our house-warming, and Emily is anxious to make things go off. *(Laughs good-humouredly.)* The dear woman is bitten by the recitation craze, and is getting up some very taking things in plantation dialect.

Lady G. (over the writing-table, murmurs below her breath). You and I are dead . . . the June roses . . .

Eugene (continuing). Don't say you can't come. For *us,* you know, you can throw over someone else. Clapham is not a long drive.

Lady G. (with closed eyes). Ah, Clapham! *(Shuts the book desperately and walks back to the tea-table, where* Eugene *stands, having gathered hat and gloves in his hand.)* Yes; tell your wife I'll come. As you say, we can dispense with the ceremonies of introduction. And many thanks, of course, and wishes for a happy and useful New Year.

Eugene. Thanks so very much. I may? *(Kisses her hands, first one, then the other.* Lady G. *flushes angrily, and standing in the light of the pink-shaded lamp looks very striking and handsome.* Eugene *looks at her closely with a certain appreciation that makes her flush deeper.)* What a fool I was, Grissel, after all!

Lady G. (simply). I expect you were wise, without meaning to be, Eugene.

Eugene. A mere fool, my dear. *(He gives her the conqueror's look.)* If you were a bad woman, Grissel, and cared . . . you could make a fool of me yet!

Lady G. (very coldly, with lowered eyes). I am not *that* sort of a woman, at least.

Eugene (in a different tone). Nor I that sort of a man, I hope. Now—we expect you Friday. This is *so* delightful, Grissel! One more favour—is it granted before asked?

[*He takes her hands again.*]

Lady G. (hurriedly). Yes, yes!

Eugene. I claim this *en artiste.* You shall wear the famous sapphires that have graced the Fairweather ladies for so long. Emily too has set her heart on having them. She has the true American sentiment about these wonderful heirlooms that *you* set so little store by.

Lady G. (hysterically laughing). Wouldn't the sapphires in a glass case content your American friends' curiosity without me?

Eugene (gently patting her hand). Now, now, Grissel! I can't have you say naughty things to an old friend! Come and look half as beautiful as you do this evening *(places a light kiss on the middle of her forehead),* and charm the heart out of young America.

Lady G. (with heroism). I'll come!

Eugene. May I have one of your roses? *(Takes one from the bowl.)* Wonderful how modern science turns winter into summer—Poetic . . . and with our hearts always young . . . eh, Grissel? Good-bye!

Lady G. Good-bye!

Eugene (at the door). A thousand, thousand thanks!

[*He gives her another look as he passes through the portière.* Lady G. *looks straight in front of her with a mechanical smile.* Eugene *goes.* Lady G. *bends over the bowl of roses, which are already drooping their frail heads; she passes her fingers tenderly over the petals. Turning to the mantelpiece she leans her forehead against the marble ledge, and looks thoughtfully into the fire. Suddenly her shoulders begin to shake with convulsive sobs, long and laboured.*]

Lady G. My beautiful, dead love! Empty, intolerable, barren life!

The door opens, and Lady Lucy Cohen *puts her head in inquiringly.*

Lady L. May one? I couldn't help coming back to hear all about it. *(Comes down the room.)* Why, Grissel! (Lady G. *stands with her forehead against the mantelpiece, gasping and struggling with her sobs.)* What has the wretch done this time? My dear, dear, soft-hearted old thing, do wake up and take things as they come!

Lady G. (raising her head). I'm wide awake now, Lucy! But my head aches and I'm a little depressed and overcome.

Lady L. You had better tell me all about it, darling.

Lady G. (fretfully). There's nothing to tell . . . He's stupid and sleek and purse-proud (Lucy *coughs*), and babbled about 'old friends' till I was sickened.

Lady L. Odious animal!

Lady G. He's got a rich American wife who recites—

Lady L. Ah!

Lady G. They live at Clapham!

Lady L. My God!

Lady G. (wearily). He came to ask me to go to a housewarming, and make a show of the sapphires for the benefit of 'young America.'

Lady L. (murmurs). Can such things go unpunished in a civilised country?

Lady G. (with a hysterical laugh). And fancy, Lucy, I lost my self-possession at that, and asked if the sapphires wouldn't do without me—in a glass case—ha! ha! ha!

Lady L. (with a horrified little gasp). Grissel! You?

[*There is a pause.*]

Lady L. What are you doing? Burning him in effigy?

[Lady G. *has taken the roses from the bowl in her two hands, and sinking on her knees by the glowing hearth, scatters them carefully on the fire. She watches the smouldering blossoms thoughtfully before speaking.*

Lady G. (absently). In the heart of the fire, where they can't decay, or rot, or grow old . . . and the dreams go with them, up into the cold thin air—not lost, but purified . . .

Lady L. I always said that young man was a cad.

Lady G. My head aches.

MAY MORRIS

Notes

Introduction

1. The year was 1910. See B. L. Reid, *The Man from New York: John Quinn and His Friends* (New York: Oxford University Press, 1968), 80.

2. Among the Manets Quinn owned were *Le Polichinelle, Paola,* and *Kneeling Figure of Woman.* Among the Matisses were *Nude Seated, L'Esclave Blanche, The Spanish Girl, Hat with Roses, Girl with Flowers, The Cyclamen, Nature Morte, L'Atelier,* and the sculpture, *Bronze Head of Boy.* This is by no means a complete listing. See Judith Zilczer, *John Quinn: Patron of the Avant-Garde* (Washington D.C.: The Smithsonian Institution Press, 1978); and Joseph Brummer & E. Weyhe, *John Quinn: Collection of Paintings, Water Colors, Drawings, and Sculpture* (New York: Pidgeon Hill Press, 1926) for information on Quinn's collection.

3. At one time, Quinn owned nearly all of Conrad's original mss. He also owned a number of Eliot's mss., including the original Eliot-Pound ms. of *The Waste Land.* See Reid, 112, 533–40, 580–81.

4. Saarinen, *The Proud Possessors: The Lives, Times, and Tastes of some Adventurous American Art Collectors* (New York: Random House, 1958), 206–237.

5. Reid, 81.

6. The letters owned by Richard Londraville are dated (M. Morris to Quinn) 26 March 1912, Easter Monday 1912, 25 April 1912, 30 September 1913, and 15 April 1914; and (Quinn to M. Morris) 4 June 1914, 10 February 1915.

Mrs. Foster, editor, poet, model, and art-buyer for Quinn, died in 1970. A good friend of the Yeats family, she met Quinn through John Butler Yeats in 1918. See Richard Londraville, "The Many Careers of Jeanne Robert Foster," *Biblion* (Winter 1968): 84–92; "Jeanne Robert Foster," *Eire Ireland* Vol. 5, #1 (Spring 1970): 38–44; and Janis and Richard Londraville, "A Portrait of Ford Madox Ford: Unpublished Letters from the Ford-Foster Friendship," *English Literature in Transition* (February 1990): 181–207.

7. Jan Marsh, *Jane and May Morris: A Biographical Story 1839–1938* (London: Pandora Press, 1986).

8. There were certainly more letters. Mrs. Foster left a note to Richard Londraville saying that she had sent back many of May's letters to her after Quinn's death (From the private collection of Richard Londraville). These May must have destroyed. The ones that were saved might have been done so by accident. Quinn left many boxes of papers, which Mrs. Foster catalogued for the New York Public Library (hereafter NYPL). Mr. Thomas Conroy had additional excerpts, typed by Mrs. Foster, from other letters from May to Quinn, which I have reprinted in this book.

9. May did write one letter to Shaw (n. d.) that indicates some intimacy with him: " . . . your resolution when we became acquainted not to make love was most judicious and worthy of all praise, having, as you say, the most entirely

satisfying results: I don't think our intercourse can have caused you more pleasure than it has me" (Michael Holroyd, *Bernard Shaw: The Search for Love* [London: Chatto & Windus], 225).

Letters from May and John Quinn to Esther Pissarro in the Pissarro Archives at the Ashmolean Museum in Oxford hint at May and Quinn's attraction to one another. "I do like your John Quinn," writes May on 9 January 1910. "He has been more heartily friendly and companiable *[sic]* than anyone I've met in this country."

10. *Lady Griselda's Dream* is reprinted in the appendix of this text. See Janis Londraville, "*Lady Griselda's Dream:* May Morris's *Man and Superman*," *The Independent Shavian* 39, no. 1: 6–14.

11. David and Sheila Latham, *An Annotated Critical Bibliography of William Morris* (London: Harvester Wheatsheaf, 1991), 15. In a contemporary review of the *Collected Works* (*Athenaeum* [30 December 1911]: 813), the reviewer says that "no one can go through these volumes without being struck by the great labour that has been spent on getting a correct reproduction of the author's thought, and the numberless minor corrections in punctuation and the like that have been made. . . . [May Morris's] descriptions of [Morris's] life and activities, while not trenching on the province of Prof. Mackail's 'Life,' have supplemented and illumined it to a remarkable degree; the William Morris of a small circle may now be seen by the world in his true light."

William Morris: Artist, Writer, Socialist, ed. May Morris (New York: Russell and Russell, 1966) was originally published in Oxford by B. Blackwell in 1936 in 2 vols.

12. May Morris in her introduction to Vol. VIII (p. xxvi) of *The Collected Works* (New York: Russell and Russell, 1966).

13. From Lily (Susan Mary) Yeats's *Scrapbook,* "My Six Years I Spent with May Morris." Ms. Yeats worked for May from 1888 until 1894 (From the private collection of Michael Yeats).

No one knew at the time that Lily Yeats suffered from a severe thyroid condition; it was not properly diagnosed until years later. Because of her poor health, she finally resigned her position with the Morris firm. Any sympathy she might once have felt for May was obviously gone: "I wrote [May] a letter saying on account of my health I would leave. . . . She wrote to me saying that she ought to have given me my congé long ago as I was so delicate. It was a very mean letter. I had never been absent more than two or three days each year, and she never paid anyone when absent from illness, and if we were even five minutes late in the morning we had to make it up during our lunch hour. Papa was so angry at her letter that he did not sleep all night. In the morning he dictated the following letter for me to write to her:

Dear May,

I have received your malicious and impudent letter and will leave at once,

which I did" (*Scrapbook*). See also William M. Murphy, *Prodigal Father* (Ithaca, New York: Cornell University Press, 1978), 164, 180.

14. One play in which May acted with her father was *The Tables Turned or Nupkins Awakened,* written by Morris. It was first performed on 15 October 1887 in the Hall of the Socialist League. In "Aristophanes in Farringdon Road: 'A Socialist Interlude,'" *Pall Mall Gazette,* 17 October 1887: 1–2, the reviewer of *The Tables Turned* states that "Miss May Morris . . . acted with grace" and sang

"pleasantly to her guitar." See reprint of *The Tables Turned; or, Nupkins Awakened,* ed. Pamela B. Wiens (Ohio University Press: 1994).

15. Marsh, *Jane and May Morris,* 16.

16. The photograph is reproduced as #39 in Marsh, *The Pre-Raphaelite Sisterhood* (New York: St. Martin's Press, 1985). Lily Yeats wrote of her first encounter with Jane Morris: "I thought her ugly. Her skin was sallow and coarse. . . . Afterwards when I saw her in the drawing room lying on the settee dressed in rich coloured brocade it was a different story. She had large hazel eyes, calf-like and without light. She never spoke and always seemed unhappy. She liked to be surrounded by people easy to talk to and flattering and admiring, and instead she was surrounded by cranks and freaks and bad tempers, people who never looked at her" *(Scrapbook).*

17. Peter Faulkner, *Jane Morris to Wilfrid Scawen Blunt* (Exeter: University of Exeter Press, 1986), ix. Jane's friendship and affair with Blunt seems strange. She must have known of his reputation and guessed that people would talk. But she was lonely, unhappy in her marriage, and vulnerable when he arrived on the scene. Even after the sexual relationship ended, they remained friends.

18. In "The Defence of Janey," *The Journal of the William Morris Society* (Autumn 1987): 20, Jan Marsh explains that "Jane knew that May did not love her prospective husband Harry Sparling, whom she seems to have picked up on the rebound from George Bernard Shaw. In many ways Jane remained a romantic believer in true love. If she warned her daughter against a loveless marriage, her advice was vindicated within a couple of years [when the marriage failed]. To some extent, Jane's morose response towards May's emotional affairs would seem to have been justified."

19. Blunt's diaries at times indicate that he did not care for May: "May is an obstinately silent woman . . . ." (29 Nov. 1896) "Her ideas were all her father's and I fancy her art too" (5 April 1897). Faulkner, *Jane Morris to Wilfrid Scawen Blunt,* 107.

After reading an article Blunt published about her father in the 8 May 1919 issue of the *Times Literary Supplement,* May wrote to the paper that Blunt gave "a somewhat misleading impression of [Morris]" that could "develop into a legend of moroseness and selfishness." "William Morris," she continued, "possessed to a marked extent the power of concentration, of shutting off the world when at work, which all men who have made their mark must possess; but he also had the talent of giving himself to his friends in holiday time. . . . I don't want the legend of a morose hermit, unwilling to hold a helping hand to man or woman, to grow around my father's memory. It is so wide of the mark" (22 May 1919: p. 280, cols. 3 and 4).

May always felt the need to defend her father and did so again in the *Times Literary Supplement* years later, on 17 May 1934: "As to the words that may be construed into finding a sort of inhumanity in him, let those to whom Morris is only a fairy-tale be told that the friends who surrounded him with their affection knew well what they were to him—knew that behind the reserve of a shy man was the need for friendship and a deep satisfaction in their love" (p. 360, col. 3).

20. For a detailed discussion of May's training and of her management of Morris & Co., see Marsh, *Jane and May Morris,* 160–62, 168–71, 217–20.

21. Isabelle Anscombe, *A Woman's Touch: Women in Design from 1860 to the Present Day* (New York: Viking Penguin Inc., 1984), 23.

22. Elizabeth Masterman, "May Morris, Some Notes for Book Collectors" (*The*

Book Collector: Summer, 1984): 170–71. May exhibited some of her work as early as 1888, when she was only twenty-six, at the Arts and Crafts Exhibition Society at New Gallery on Regent Street. See *Arts and Crafts Exhibition Society Catalogue of the First Exhibition* (London: The New Gallery, 1888): 104, 145. She exhibited a Screen of tulip and pomegranate embroidered with floss silk and a silk embroidered cover for *Love is Enough.*

23. See Marianne Carlano, *Early Modern Textiles from Arts and Crafts to Art Deco* (Boston: Museum of Fine Arts, 1993); and Helen Sloan, *May Morris, 1862–1938: An Exhibition at the William Morris Gallery, 10 January–11 March 1989* (London: The William Morris Gallery, 1989).

24. May Morris, "Embroidery," in *Plain Handicrafts,* ed. A. H. Mackmurdo (London: Percival & Co., 1892), 47–48.

25. In a letter to the *Times,* Philip Burne-Jones wrote that "It is many a day now since students have been sedulously advised to ignore the wisdom and experience of the past, to despise correct drawing, to shun beauty in any form, and to seek their inspiration in the tavern and the gutter. Such advice could have only one result—anarchy and degradation of art exemplified to-day by the Post-Impressionists.

" . . . One is tempted to suspect that it is a huge practical joke, organized in Paris at the expense of our countrymen." See the *Times* 17 Nov. 1910: p. 4, col. 1.

See also Burne-Jones's "The Cult of the Hideous and the Modern Iconoclasts: An Address Delivered at the Author's Club, 19 February 1912" (London: Chiswick Press, 1912).

26. For a discussion about Morris's activities, see Peter Faulkner, *Against the Age: An Introduction to William Morris* (London: George Allen & Unwin, 1980).

27. See May's letter to Quinn dated 31 December 1915 (chapter 6) for her views about the necessity of art during war.

28. Sally Peters, "From Mystic Betrothal to Ménage à Trois: Bernard Shaw and May Morris," *The Independent Shavian,* Vol. 28, #1–2 (1990): 6.

29. Lily Yeats was not taken with Mr. Sparling's physical stature: "[May] had just become engaged against all their wishes to a reporter, a freak to look at, very tall, no chin, and very large spectacles" *(Scrapbook*). In another notebook titled *Draft Scrapbook,* Ms. Yeats goes on to say that Sparling was "the queerest looking young man, very tall, thin, stooped. . . . Her people did not like the engagement" (From the private collection of Michael Yeats). In *Prodigal Father,* Murphy suggests that May chose Sparling "partly to spite her parents" and that "he was a convenient stick for May to beat her parents with" (156–57).

30. When Shaw's home on Fitzroy Square was being redecorated, he moved in with the Sparlings to avoid the paint fumes (Holroyd, 227).

31. Shaw, *Morris As I Knew Him,* (London: The William Morris Society, 1966), 32–33. Shaw's 1893 diary details some of his time with May: [21 May] ". . . Sparling being in France . . . May and I walked to Richmond by way of Strand-on-the-Green, Kew Gardens and the towpath. We came back by train and I played *Die Walküre* to her after tea. I slept at the Terrace." [30 June] ". . . I went to the Terrace with May and slept there." [10 July] "May came back with me. After tea she and I went for a walk over Primrose Hill where we sat for a while. . . . I slept at the Terrace" (Holroyd 228).

32. Lucy Carr Shaw to Janey Crichton, 27 July 1901. Shaw actually married Charlotte Payne Townshend on 1 June 1898, several months before May's divorce became final (Marsh, *Jane and May Morris,* 237).

33. Longmans, publishers of *The Collected Works,* often urged May to work

more quickly and did not always treat her well. When visiting her in London in 1911, Quinn wrote in his journal that he was shocked to learn May was only receiving £10 for each volume: "so she gets less than a typewriter . . ." (Reid, 99). See Henry Curwen (1845–1892), *A History of Booksellers, the Old and the New* (London: Chatto and Windus, 1873) for a discussion of the Longman family.

34. J. W. Mackail letter quoted in Eugene D. Lemire's *The Unpublished Lectures of William Morris* (Detroit: Wayne State University Press, 1969), 21.

35. Quinn writes to Esther Pissarro on three occasions: "I got a note from [Miss Morris] from Chicago the other day. She expects to return to New York for a few days in December. I have just written her a note telling her I should be glad to show her something of the city. . . ." [27 Nov. 1909]. "Miss Morris has been quite successful lecturing. She expects to go presently into Canada and expects to return about the end of March or early in April" [7 March 1910]. "Miss Morris's trip here was a great success, although she worked very hard" [15 Nov. 1910] (Pissarro Archives, Ashmolean Museum, Oxford).

36. Reid explains that May and Quinn "toured the city, dined out, and were much together at Quinn's apartment" (80).

37. Woodrow Wilson, whom Quinn disliked, was nominated instead of Underwood. Underwood remained in the House and continued to be a strong ally. He helped Quinn repeal the Tariff Act of 1909, which taxed imported art less than twenty years old. Quinn wrote two briefs he presented to the House entitled *Memorandum Against Taxing Sales of Works of Art* (n. d.) and *Memorandum Against the Imposition of Any Duty on Original Works of Art* (1921). See chapter 4, Quinn to May Morris, 18 June 1913.

38. On 26 March 1923, Quinn wrote to Percy Moore Turner explaining that "I have never been a Tammany lawyer nor have I ever been a member of Tammany Hall. . . . While I went to National and State Conventions, I never was a member of Tammany Hall, never served on any of its committees, never held any office under it. . . ." (Reid, 573–74).

39. Quinn argued that if a person could not comprehend *Ulysses,* the book could not corrupt him because one cannot be corrupted by something one doesn't understand. Although Quinn lost the case—largely because Joyce did not take his advice on several occasions—Reid says that Quinn's arguments "formed much of the grounds of decision twelve years later when *Ulysses* was cleared for American publication—in a judgment which is generally taken as a model of enlightened jurisprudence" (Reid, 455–56). See Reid, 439–58; and Jackson Bryer, "Joyce, *Ulysses,* and the *Little Review,*" *The South Atlantic Quarterly,* LXVI (Spring 1967): 148–64.

40. From "Notes of Conversations with Jeanne Robert Foster," Richard Londraville, private diaries, 1966.

41. Reid, 80.

42. See May's 5 December 1914 letter to Quinn (chapter 5) for her impressions of Shaw's 14 November 1914 *New Statesman* article, "Commonsense about the War." During World War I May became involved in the Women's Institutes and helped make clothing and find supplies for Belgian refugees. At the same time, she studied Lloyd-George's views on rural reform, a chief interest of hers, and was impressed with George Russell's (AKA "A. E.," 1867–1935) ideas for agricultural reform in Ireland. See May Morris to Quinn, 14 October 1914 (chapter 5).

43. Reid, 81.

44. Reid, 104.

45. Reid, 13.

46. See Quinn to Yeats, 23 August 1907, in The John Quinn Memorial Collection, NYPL.

47. Janis and Richard Londraville, "Stage Irishmen and Pseudo-Celtic Drama: Selections from the Correspondence between Frank High O'Donnell and John Quinn," *Yeats: An Annual of Critical and Textual Studies* (1991): 80.

48. Quinn often used his business frustrations as an excuse to be left alone by artists and writers who were hounding him for support. Forestalling such pleas from Wyndham Lewis, for instance, Quinn wrote to him on 15 November 1919 that "(a) a senior lawyer in the office has been knocked endways by his wife going off her nut and his postponing a decision in a situation which has grown steadily worse, and as a result he has been of practically no use to me for two months; (b) the next lawyer in the office left me with no notice to take a place in the Government after he had been 'soldiering' in my office for over three months. . . . I have been trying to do all the work and have never been so driven and overworked. I have had no time to attend to personal matters. The fact that your letter asked me to give early attention to your things worried me, but it was a physical impossibility for me to do it" (Richard and Janis Londraville, "Two Men at War with Time: The Unpublished-Correspondence of Wyndham Lewis and John Quinn, Concluded," Vol. 39, #165, *English* [Autumn, 1990]: 229).

49. It is Shaw himself who connects May to *Man and Superman.* In *Morris as I Knew Him* (William Morris Society, 1966), Shaw writes of his early days with her: "I was a bachelor then, and likely to remain so; for I not only felt about marriage very much as Jack Tanner does in *Man and Superman,* but I was so poor that I could hardly have supported Morris's daughter. . . . . But these material considerations only made the Morris paradise more celestial and my part in it quite irresponsible. For if I could not immediately marry the beautiful daughter I could all the more lightheartedly indulge my sense of her beauty" (29).

50. For a history of some of Quinn's relationships, see Reid. It was important to Jeanne Robert Foster that Quinn's reputation with women not be exaggerated, and she tried to persuade B. L. Reid to moderate some of his opinions. In a letter to Richard Londraville dated 24 December 1968, she wrote, "I persuaded Reid to do Quinn justice in certain ways by giving him my intimate handwritten diaries of his last days. After reading that, Reid changed his mind and knew that Quinn was not 'a conqueror or a crusher of women'" (Londraville private collection).

51. Reid, 81.

52. Shaw, *Man and Superman,* in *Seven Plays by George Bernard Shaw* (New York: Dodd, Mead & Co., 1951): Act III, pp. 638–39.

53. J. B. Yeats to Quinn, 27 October 1912. See The John Quinn Memorial Collection, NYPL.

54. *Lady Griselda's Dream,* Appendix to this text, 183–184. The play was originally published in *Longman's Magazine,* Vol. 32 (June, 1898): 145–157.

55. Appendix, 184.

56. Appendix, 179.

57. See n. 10.

58. Appendix, 190.

59. *Man and Superman,* III, pp. 630–31.

60. Marsh, *Jane and May Morris,* 278–79.

61. Elfrida Manning, "A Visit to May Morris, 1925," *The Journal of the William Morris Society* (Summer, 1980): 18.

62. Marsh, *Jane and May Morris*, 277.

63. Sir Basil Blackwell, "More about Miss Lobb," *The Bookseller* (October 1962): 1736.

64. Even if Mary Lobb did not understand May's dedication to her father's works, she supported her endeavors. In the introduction to Shaw's *Morris As I Knew Him* (7, 8), Basil Blackwell explains that he had suggested to May in 1934 that if any "scrap" of her father's writing remained unpublished, he would be interested in printing it. When publication was held up, Miss Lobb confronted him: "Look here, you are worrying May, and I won't have her worried. You've got to publish that stuff. Don't think that I care a snap for the writings. I hate old William Morris—dreadful old bore; but I'll not have May worried. You go home and write to-night telling her you'll publish *everything*. I've no money—I've only got £50 in the world, but you shall have that, and welcome, if you do as I tell you."

Blackwell undertook the task and asked Bernard Shaw to write an introduction for one of the proposed volumes ("Morris as I Knew Him," Vol. 2, ix–xl). The two volumes were finally published as *William Morris: Artist, Writer, Socialist*.

65. Appendix, 181.

66. May Morris to G. B. Shaw, 5 May 1936, quoted in Marsh, *Jane and May Morris*, 297.

Chapter 1. The Letters of 1910

1. The Synge book was *The Aran Islands* with drawings by Jack B. Yeats (Dublin and London: Maunsel & Co. Ltd.and Elkin Mathews, respectively, 1906).

Henry James, like William Morris, was one of Quinn's literary heroes. Leon Edel, in *Henry James, The Master: 1901–1916* (New York: J B. Lippincott Co., 1972), relates: "On October 17, 1910, John Quinn, the wealthy Irish American lawyer and patron of the arts, friend of Yeats and Lady Gregory, future friend of Conrad, Joyce, Eliot, Pound, and collector of their works and manuscripts, dining at Hotel Belmont, suddenly had one of the 'moments' of his life which he recorded. An enthusiast, a lover of literary celebrity, he recognized Henry James, massive, slow-moving, awe-inspiring, at dinner with two gentlemen and a lady" (450). They were Walter Berry, W. Morton Fullerton, and Edith Wharton. It was a moment Quinn never forgot.

2. Quinn served as May's publicity agent on occasion during her tour and set up places for her to speak. When May finally spoke in Buffalo, Dard Hunter was sent as an emissary from Elbert Hubbard of the Roycroft Library to invite May to visit Roycroft. Hunter later related that May, "not very attractive, and . . . at least twice my age . . ." unfolded the letter from Hubbard and flashed her eyes: "I most certainly will not go to East Aurora, nor do I have any desire to see that obnoxious imitator of my dear father." "With an air of disdain," writes Hunter, "she crumpled the note in her hand and gave it back to me" (Freeman Champney, *Art and Glory: The Story of Elbert Hubbard* (New York: Crown Publishers, 1968), 119.

3. Quinn is probably referring to a letter lost from the correspondence.

4. *Don*, a three act comedy by Rudolf Besier, was reviewed in the *New York Times* on 31 December 1909 (p. 9, col. 3). The play was performed at the New Theatre, and the starring role of Don was played by Matheson Lang. The reviewer said that the main character had "a specialty of rescuing unhappy wait-

resses in distress" and that though the first two acts had an "amusing force," the final act fell into "melodrama."

5. Douglas Hyde (1860–1949), playwright, poet, President of Ireland. Hyde, who also published under the name An Chraoibhin Aoibhinn, and Quinn were good friends, and each visited the other in his respective country. In Ireland, Hyde, Quinn, and W. B. Yeats once attended a feis in County Galway, Quinn's account of which is printed in Lady Augusta Gregory's *Our Irish Theatre* (Gerrards Cross: Colin Smythe, 1972), 248: "There was an old man there and it took much persuasion to get him to mount the platform and tell his story. He hung back diffidently for a long time, but finally a lane was opened in the crowd and he got his courage up and . . . made a great speech in Irish. Hyde translated parts of it for Yeats and me, and told us how the old man had boasted that he had been at [the Irish bard] Raftery's dying. . . ."

6. Alice Thursby, Arthur Brisbane's sister, was romantically linked to Quinn as well.

7. Arthur Brisbane (1864–1936), American journalist. Brisbane served as London correspondent for the *New York Sun,* managing editor of the *Evening Sun,* managing editor for the *New York World,* and editor of Hearst's *Evening Journal (The National Cyclopaedia of American Biography,* s.v. "Brisbane, Arthur").

8. The book was *Deirdre of the Sorrows,* printed in New York for John Quinn in 1910. Fifty copies were printed, five on vellum. Quinn had also previously printed fifty copies of Synge's *Poems and Translations* in New York in 1909 (*National Union Catalog* [hereafter *NUC*] Vol. 580, p. 255).

9. The Cuala Press, originally the Dun Emer Press, was run by Lily (Susan Mary) and Lolly (Elizabeth) Yeats.

10. Marsh mentions that May's tour included stops in New York, Minneapolis, Madison, Chicago, and Canada. She doesn't mention Cleveland (Marsh, *Jane and May Morris,* 252).

11. Hackett, who was born in Ireland, was a long-time friend of Quinn, and, as a favor, helped promote May and the *Collected Works.* He and Quinn ended their friendship in 1912 after Quinn, who had invited Hackett to the Democratic Convention in Baltimore to campaign for Underwood, turned on Hackett during a convention floor battle and called him "yellow" and a "quitter" (Reid, 49, 66, 97, 131).

12. In April 1910 Quinn took John Butler Yeats to Thomas Fortune Ryan's estate in Virginia for a vacation, and in May he bought Manet's *L'Amazone* for $4,000 (Reid, 91).

13. Quinn commissioned American sculptor Jo Davidson (1883–1952) to make a bust of May. On 25 December, the *New York Times* reviewed Davidson's work, mentioning his bust of May Morris. The reviewer writes that "Davidson manages to give his portraits the impression one gets from the muscular action of a person's face. His work doesn't keep still. . . ." (25 Dec. 1910: pt. 5, p. 7). Quinn disliked Davidson intensely (Reid, 112).

14. Elisabeth Luther Cary, *William Morris, Poet, Craftsman, Socialist* (New York and London: G. P. Putnam's Sons, 1902).

15. Sir Emery Walker (1851–1933) was a long time friend of the Morris family. In 1888, William Morris, Walter Crane, and he founded the Arts and Crafts Exhibition Society. Eleven years older than May, he not only helped Morris begin the Kelmscott Press but also was instrumental in the founding of the Doves Press. He was married to Mary Grace from 1877 until her death in 1920 and

had one daughter (*Dictionary of National Biography 1931—1940,* s.v. "Walker, Sir Emery").

16. Frederick James Gregg, the New York literary journalist who wrote for the *Evening Sun,* was an old school friend of J. B. Yeats and one of Quinn's closest friends. See Gregg's 1867 article on Morris ("The Personality of William Morris") in *The Book Buyer* (November 1896): 619–21. Jo Davidson was the American sculptor; Charley Fitzgerald and Miss Grigsby are unidentified.

17. King Edward VII (1841–1910) died on Friday, 6 May 1910.

18. Charles Fairfax Murray was an illustrator and painter. See Murray's correspondence with William Morris in Norman Kelvin's *The Collected Letters of William Morris, Vol. 1 1848–1880* (Princeton: Princeton University Press, 1984). Murray was in Genoa with the Morris family in 1878. Even though he didn't completely agree with Morris about his type of socialism, they always seemed to remain friends. See Philip Henderson, *The Letters of William Morris to his Family and Friends* (London: Longmans Green & Co., 1950), 123. Murray also catalogued the art collection of J. Pierpont Morgan and others.

19. Sir William Blake Richmond (1842–1921) is perhaps best known for his paintings, *The Death of Ulysses, Song of Miriam,* and *An Audience at Athens during the Performance of Agamemnon,* and for his portraits of Gladstone, Darwin, Browning, and Prince Bismark. He was commissioned to decorate Saint Paul's Cathedral in mosaic and succeeded Ruskin as the Slade Professor of Fine Art at Oxford from 1878–1883. His home was Beavor Lodge, Hammersmith. See the *Times,* 14 February 1921: p. 13, col. 5 for obituary.

20. Quinn probably refers to the 1910 edition of Douglas Hyde's book: *A Literary History of Ireland from Earliest Times to Present Day* (London: Unwin, 1910); and to Samuel Dill's *Roman Society in the Last Century of the Western Empire* (London: Macmillan, 1898) or *Roman Society from Nero to Marcus Aurelius* (London: Macmillan, 1904).

21. *The Works of George Meredith: Memorial Edition* (New York: C. Scribner's Sons, 1909–1912) in 29 vols.

22. The portrait of Quinn, painted by John in 1909, is entitled *The Man from New York.* Quinn paid John $785 for it. It is currently owned by the New York Public Library, Astor Lenox and Tilden Foundations. See Zilczer, 163.

23. Quinn probably refers to Yeats's 1902–1903 American lecture tours. See Richard Londraville, "Four Lectures by W. B. Yeats, 1902–1904," *Yeats Annual* 8 (1991): 78–122.

24. Il'ia Il'ich Mechnikov (1845–1916), also known as Elie Metchnikoff, wrote *Scientifically Soured Milk; Its Influence in Arresting Intestinal Putrefaction . . .* (New York: The Lactobacilline Co. of New York, 1907).

25. *Orkney and Shetland Old-Lore Series of the Viking Club* began in 1892 and was issued quarterly by the Viking Society for Northern Research, London. See *NUC,* Vol. 637, p. 333.

26. Wilfrid Scawen Blunt (1840–1922). See his "Letter to Egyptian Nationalist Congress at Brussels," *Times* 23 September 1910: p. 3, col. 3. and his book, *Atrocities of Justice Under British Rule in Egypt* (London: Unwin, 1907). Besides his affair with Jane Morris, Blunt also had a liaison with Lady Gregory. See Marsh, *Jane and May Morris,* chapters 9 and 17, passim; and Faulkner, *Jane Morris to Wilfrid Scawen Blunt,* 1986.

27. J. W. Mackail, son-in-law of Ned and Georgiana Burne-Jones and Morris's first biographer. Jane Morris gave Mackail some trouble about publishing the truth about her origins. She felt Morris should not look as if he married someone

from a low station. Mackail wrote to Sydney Cockerell on 22 September 1898 that "I have been obliged in some degree to slur it over and the less will be the book's worth." Other areas of the book, especially concerning the relationship between Morris and his wife, were also white-washed. See Marsh, *Jane and May Morris,* 242–245. John William Mackail, *The Life of William Morris* (London: Oxford University Press, 1950) [originally published in 1899].

28. George Saintsbury, *Historical Manual of English Prosody* (London: Macmillan, 1910).

29. Jo Davidson, the sculptor. I have not located any information about a bust of William Morris by Davidson.

30. Marsh says that "In May's case, those who met her for the first time in the years after 1914, usually did so in search of her father . . . ; that is, they were primarily interested in learning more about Morris rather than becoming acquainted with May" (Marsh, *Jane and May Morris,* 272). It appears from May's letters to Quinn that she was being bothered by visitors as early as 1910.

31. Quinn's Japanese houseboy, Sadajiro Kumatani (Reid, 20).

32. Quinn took John Butler Yeats with him to Fisher's Island at the head of Long Island Sound. They returned on 6 July (Reid, 86).

33. Charles D. Norton (1871–1923) resigned as Secretary to President Taft to assume duties of the Vice-President of the First National Bank of New York. He was active in the reorganization of the Red Cross, and was a member of the Red Cross War Council in 1917 (appointed by President Wilson). *The National Cyclopedia of American Biography,* s.v. "Norton, Charles D."

34. Quinn is referring to Kuno Meyer's (1858–1919) *Four Old Irish Songs of Summer and Winter* (London: Nutt, 1903).

35. For an English translation of *The Tinker and the Fairy,* see Miss Butler's translation: M. H. Gill, 1902. The Gaelic title is *Tincéar agus an t-sídeog.*

36. The fight was between J. J. Jeffries and J. Johnson on 4 July 1910. Johnson won in the 15th round and was crowned heavyweight champion. See the *New York Times* Jul 4 p. 4, col. 3; p. 6, col. 4; p. 14 col. 1; and Jul 5 p. 1, col. 7; p. 4, col.1; p. 7, col. 3; and p. 12, col. 3.

37. Quinn refers to Charles Evans Hughes (1862–1948), Republican, elected Governor of New York in 1906, reelected in 1908, resigned on 6 October 1910 on his appointment to the Supreme Court by President Taft. He resigned from the Court in 1916 and unsuccessfully bid for his party's presidential nomination, after which he returned to private law practice. *The National Cyclopaedia of American Biography,* s.v. "Hughes, Charles Evans."

38. Francis Thompson (1859–1907), *A Renegade Poet, and Other Essays* (Boston: The Ball Publishing Co., 1910). See his chapter entitled "Paganism: Old and New."

39. See n. 21.

40. William Morton Payne, *The Greater English Poets of the Nineteenth Century* (New York: H. Holt & Co., 1907), 316–48. The book was a compilation of lectures Payne (1858–1919) gave at the Universities of Wisconsin, Kansas, and Chicago.

41. James Gibbon Huneker (1857–1921), journalist and critic for the *New York Sun,* was one of Quinn's closest friends. Huneker often helped promote Quinn's favorites, including Yeats, Synge, and even May (specifically her introductions to the *Collected Works*) in his articles and among his journalist friends. Huneker wrote *Promenades of an Impressionist, Painted Veils* (a novel which Quinn privately called "Painted Whores"), and *Ivory Apes and Peacocks,* which he dedicated to Quinn (Reid, 79, 210, 443).

42. Hone, the Irish landscape artist of the Barbizon School, was one of Quinn's favorite landscape artists. Reid documents that Quinn owned Hone's *Bundoran Rocks* and Charles Shannon's *Portrait of W. B. Yeats, Sapphire Bay,Summer,* and *Portrait of Lilah McCarthy as Dona Ana.* In *Portrait of Lilah McCarthy,* the model wore the gown that Charles Ricketts (British printmaker, engraver, and sculptor, 1866–1931) designed for a performance of Shaw's *Man and Superman* at London's Court Theatre (Reid, 61–62, 70, 90). Zilczer lists a number of Russells (George William Russell, AKA "A. E.") that Quinn owned, including *Starling Lake, Lovers in Tirnan-Og, Across the Ridge, The Lowlands in the Hills, The Women of the Sidhe,* and *The Herd Boy Goes Forth to Find His Poetry.* Quinn is probably referring to Jack Butler Yeats here, although he also owned a number of John Butler Yeats's paintings as well. Zilczer lists *Race Course, Town, Galway, The Bay Pilot, The Ganger, The Gang, Fortune and her Wheel, Portrait Figure of an Irish Gentleman, The Crest of the Hill, Political Meeting, The Car is at the Door,* and *The Stevedore* as some of the Jack Butler Yeats drawings Quinn owned (Zilczer, 183,190–91). See also Brummer and Weyhe.

43. Earlier in August, Quinn held a gathering for some of his artist and writer friends, including John Butler Yeats, John Sloan, and Ezra Pound (Reid, 86).

44. Augustus John (1878–1961), British painter. See Holroyd, *Augustus John* (New York: Holt, Rinehart and Winston, 1975).

45. Charles H. Shannon, the artist. See this chapter, n. 42. Quinn convinced W. B. Yeats to pose for an oil portrait by Shannon, which Quinn purchased. Yeats told Quinn that he felt it brought out his resemblance to his mother, Catherine Pollexfen. Shannon also did a drawing of the poet, but Yeats said it looked "damnably like Keats" (Reid, 31, 61, 70, 74, 90). See the Quinn-Shannon correspondence in the John Quinn Memorial Collection, NYPL.

46. T. W. Rolleston, Irish author and political activist who wrote for the *Dublin Express.* Quinn often visited his home while in Ireland and was godfather to Rolleston's daughter, Aideen. See the unpublished Rolleston-Quinn correspondence in the John Quinn Memorial Collection, NYPL.

47. Quinn had become the chief counsel for tycoon Thomas Fortune Ryan. Although he continued to work for insurance companies and banks, Quinn received a lucrative annual retainer from Ryan, who became Quinn's most important client. See Reid, 34–35, 84, 133.

48. Paul Kieffer, the only law partner Quinn seemed to be able to respect. At first Kieffer avoided working for Quinn because of Quinn's rumored Tammany connections. But Reid says that when Kieffer finally did join the firm, he "found in Quinn a brilliant tutor and performer in the law, a fair if strenuous and exacting colleague, and a staunch friend" (Reid, 84). Kieffer continued to carry on Quinn's business affairs for many years after Quinn's death from cancer in 1924.

49. Arthur Symons(1865–1945), *The Romantic Movement in English Poetry* (London: A. Constable & Co. Ltd., 1909 and New York: E. P. Dutton, 1909).

50. W. J. Courthope (1842–1917), *A History of English Poetry* (New York and London: Macmillan, 1895–1910). Reprinted in New York by Russell and Russell (1962) in 6 vols.

51. Anne Isabella (Thackeray) Ritchie [1837–1919], *The Works of William Makepeace Thackeray; with Biographical Introductions by His Daughter* (New York and London: Harper & Bros., 1910).

52. May changed some punctuation from this copy to Quinn to the one published in Morris's *Collected Works* (Vol. 24, 343–44). For a detailed explanation,

see Janis Londraville, "May Morris's Editing of 'So Many Stories Written Here,'" *The Journal of the William Morris Society* (Autumn, 1992): 31–34. The location of May and Jenny's copy of *The Earthly Paradise* is not known.

53. Frederick Hollyer, British portrait photographer. See Jean-Claude Lemagny and André Rouillé, *A History of Photography* (Cambridge: Cambridge University Press, 1987), 88, 98.

54. E. T. Cook and Alexander Wedderburn, eds., *The Works of John Ruskin* (London: G. A. Allen and New York: Longmans, Green, & Co., 1903–1912).

55. Harry Buxton Forman, *The Books of William Morris, Described with Some Account of His Doings in Literature and in the Allied Crafts* (Chicago: Way & Williams, 1897 and London: F. Hollings, 1897). Temple Scott, *A Bibliography of the Works of William Morris* (London: G. Bell & Sons, 1897).

56. May published "How I Became a Socialist" in Volume XXIII of *The Collected Works of William Morris.* See the 1966 New York edition of *CW* published by Russell & Russell, 277–81.

57. Jean Lahor (pseu. for Henry Cazalis), *William Morris et le Mouvement Noveau de L'Art Décoratif* (Genève: Eggimann, 1897).

58. Lewis Melville (pseudonym for Benjamin Saul Lewis), *William Makepeace Thackeray; A Biography including hitherto Uncollected Letters and Speeches and a Bibliography of 1300 Items* (London: John Lane, 1910).

59. William Morris, *The Pilgrims of Hope; A Poem in XIII Books* (Portland, Maine: T. B. Mosher, 1901). The *NUC* notes that *The Pilgrims of Hope* was "originally written for and contributed . . . to . . . the *Commonweal* . . . during 1885–86" and that "400 copies of [the Mosher edition] have been printed. . . ." (*NUC*, Vol. 396, p. 153).

60. Benjamin Jowett (1817–1893) was Master of Balliol College, Oxford. See Evelyn Abbot and Lewis Campbell, eds., *The Letters of Benjamin Jowett* (London: J. Murray, 1899).

61. This sentence is handwritten by Quinn, apparently added by Quinn after his stenographer had typed the letter.

62. May took Quinn's advice. The "March" poem is printed in May's introduction to *Volume VI: The Earthly Paradise* of Morris's *Collected Works* (xxx–xxxi). May explains that "March" was "written on half sheets of note paper" and "left aside as the book grew" (May Morris, *The Introductions to the Collected Works of William Morris* [New York: Oriole Editions, 1973], 170).

63. Lechlade, near Kelmscott, is approximately twenty-five miles west of Oxford, on the Thames.

64. May refers to her father's *Queen Guenevere* (AKA *La Belle Iseult),* the only known painting he did of Jane. Morris also did a drawing of Jane entitled *Iseult on the Ship* (Marsh, *The Pre-Raphaelite Sisterhood,* 126, 210, 245). The drawings of Jenny and May to which May refers in this letter are at Kelmscott Manor/Society of Antiquaries. Marsh says that May was the model for DGR's *Rosa Triplex* and that he did chalk portraits of both May and Jenny. May sat again for DGR in 1872 for a picture of a girl holding a pansy (Marsh, *Jane and May Morris,* 100, 120).

It is worth noting here that, when May was a small child, DGR expressed interest in adopting her. May resented having the request denied, feeling that she would always be second best to her sister Jenny (Holroyd 224). Considering the strain in the Morris marriage, this request was probably not well-received by May's father.

65. Thomas Fortune Ryan. See n. 47.

66. I have been unable to locate this collection, nor have I found any reference to it.

67. Edward William Bok (1863–1930), journalist, editor of *Ladies Home Journal,* and author of *A Story of Some Pictures* (Philadelphia, 1896), *Successward* (New York, 1896), and *Explaining the Editor* (Philadelphia, 1901).

68. Arthur Clutton-Brock (1868–1924) wrote *William Morris, His Work and Influence* (London: Williams and Norgate, 1914), which May gave to Quinn as a gift. See Quinn's letter to May, 4 June 1914.

69. Sir Henry Francis Herbert Thompson (1859–1944), Egyptologist. See his account of demotic papyri in Petrie's *Gizeh and Rifeh* (1907) and *The Coptic (Sahidic) Version of Certain Books of the Old Testament* (1908). Thompson's obituary appeared in the *Times* 29 May 1944, p. 6, col. 6.

70. The year of 1910 was a busy one for the women's movement. Injuries, assaults, arrests, demonstrations, fines, raids, picketing, and vandalism were all results of activists' activities. See letter from Quinn to May, 16 December 1913.

71. Quinn also owned some of Rossetti's manuscripts at one time, which were among the mss. he sold to Henry Huntington in 1913 (Reid, 197). See chapter 4, Quinn to May Morris, 4 March 1913.

72. See n. 25, Introduction to these letters, for excerpts from Burne-Jones's article; and n. 19 this chapter for Richmond.

73. Robert Baldwin Ross, 1869–1918, art critic, author, and literary executor for Oscar Wilde. Ross edited the *Complete Works of Oscar Wilde* (New York: Bigelow, Brown and Co.) in 1921. Ross contributed to many journals and was a staff writer for the *Morning Post.* See his "Present and Future Prospects for English Art" (Liverpool: Sandon Studios Society, 1911) and his obituary in the *Times,* 7 October 1918: p. 5, col. 4.

74. May refers to Alfred Noyes (1880–1958), *William Morris* (London: Macmillan, 1908). See n. 68 this chapter for Clutton-Brock.

75. Eiríkr Magnússon, who taught Morris the Icelandic language.

76. John Knewstub, art dealer. See his correspondence with Quinn in the John Quinn Memorial Collection, NYPL.

77. The following reviews did appear, probably at Quinn's continued urging: *Nation* 92: 16 Mar 1911, 268; 93: 10 Aug 1911, 125; 94: 18 Jan 1912, 64; 95: 5 Dec 1912, 538–39; 98: 19 Feb 1914, 189. *New York Times* 7 Jan 1912 pt. 6, p. 1, col. 3; 1 Dec 1912 pt. 6, p. 730, col. 1; 13 June 1915 pt. 6, p. 217, col. 1.

78. Elkin Mathews Ltd, booksellers, Bishop's Stortford, England.

79. Theodore Watts-Dunton (1832–1914). See *The Catalogue of the Library of Walter Theodore Watts-Dunton* (London: Dryden Press, 1917). Watts-Dunton edited *The Letters of Algernon Charles Swinburne with some Personal Recollections, by Thomas Hake and Arthur Compton-Rickett* (London: J. Murray, 1918). Lily Yeats said that May "basked in Watts-Dunton's admiration" when he visited the Morris home *(Scrapbook).*

80. See the *New York Times,* 25 December 1910: pt. 5. p. 7.

81. John Boyd Thacher(1847–1909), *Christopher Columbus: His Life, His Work, His Remains . . .* (New York: G. P. Putnam & Sons, 1903–4). See also Thacher's *The Continent of America: Its Discovery and Its Baptism* (New York: W. E. Benjamin, 1896).

82. I have found no record of Quinn's letter to Jane Burden Morris.

Chapter 2. The Letters of 1911

1. May Morris comments that this poem was struck out at the beginning of her father's "Bellerophon in Lycia." In *Collected Works,* May added a nineteen-

line stanza at the beginning and a six-line one at the end. Perhaps she only sent her favorite part to Quinn. See *CW*, Vol. 6, xiv–xvi.

2. May wrote several articles for the *Burlington*. See the bibliography at the end of this text.

3. Charles John Holmes (1868–1936), *Notes on the Post-Impressionist Painters, Grafton Galleries, 1910–1911* (London: P. L. Warner, 1910).

4. Elizabeth Bisland, *The Life and Letters of Lafcadio Hearn: 1850–1904* (Boston and New York: Houghton, Mifflin & Co., 1906).

5. The book was probably Gilbert Murray's (1866–1957) translation of Euripides: *The Iphigenia in Tauris of Euripides* (London: G. Allen and Sons, 1910).

6. See "The Works of J. M. Synge," 23 February 1911: *Times* LS p. 73, col. 2. Gregg was Quinn's friend, Frederick James Gregg of the *New York Sun*. See chapter 1, n. 16 and this chapter n. 16.

7. Francis Hackett of the Chicago *Evening Post*. See chapter 1, n. 11.

8. Paul Elmer More (1864–1937). His *Shelburne Essays*, written for magazines and newspapers, were first collected in 1904. Quinn probably owned a copy—and the updated versions as released over the years. *NUC*, Vol. 394, p. 237.

9. See chapter 1, n. 77.

10. Quinn liked the work of Br. sculptor Eric Gill (1882–1940), but Augustus John did not and convinced Quinn to turn his attentions elsewhere (Reid, 96–97). See Eric Gill, *Autobiography* (New York: The Devin-Adair Co., 1941).

11. Marie Claire, *The Trial* (Albany: E. H. Pease & Co. and P. L. Gilbert, 1851). Lauren Housman, *An English Woman's Love Letters* (Chicago: W. B. Conkey Co., 1901).

12. Quinn did buy Manet's *Le Polichinelle* (1874) in 1911 from art dealer Durand-Ruel for F.fr. 1,500 (Zilczer 171; Reid 91, 508).

13. During April, Quinn spent some time at Oak Ridge, the Virginia estate of financier Thomas Fortune Ryan. For companionship, he brought along John Butler Yeats, whom he had outfitted with a new set of clothes for the occasion (Reid, 91).

14. A week before King George's coronation, seamen and firemen in Southampton went on strike. The unrest quickly spread to ship repairers, laborers, engineering laborers, dockers, and coal porters. The upheaval did not seem directed at any one complaint, and the strike was finally settled by raising wages. See E. H. Phelps Brown, *The Growth of British Industrial Relations* (London: Macmillan, 1960), 321–22.

15. Esther Pissarro told May about Quinn's plans, which irritated him greatly. He was not looking forward to seeing May again, preferring to carry on the liaison with her from afar. Pissarro's husband, Lucien, was the son of the French impressionist Camille Pissarro (Reid 31). See also Introduction, n. 9.

16. Gregg, "The Personality of William Morris," *The Book Buyer:* 621. See chapter 1, Quinn to May Morris, 13 May 1910, n. 16.

17. After Quinn returned to the United States that autumn, he was again confronted with a task he hated: buying Christmas presents. May was not on his primary list. Among the purchases were a $550 watch at Tiffany's for his sister, Julia Anderson; a $260 watch for a girlfriend, Ada Smith; and a $45 jewel case for his first love, Annie Foster (Reid, 91). May received pippin apples from him. At this time, Quinn was also busy with the legal battle over the American production of Synge's *Playboy of the Western World.* He wrote to Frank Hugh O'Donnell on 23 February 1912 about the case: "In Philadelphia they tried riots and were chucked out, and then they had the actors arrested. . . . I had a writ

of habeas corpus sued out before Judge Carr and cross examined the complainant (the liquor-dealer), and his brother (the priest), and another priest. The Judge took the book under consideration and sustained the writ and dismissed the charge" (Londraville, "Stage Irishmen," *Yeats: An Annual* (1991): 79–80).

Chapter 3. The Letters of 1912

1. Morris Hilquit (1869–1933), socialist. See his *History of Socialism in the United States* (New York and London: Funk and Wagnalls, 1903); and *Socialism in Theory and Practice* (New York: Macmillan, 1912).

2. John Sloan (1871–1951), artist, illustrator of Max Miller's book, *The Beginning of a Mortal* (New York: E. P. Dutton, 1933). See also John Sloan, *The Gist of Art* (New York: The American Artists Group, 1939).

3. P. Lubbock, "The Poetry of William Morris," *Quarterly Review* Vol. 215 (October 1911): 482–504.

4. Quinn finally did get *On the Way Down to the Sea,* an oil on canvas, 79 X 67, which is now in the collection of the Phillips Exeter Academy in Exeter, New Hampshire. Quinn's relationship with John deteriorated over the years, even though Quinn continued to support John's artist sister, Gwen. On 15 August 1920, Quinn wrote to Wyndham Lewis that "John did not play fair with me. I began to buy his work in 1908 and 1909 when his prices were low, and I paid him more for it than Sir Hugh Lane was paying him and others, and advanced him money and encouraged him to put up his prices. The year that he was in the south of France and did not paint, I advanced him money to carry him through. I responded for years to his calls for advance of money, and he promised me the first chance at his best work, but he constantly broke his word and sold it to Sir Hugh Lane and to others who paid him less than I would have paid but who were on the ground and tempted him with cash. He broke his word with me repeatedly, so I finally broke with him" (Richard and Janis Londraville, "Two Men at War with Time: Concluded," *English* Vol. 39, #165 [Autumn 1990]: 236–37).

5. Probably Louis Hourticq's *Art in France,* published in the U.S. by Scribner as part of the "Ars Una" series, 1911.

6. Durand-Ruel, the art dealer, sold Quinn his first Manets. One of them, *L' Amazone,* Quinn later traded back to him as one third of his purchase price for Puvis de Chavannes's *Beheading of St. John the Baptist.* The total price was the Manet plus $8,000 (Reid, 105).

7. In 1913, Quinn sold his Morris manuscripts, except the *House of the Wolfings,* to Mr. Henry E. Huntington, who founded the Huntington Library in San Marino, California. The sale is discussed in Quinn's letter to May, dated 18 June 1913. The Huntington's records indicate that Mr. Huntington bought *An Account of Three Socialist Lectures, Address on behalf of the work of the S. P. A. B., Child Christopher* (and *Goldilind the Fair), Home Rule or Humbug, Hopes and Fears for Art,II: The Art of the People, Notes on Passing Events, Notes relating to the S. P. A. B.'s efforts to save Magdalen Bridge, Sigurd the Volsung:* fragment, *The Story of the Glittering Plain* (final and original drafts), *True and False Society, To the Editor of the Athenaeum* (c. 1880), *To the Editor of the Pall Mall Gazette* (16 July 1881), *Letter to Thomas Wise* (16 January 1882), *Letter to Thomas Wise (?)* (12 January 1882). The ms. of the *House of the Wolfings* is located at the Pierpont Morgan Library in New York. Quinn owned the *Aeneids of Virgil* and the *Odyssey of Homer* mss. as well, but they are not among the Huntington collection. There is a ms. of the

Odyssey of Homer at the University of Texas, Austin, which may well be the one that Quinn owned.

8. See *The Library of John Quinn* (New York: The Anderson Galleries, 1924). Reid explains that Quinn later "told [W. B.] Yeats he was resolved to buy no more manuscripts except those of a few living men whom he cared about personally, such as Conrad, Symons, James Stephens, and Yeats himself. In testimony to his new emphases he had, in the process of raising $28,000 to buy *La Rivière* and *Le Vendage* of Puvis de Chavannes, sold manuscripts of Meredith, Morris, Swinburne, Gissing, Henley, Rossetti, and others to Henry E. Huntington. . . . The connoisseur's career which had begun with an Ohio schoolboy buying contemporary first editions was beginning to find its ultimate direction" (Reid, 197).

9. Sir William Rothenstein (1872–1945), British artist. See his *English Portraits,* a series of lithographed drawings (London: G. Richards, 1898); "An Address . . . on the occasion of the distribution of prizes to the students" (Birmingham: Birmingham Municipal School of Art, 13 February 1908); *Manchester Portraits* (Manchester: J. E. Cornish, 1900); and "A plea for a wider use of artists and craftsmen" (London: Constable, 1917). Quinn particularly liked Rothenstein's portrait drawing of Joseph Conrad, which appeared in a 1911 issue of *The English Review,* and had Conrad autograph a copy for him (Reid, 113).

10. Charles Conder (1868–1909), British printmaker, engraver, and lithographer. Quinn bought three Conders in 1912: *La Belle Antonia* (1905) from the Goupil Gallery for $750; and *Fantasia* for $1,500 and *Casino de Paris* for $628 from the Berlin Photographic Gallery (Zilczer, 153).

11. Reid adds a little more to the story of the chest: "In November [1911] [Quinn] wrote to Epstein [the sculptor] of his rage at Parkenthorpe's for sending over a heavy oak chest [the one he purchased with May] empty and his delicate Queen Anne chest filled with fragile or heavy objects, damaging them and the chest itself (Reid, 111).

12. T. W. H. Rolleston (1857–1920), *Myths and Legends of the Celtic Race* (London: G. G. Harrap and Co., 1911).

13. The book may have been Lucien Pissarro's *Rossetti* (London: T. C. and E. C. Jack; New York: F. A. Stokes, 1908). The only book Esther Pissarro did herself was *Songs by Ben Jonson* (Hammersmith: The Eragny Press, 1906).

14. Walter Crane (1845–1915), *William Morris to Whistler* (London: G. Bell and Sons, Ltd., 1911).

15. Kelmscott Press, which William Morris founded.

16. May refers to the Arts and Crafts Movement. She showed some of her embroidery and jewelry work at Arts and Crafts exhibitions from 1888 on (Marsh, *Jane and May Morris,* 168–71).

17. Henry Mayers Hyndman, one time leader of the Social Democratic Federation. Holroyd says that Hyndman's "majestic head teemed with insurrectionary dreams. He saw himself, in his immaculate frock-coat, fine gloves, silk hat and other grand insignia of the class he fiercely denounced, as leading his rough proletarian army through a revolutionary dawn into the clear light of national regeneration." His failure as a leader was that he was not a team player. As Holroyd explains, "he would not have shared the leadership with God Almighty. His famous temper was responsible for driving away many socialists—among them Edward Aveling, Belfort Bax, Walter Crane, Eleanor Marx and William Morris. . . ." (129–31).

18. Probably Mary A. Sloane, one of May's closest friends. One of Ms. Sloane's

paintings was exhibited at the Arts & Crafts Exhibition at the Royal Academy in 1916 *(May Morris, 1862–1938: An Exhibition* [London: William Morris Gallery, 1989], 2).

19. Morris dances originated with the Moors in Spain around 1500. They had a "varied development in England where bells, kerchiefs, hobby horses, and blackamoors were part of the dance. . . ." (*The Dance Encyclopedia* [New York: Simon and Schuster, 1967], 644).

20. Sir Edward Tyas Cook (1857–1919), *The Life of John Ruskin* (London: G. Allen, 1911).

21. Charles Eliot Norton (1827–1908). See *The Letters of John Ruskin to Charles Eliot Norton* (Boston and New York: Houghton, Mifflin & Co., 1904). Norton, whose interests included church buildings of the middle ages, also authored books on Dante, de Tocqueville, Goethe, and Carlyle.

22. Philip Webb, a distinguished architect and friend and associate of the Morris family, built the Red House in Upton, Kent for Morris in 1860. Following Morris's death, Jane Morris commissioned Webb to design two cottages, which were built as a memorial to her husband. She also commissioned him to design the Morris gravestone. (Marsh, *Jane and May Morris,* 242, 269).

23. In *The Collected Letters of William Morris* Vol. II (Princeton: Pinceton University Press, 1987) Norman Kelvin explains that the White Horse is "374 feet in length [and 130 feet high] and was the national symbol of the Saxons." It is "said to commemorate the victory of Alfred the Great over the Danes in the Battle of Ashdown in 871. . . ." (574). However, archaeologists believe that although the Alfred story is the conventional one, the White Horse may originate in the Iron Age. The hill itself is 856 feet high and is near Dragon Hill, where St. George, according to mythology, killed the dragon (*The Shell Guide to England* [Rainbird Reference Books Ltd., 1970], 298).

24. Probably Charles Montagu Doughty (1843–1926). See his epic poem *The Dawn in Britain* (London: Duckworth, 1906); and his play *The Cliffs* (London: Duckworth, 1914).

25. Morris dancers. See n. 19.

26. A few days before May wrote this letter, on 12 July, Quinn served as lawyer in the incorporation proceedings of the Association of American Painters and Sculptors, which was to sponsor the famous February-March Armory Show in 1913 (Reid, 142).

27. Sir Edward Grey, lst Viscount (1862–1933). See "Colonial and Foreign Affairs; report of speeches delivered by Lord Coleridge, R. Hon. Sir Edward Grey, et. al. on 3 May 1905" *(NUC, Vol. 218, p. 158.).* Also read Grey in *European War* (Ottawa: J. de L'Tache, 1914) and *The War of Democracy* (Garden City, 1917), 39–51.

28. Robert Bontine Cunninghame Graham (1852–1936), scholar, Scottish nationalist, socialist devoted to Morris. Graham was imprisoned in 1887 after the Trafalgar Square riots. He died in Argentina, where the new city of Don Roberto was named after him (*Dictionary of National Biography,* s.v. Graham, Cunninghame). Lily Yeats writes in her journal that Cunninghame Graham often visited the Morris house while she was working there. "He looked a dashing desperato [*sic*]—in riding dress, a wide-brimmed hat, his manners gracious and courteous, he never stayed as long as he came on horseback and had left some strange passer by to hold his horse. The gloom of the house felt deeper after his flashing coming and quick going" *(Draft Scrapbook).*

29. George Lansbury was the editor of *The Herald,* a national labor weekly, and the author of *The Principles of the English Poor Law* (London: Twentieth Cen-

tury Press, 1897), *Socialism for the Poor* (London: The Clarion Press, 1908), and *In France* (London: Limit Printing and Publishing Co., 1915?) among others.

30. John Burns (1858–1943) was President of a local government board in England, an engineer and member of both the Amalgamated Society of Engineers (joined 1879) and the Social Democratic Federation (joined 1883). In 1887, on Bloody Sunday, he was arrested with Cunninghame Graham. A Labour M.P. (1892–1918), Burns became President of the Board of Trade in 1914 (Brown, *Growth of British Industrial Relations* [1960], 370).

31. Yeats rewrote much of *The Countess Cathleen* after the furor it caused in 1899 in Ireland, and so May certainly saw the revised version. For a discussion about the problems surrounding the play, see Janis and Richard Londraville, "A First Class Fighting Man: Frank Hugh O'Donnell's Correspondence with John Quinn," *Eire Ireland* XXVI 3 (Fall, 1991): 60–81. O'Donnell, who despised Yeats, was the force behind *The Countess Cathleen* riots in 1899. He met Quinn in 1907, and although the two disagreed on many things—including Yeats, Synge, and Irish politics—they remained friends until O'Donnell's death in 1916.

32. William Paton Ker (1855–1923), *English Literature, Medieval* (London: Williams and Norgate for Home University Library of Modern Knowledge, 1912).

33. H. G. Wells, et. al., *Socialism and the Great State: Essays in Construction* (Ayer, 1972. Reprint of 1912 edition).

34. John Bruce Glasier was a Scottish socialist friend of Morris. In his *William Morris and the Early Days of the Socialist Movement* (London, 1921), he includes an account of the "Huck Finn" incident.

35. Herbert Spencer (1820–1903) is known for his theories of evolution and is the author of *Principles of Psychology* (1855) and *The System of Synthetic Philosophy* (1862–93), among others.

36. John Drinkwater (1882–1937), *William Morris, A Critical Study* (London, M. Secker, 1912).

37. Quinn wrote to Joseph Conrad that his "experiment in partnership" with Shoemaker had cost him more than $10,000 (Quinn to Conrad, 20 July 1912 in Reid, 131–32).

38. Thomas Fortune Ryan.

39. George Brinton McClellan Harvey (1864–1928) was editor of *Harper's Weekly* and author of *Women, etc.; Some Leaves from an Editor's Diary* (New York and London: Harper & Bros., 1908); *"The Power of Tolerance," and other speeches* (New York and London: Harper & Bros., 1911); and *Hughes or Wilson* (New York: North American Review Corp., 1916?).

40. Francis William Bain, *A Syrup of Bees* (Stories translated from Hindu) (London: Phillip Lee Warner, 1914).

41. Abulqasem Ferdowsi (also Firdawsi or Firdausi), *Shahnameh* (The Book of Kings). Before Morris's attempt, the *Shahnameh* was translated from its original Persian by James Atkinson for the Oriental translation fund of Great Britain and Ireland, 1832 (London). Atkinson's version was abridged, so perhaps Morris's intent was to do a complete translation.

42. See this chapter n. 23.

43. As Christmas approached, Quinn sent May her usual barrel of apples as a gift (Cable from Quinn to May, December 1912, NYPL).

Chapter 4. The Letters of 1913

1. Pierre Puvis de Chavannes (French painter 1824–1898) was Quinn's favorite at the time. In addition to the two mentioned here and *Beheading of St. John*

the Baptist mentioned in chapter 1, Quinn also owned *Study for War* (1861), *Study for Ave Picardia Nutrix* (1865), *Child Carrying Flowers* (1884), *Male Nude with Lyre* (1889), *Female Nude with Lyre* (1889), *Summer: Study for the Mural Painting at the Hotel de Ville, Paris* (1891), and *Seated Man* (n.d.). Quinn spent around $20,000 for this collection (Zilczer, 179–80).

2. The Huntington Library catalog lists fifteen mss. poems by Rossetti that were bought from Quinn in the 1913 sale, including "Broken Music" and "Bella's Bullfinch."

3. Quinn bought a Gauguin lithograph for girlfriend Dorothy Coates at the show (Reid, 149).

4. Quinn did not own any paintings by Francis Picabia (French, 1879–1953). Zilczer does list twenty-seven Picassos that Quinn had purchased before his death in 1924, including *Three Women at the Spring* (1921, purchased for $6,832 in 1922), and *Girl with a Hoop* (1919, purchased for French francs 25,000 in 1920) (Zilczer, 153–78). This is by no means a complete list. Reid notes that at one dispersal auction after Quinn's death, thirty-two paintings and thirty pieces in other media by Picasso were sold (660). Six Cezannes, four Gauguins, thirty-four Matisses (including *The Blue Nude*), two Pissarros, and one Van Gogh (*Self Portrait*, 1886–1890) are listed by either Zilczer or Brummer & Weyhe as belonging to Quinn.

5. Probably the most important art show in America to that date, the Armory Show displayed about eighty of Quinn's purchases. In his opening speech, Quinn said that the show was "epoch making in the history of American art, . . . the most complete art exhibition that has been held in the world during the last quarter century" and that "American artists—young American Artists, that is—do not dread . . . the ideas of the culture of Europe" and that the Show was the first chance for Americans "to see and judge for themselves the work of the Europeans who are creating a new art." For a detailed explanation of Quinn's role in the Armory production, see Reid, 142–47.

6. See the Special Exhibition Number [illus.] of *Arts and Decoration* 3 (March 1913): 149–82 for information related to the Armory Show and for Quinn's article (pp. 155–58). Jeanne Robert Foster wrote to Richard Londraville on 13 April 1970 about Quinn's lack of published material: "The articles he did were embodied in long letters to Yeats, to Eliot, to Lady Gregory, to Pound, to Epstein, etc." (Londraville private collection)

7. Maggs Bros. booksellers dealt with rare books, bindings, prints, and autographs and were located on Conduit Street and New Bond Street, London, and at 93–95, rue La Boetie, Paris.

8. Reid explains that "Quinn was now [1913] counsel on matters of tax law for the New York Stock Exchange. In the spring and summer of 1913 the Exchange was under federal and state attack, which meant repeated trips to both Albany and Washington" (156).

9. Sydney and Beatrice Webb founded *The New Statesman*, the first issue appearing on 12 May 1913. See S. K. Ratcliffe, "The New Statesman," in *The Webbs and Their Work*, edited by Margaret Cole (Connecticut: Greenwood Press, 1985), 131–44.

10. M. F. Roberts, "Science in Art, as Shown in the International Exhibition of Painting and Sculpture," *Craftsman* 24 (May 1913): 216–18.

11. Morris's *House of the Wolfings* is now located at the Morgan Library in New York, but I don't know the history of its travels from Quinn to the library. It is possible that the long autobiographical letter from Swinburne to Stedman

quoted on pages 190–91 of Philip Henderson's *Swinburne: Portrait of a Poet* (New York: Macmillan, 1974) may have been one that Quinn owned. Edmund Clarence Stedman (1833–1908) wrote numerous books, including *Victorian Poets* (Boston: Houghton, Mifflin, 1886). I am not able to locate other Swinburne's letters to Stedman that Quinn owned or Quinn's ms. of Meredith's *Ode to Napoleon.*

12. Quinn is referring to the two Pierre Puvis de Chavannes paintings he bought in March 1913, *Le Vendage* and *La Rivière.*

13. Although I have been unable to locate the text for May's talk, it is possible that it was similar to several she gave later in her life. See *Philobiblon* VII #4 (1934): 169–72 and other pages not numbered for May's articles, "Reminiscences about My Father" and "A Talk on William Morris, by May Morris, broadcast by the British Broadcasting Corporation on Friday, February 9th, 1934," respectively.

14. In the undated brief Quinn prepared *(Memorandum Against Taxing Sales of Works of Art),* he argued that "Today it is the artist and the craftsman who stand between the harshness and the crudeness of machines and their unlovely, if necessary, products, and a fine life. Art is needed more now than it was needed in the Middle Ages before the steam engine was invented, when nearly all workmen were artists" (4). Quinn's battle for duty-free art would take up much of his time and interest over the next ten years of his life. The two briefs are owned by Richard Londraville and were displayed at the June 15–September 4, 1978 exhibition, "The Noble Buyer: John Quinn: Patron of the Avant-Garde" at the Hirshhorn Museum, the Smithsonian. See Introduction, n. 37.

15. John Masefield (1878–1967), *The Daffodil Fields* (London: William Heinemann, 1913); and *The Everlasting Mercy* (London: Sidgwick, 1911).

16. Sir Rabindranath Tagore (1861–1941), *Gitanjali (Song Offerings)* (Boston: International Picket Library, 1912). The introduction was written by W. B. Yeats.

17. Laurence Binyon, aka Robert Laurence (1869–1943), British poet, playwright, and art critic, complied *Guide to an exhibition of Chinese and Japanese Paintings. . . . (4th–9th Centuries)* (London: Printed by the order of the Trustees, British Museum Dept. of Prints and Drawings, 1910). See also *Japanese Art* (London: International Art Publishing Co., 1910 and T. F. Unwin, 1909).

18. The originals of the two letters that follow have apparently been lost. Jeanne Robert Foster prepared a typescript of excerpts—sometimes only pieces of sentences—of portions she must have felt were interesting. These are reprinted here. The transcripts are in the private collection of Mr. Thomas Conroy, Quinn's grandnephew.

19. Reid explains the situation: "Quinn involved himself heavily on behalf of his old Irish and Tammany friend Daniel F. Cohalan, whose appointment to the Supreme Court of New York Quinn had engineered after declining the post himself in 1911. One John A. Connolly . . . claimed . . . that between October 1904 and November 1906 he had paid nearly $4,000 to Cohalan, who was then rising to be the chief lieutenant of Boss Charles F. Murphy of Tammany Hall, for Cohalan's use of his influence in getting Connolly contracts for work for the city. . . . *The New York Times* demanded that Cohalan clear himself of the nasty charges or resign from the Supreme Court" (Reid, 156). Quinn convinced Cohalan and his lawyers to ask for an investigation by the New York State Legislature. The investigation did not exactly clear Cohalan, but it turned up evidence that Connolly, who had been in a mental institution for a time, was at least untrustworthy. The matter was finally dropped.

20. In his undated brief *(Memorandum Against Taxing Sales of Works of Art),*

Quinn cites Ruskin and Morris as leaders in "bringing art to the people" and quotes Morris: "I do not want art for a few, any more than education for a few, or freedom for a few" (Londraville, private collection), 3.

21. It may be that Quinn's doctor did recommend a vacation, but Quinn's major reason for going to the Adirondacks at this time was to be near his favorite mistress, ex-schoolteacher Dorothy Coates, who was ill with tuberculosis in Saranac, New York. Although May Morris did not know about Ms. Coates, others of Quinn's friends did. He received a letter on 4 September, for instance, from Maud Gonne, who told him that Ms. Coates could indeed survive the dreaded disease, that she herself had almost died of TB at one time but was now perfectly well. She told Quinn that W. B. Yeats had even written her epitaph [See Yeats's "I dreamt that one had died in a strange place"] (Reid, 166–67).

22. Probaby Phillip Webb, an old friend of the Morris family. See chapter 3, n. 22 and chapter 6, May Morris to Quinn, 4 June 1915.

23. Sydney Carlyle Cockerell was Morris's librarian and secretary and had charge at one point of the Kelmscott Press. After Morris died, Cockerell was a trustee of the estate, a secretary to Wilfrid Blunt, and then Director of the Fitzwilliam Museum, Cambridge from 1908–37. Philip Henderson, *The Letters of William Morris to His Family and Friends* (London: Longmans, Green, and Co., 1950), 350.

24. George Russell, "The Co-Operative Movement," *The New Statesman*, Irish Supplement (12 July 1913): 2–5.

25. Mrs. Emmeline Pankhurst (1858–1928) was a major figure in the Women's Suffrage Movement. See Emmeline Pankhurst, *My Own Story* (New York: Source Book Press, 1914).

26. See chapter 1, n. 42 for Shannon and Ricketts.

27. Jacques Anatole Thibault (aka Anatole France) spoke to the Fabian Society at the galleries of the Royal Society of British Artists in Suffolk St. at 8:30 PM on 11 Dec. on "The Dangers of Militarism and Uselessness of War." George Bernard Shaw presided and, besides May, H. M. Hyndman and Keir Hardie, M. P., attended, among others. Much of France's speech is quoted in the*Times*, 12 December 1913: p. 7, col. 2.

28. See Hyndman's *The Historical Basis of Socialism in England* (London: K. Paul, Trench & Co., 1883) and *Further Reminiscences* (London: Macmillan, 1912). James Keir Hardie (1856–1915), M. P., was a political writer and a supporter of the Women's Suffrage Movement. See his *After Twenty Years: All about the I. L. P.* (London: Independent Labour Party, 1913) and *The Queenie Gerald Case* (Manchester: Independent Labour Party, 1913).

29. Charles Conder, British decorative artist (1868–1909). See chapter 3, n. 10.

30. This lecture was probably a draft of the one that Yeats gave during his 6 February–2 April 1914 North American lecture tour. He entitled it "John M. Synge and the Ireland of His Time." See Karin Strand's 1978 dissertation, *W. B. Yeats's American Lecture Tours* (Ann Arbor: University of Michigan Press, 1991), 70.

31. Maurice Bourgeois, *John Millington Synge and the Irish Theatre* (London: Constable & Co., 1913).

Chapter 5. The Letters of 1914

1. Jane Burden Morris died unexpectedly while on a trip to Bath in January 1914. Her obituary stated that she was one of the last survivors of the Pre-Raphaelites, "who lived, almost unconsciously and always without the least

trace of self-consciousness, at an extraordinary tension of high idealism combined with unpretending simplicity." The article also called May a "designer and executer of embroideries," who had written "pleasant biographical notes" to the *Collected Works.* See *New York Times* 28 January 1914: p. 9, col. 6. An article about Jane's career appears in the same newspaper, 1 February 1914, Sec. 3, p. 3, col. 4.

2. While Quinn was in Ohio at his cousin's funeral, Standish O'Grady arrived in New York, and Quinn arranged to have him stay at his apartment. When Quinn returned, he arranged for O'Grady and J. B. Yeats—old friends—to have a reunion. O'Grady left for his return voyage to Ireland in late January (Reid, 175).

3. Bernhard Berenson (1865–1959), an art scholar and critic, wrote *The Venetian Painters of the Renaissance* (New York and London: G. P. Putnam's sons, 1894) and *The Study and Criticism of Italian Art* (London: G. Bell & Sons, 1901), among others. Wilhelm Von Bode (1845–1929) wrote *Florentine Sculptors of the Renaissance* (New York: Charles Scribner's Sons, 1909) and *The Collection of J. Pierpont Morgan* (Paris: Librairie Centrale des Beaux Arts, 1910), among others.

4. Quinn and Yeats had a falling out in 1909 when Quinn thought that Yeats was flirting with Dorothy Coates, Quinn's mistress. Reid explains: "Quinn and Yeats had come to bitter words and a loud parting over Dorothy Coates. Quinn thought Yeats had been gossiping loosely and injuriously about his relationship with her, and he charged Yeats with trying to take over his mistress for himself. Their friendship ceased at once" (74). In 1914 Quinn, on hearing Yeats was coming to America, wrote to the poet on 9 February and offered an olive branch: " . . . you were always generous in your sympathies and full of humanity. . . . So if the suggestion appeals to you, I should be glad to shake hands with you and let by-gones be by-gones" (The John Quinn Memorial Collection, NYPL). Quinn and Yeats reconciled and Yeats moved into Quinn's apartment for a ten-day stay in March (Reid, 176).

5. Quinn is probably referring to Thomas Fortune Ryan. Even though this letter indicates a rift, Quinn remained Ryan's corporation attorney for many years.

6. Neither the March 1913 nor March 1914 issues contains the information to which Quinn refers. Perhaps he mistook the date or the journal.

7. Clutton-Brock, *William Morris, His Work and Influence* (London: Williams and Norgate, 1914).

8. Belle da Costa Greene, librarian to J. P. Morgan, and Quinn were good friends. Quinn persuaded her to use her influence with her employer to get a position as librarian of the Institut Francais for painter Marcel Duchamp. Quinn owned four Duchamps, including *Nude Descending a Staircase (No. 1)* (Reid, 210).

9. Woodrow Wilson served as President of the United States from 4 March 1913—3 March 1921.

10. Quinn was Moore's friend and patron and was responsible for Boni & Liveright's publication of Moore's *A Story-Teller's Holiday* and *Avowals* (Reid 484). *Vale* (Collection of British Authors, Vol. 4490) was published in 1914 and was Vol. 3 of *Hail and Farewell,* with *Ave* and *Salve* comprising the first two volumes. The thirteen-year-long Quinn-Moore correspondence is located in the John Quinn Memorial Collection, NYPL.

11. See chapter 6, n. 17. May showed her work in and helped organize the 1914 Paris Exhibition of the Decorative Arts of Great Britian.

12. Clutton-Brock, *Thoughts on the War* (London: Methuen & Co., 1914), published from the *Times Literary Supplement.*

13. In *The New Statesman Supplement* (14 November 1914), Shaw contradicted himself on several occasions, especially when speaking about military buildup and England's obligations to Belgium. In the *New Statesman* IV, 21 November 1914, many readers reacted, most of them negatively, to Shaw's essay. Shaw responded defensively in the same magazine, 19 December 1914.

14. Mrs. Marie Spartali Stillman, painter and model, took her training with Ford Madox Brown (Marsh, *Jane and May Morris,* 164–65). She married W. J. Stillman, an American journalist. Wilfird Scawen Blunt once tried to seduce her, according to Marsh (*Pre-Raphaelite Sisterhood,* 285, 351).

15. Only twenty-four volumes of the *Collected Works* were published.

16. Quinn sent May the apples and a gift of £20 (Cable, Quinn to May Morris, December 1914, John Quinn Memorial Collection, NYPL).

Chapter 6. The Letters of 1915

1. Bain, *A Syrup of the Bees.* See chapter 3, n. 40.

2. Laurence Binyon, *The Winnowing Fan: Poems on the Great War* (London: Elkin Mathews, 1914).

3. Quinn might be referring to his position as Special Counsel for the Comptroller of the State of New York in the "inheritance tax proceedings against the estate of John Jacob Astor, drowned on the Titanic. . . . [Quinn] was furious when his large anticipated fee was reduced by more than a third" (Reid, 193).

4. By this time, Reid explains, "it was now generally assumed that . . . Kuno Meyer was an outright German agent" and that his American lectures "were only a thin screen for systematic German propaganda." John Redmond was a Roman Catholic politician who led the Parnell party after Parnell's death in 1891. Alan Ward, in *Ireland and Anglo-American Relations: 1899–1921* (Toronto: University of Toronto Press, 1969), says that Redmond, "[t]hough courageous . . . pursued objectives for Ireland which were essentially moderate but which ultimately failed to satisfy the great bulk of his followers in Ireland and America" (11). For a more thorough explanation of the Irish controversy with Redmond, see Janis and Richard Londraville, "A First Class Fighting Man: Frank Hugh O'Donnell's Correspondence with John Quinn," *Eire Ireland* XXVI, 3 (Fall 1991): 60–81. See the Meyer-Quinn and Redmond-Quinn correspondence in the John Quinn Memorial Collection, NYPL.

5. During 1914, the year Casement (1864–1916) visited Quinn, he also published *Ireland, Germany and Freedom of the Seas* (New York: Irish Press Bureau, 1914) and was probably finishing *The Crime Against Europe* (Philadelphia: The Celtic Press, 1915). Casement, an associate of Kuno Meyer, insisted that he was not a German agent and asked Quinn to serve as his lawyer in a law suit against the *New York World* for accusing him as such. Quinn turned him down because he was not convinced of Casement's innocence. Casement never wrote again (Reid, 226–228). In 1916 Casement landed from a German submarine at Tralee and was ultimately arrested and hanged as a traitor *(Concise Dictionary of National Biography: 1905–1950,* s. v. "Casement, Roger.") See his correspondence with Quinn in the John Quinn Memorial Collection, NYPL, and Quinn's article on Casement in the *New York Times,* 13 August 1916 (listed in the Quinn bibliography in this text).

6. See the *New York Times* 11 January 1915, p. 1, col. 6 and 31 January pt. 5,

p. 19, col 1 for an articles about Barker's production of "Androcles and the Lion"; and for reactions to Barker's theater company and criticism of his production. Shaw had originally planned a trip to the U.S. but canceled at the last moment.

7. Quinn called Crowley, a black magician, "the wickedest man in England." Even so, he bought several of Crowley's mss. and all of his books (which he didn't read after his clerk told him they were "both erotic and blasphemous"). Quinn also owned the portrait of Crowley painted by Augustus John. W. B. Yeats also had some connection with Crowley as his own interest in the occult grew, but Yeats wrote Quinn and told him that he had "dropped Crowley" after he found Crowley had lied to him (Reid 101, 194).

8. Padraic Colum (1881–1972), Irish poet. See his correspondence with Quinn in the John Quinn Memorial Collection, NYPL. Many of Colum's papers are housed at The State University of New York at Binghamton.

9. Cecil Chesterton (1879–1918), historian, critic, and author. See his *The Prussian Hath Said in His Heart* (London: Chapman & Hall, 1914), which is reviewed in the *New York Times* 7 February 1915: pt. 6, p. 42, col. 3.

10. See Emmet J. Larkin, *James Larkin: Irish Labour Leader, 1876–1947* (Cambridge: MIT Press, 1965).

11. William Jennings Bryan (1860–1947), American author, politician, and orator.

12. See the *Times,* 20 April 1915, p. 12, col. 4 for Webb's obituary. He died on 17 April 1915. See chapter 3, n. 22.

13. Alfred Charles William Harmsworth, Lord Northcliffe (1865–1922) was a powerful newspaper proprietor who wrote *At the War* (New York: George H. Doran, 1916) and *Newspapers and Their Millionaires . . . with some further Meditations about Us* (London Assoc. Newspapers Ltd., 1922), among others.

14. The Lusitania tragedy brought the United States into the war. Quinn was especially affected by the ship's sinking. Hugh Lane—art collector, Lady Gregory's nephew, and good friend of Quinn—was one of the passengers who was killed. Quinn had tried to stop Lane from boarding the Lusitania after he had heard the German ambassador boasting that it would be torpedoed (Reid, 214). Perhaps Lane is best known for his superb art collection and the controversy it caused. For an explanation, see W. B. Yeats's notes in *The Collected Poems of W. B. Yeats,* edited by Richard Finneran (New York: Macmillan, 1989), 457. Lane, generally viewed as one of the first who saw the value in modern art, called Quinn's Picassos "rubbish" and told Quinn that he felt the "new experiments" resulted from "disordered imagination" (Reid, 213).

15. The book was issued in 1915 as *The Pilgrims of Hope and Chants for Socialists* (London and New York: Longmans, Green & Co.; Longmans Pocket Library).

16. Cromarty is located near Inverness, Scotland.

17. May showed her work in and helped organize the 1914 Paris Exhibition of the Decorative Arts of Great Britain and did likewise for the 1916 Arts and Crafts Exhibition in England (Marsh, *Jane and May Morris,* 270, 274). Marsh says that May might have been criticized for these activities during a dark time for Great Britain. If so, she chose to fight such opinions. May's letter to Quinn shows that, like Quinn, she feared the death of art. She felt that it was art that would maintain a cultural sanity in the midst of the bloodletting and thus continued to plan shows even through the bleak nights of the London Zeppelin raids.

18. During the raids, Jeanne Robert Foster, Quinn's companion during the final years of his life (1919–24), was also in London serving as a war correspon-

dent for *The Review of Reviews.* She would not meet Quinn until 1919, when John Butler Yeats would bring them together (Jeanne Robert Foster journals, Richard Londraville private collection).

19. Katherine Adams (sometimes Katharine [*sic*]), daughter of the Reverend Adams (Rector of Little Faringdon and an old college friend of William Morris), was a childhood friend of May's who later did embroidery and jewelry work as well as bookbinding (Marsh, *Jane to May Morris,* 95, 248). In the U.S., the only known copy of Adams's edition of *An Earthly Paradise* (30 copies printed on an Albion handpress) is at the University of California: Berkeley. Included in the Berkeley copy is a transcript of a memorial address given at the Women's Guild of Arts (n.d.).

Chapter 7. The Letters of 1916–1917

1. Quinn had already sent May a copy of his corrected version of Synge's *Deirdre of the Sorrows,* but he found errors in that version as well and had yet another corrected version printed. See chapter 1, n. 8.

2. The book to which Quinn refers was Theodore Watts-Dunton's (1832–1914) *Old Familiar Faces* (London: H. Jenkins Ltd., 1916). The writer of the introduction is not identified, but he says that Watts-Dunton called Mrs. Morris "a remarkable woman, a most remarkable woman; superior to Morris intellectually, she reached a greater mental height than he was capable of, yet few knew it. . . . She was the most lovely woman I have ever known, her beauty was incredible" (10).

3. See "The Collected Works of William Morris" review in the 13 June 1915 issue of the *New York Times:* pt. 6, p. 217, col. 1. See chapter 1, n. 77 and this chapter n. 6 for further information.

4. Sir Norman Angell (1874–1967), *The Great Illusion; A Study of the Relation of Military Power in Nations to Their Economic and Social Advantage* (London: W. Heinemann, 1910).

5. Dedicated to Quinn, James Gibbons Huneker's *Ivory, Apes and Peacocks; Joseph Conrad, Walt Whitman, Jules Laforgue, Dostoievsky and Tolstoy, Schoenberg, Wedekind, Moussorgsky, Cézanne, Vermeer, Matisse, Van Gogh, Gauguin, Italian Futurists, Various Latter day Poets, Painters, Composers and Dramatists* was published by T. W. Laurie in 1915. The essay by Amy Levy (1861–1889) is unidentified, but she did write *A Minor Poet and Other Verse* (London: T. F. Unwin, 1884) and *Xantippe and Other Verse* (Cambridge: E. Johnson, 1881), among others. The A. E. (George Russell) book was probably his *Collected Poems* (London: Macmillan, 1913). It is worth mentioning here that in 1917, Russell, Sir Horace Plunkett, and Quinn together published their *The Irish Home-Rule Convention* (New York: Macmillan, 1917). Russell's contribution was "Thoughts for a Convention," and Quinn's was "An American Opinion." The book on war was by George Washington Crile (1864–1943), *A Mechanistic View of War and Peace* (New York: Macmillan, 1915).

6. Richard Le Gallienne (1866–1947), novelist, poet, critic, and translator, author of *George Meredith* (London: E. Mathews, 1890), among others, was known as a "man of the Nineties," and made his reputation with works such as *The Book-Bills of Narcissus* (Derby: F. Murray, 1891). He translated Wagner's *Tristan and Isolde* into English Verse (New York: F. A. Stokes) in 1909.

7. Richard Le Gallienne.

8. André Suares (1868–1948) wrote several books on Dostoievsky, Tolstoy,

and Ibsen. See his *Tolstoi* (Paris, Union pour l' action morale, 1898), *Tolstoi Vivant* (Paris: J. Crémieu imprimeur, 1911), and *Trois Hommes: Pascal, Ibsen, Dostoievski* (Paris: Editions de la Nouvelle Revue Francaise, 1913).

9. See n. 5.
10. See chapter 6, n. 19.
11. See May Morris to Quinn, 23 April 1916.
12. The letter has been lost.
13. Marsh says that "During the war, the network of Women's Institutes was formed to assist women in rural areas and contribute to the war effort, and May became the chief promoter and supporter of the Kelmscott branch. . . . ." She also says that "There is no evidence that [May] gave particular support to the war effort" (Marsh, *Jane and May Morris,* 275). May's letters to Quinn, though, seem to indicate otherwise. May was at the very least concerned with helping the refugees. Besides making clothing, May sent food, including Quinn's Christmas gifts of apples, to refugees and wounded soldiers.

Bibliography of the Works of May Morris

1888	Chain Stitch Embroidery. *The Hobby Horse* 3, #12: 24–29.
1892	Embroidery. In *Plain Handicrafts,* edited by A. K. Mackmurdo, 46–54. National Association for the Advancement of Art, 1892.
1893	*Decorative Needlework.* London: Joseph Hughes.
1893	Of Embroidery (212–23); Of Materials (365–75); Colour (376–86). In *Arts and Crafts Essays by Members of the Arts and Crafts Society.* New York: Scribner's. [Reissued in 1977 by Garland Publishing Co, N.Y.]
1893–94	Of Church Embroidery. *The Building News* LXV and LXVI, Nos. 2023, 2025, 2027, 2031, 2033, 2035, 2037, 2040, 2042, 2063, 2066, and 2069 (13 October–31 August).
1895	Embroidery and Tapestry. *Journal of the Society of Arts* 43: 384.
1898	*Lady Griselda's Dream.* In *Longman's Magazine* 32 (June): 145–57. [Reprinted in the appendix of this text.]
1899	'Coptic Textiles' Illustrated from the Collection in the South Kensington Museum. *Architectural Review* V (May): 274–287.
1902	Masques and Pageantry. *Journal of the Society of Arts* 50: 670.
1903	*White Lies, A Play in One Act.* Privately Printed. Chiswick Press.
1905	Opus Anglicanum—The Syon Cope. *Burlington Magazine VI* (January): 278–285, 2 plates.
1905	Opus Anglicanum II—The Ascoli Cope. *Burlington Magazine VI* (March): 440–48, 2 plates.
1905	Opus Anglicanum III—The Pienza Cope. *Burlington Magazine VII* (April): 54–65, 3 plates.
1905	Opus Anglicanum at the Burlington Fine Arts Club. *Burlington Magazine* (July): 302–9, 2 plates.
1906	How to Make the Home Pretty. In *Domestic Economy for Teachers,* edited by John C. Horobin, 427–40. London: T. Nelson and Sons.
1910–1915	*The Collected Works of William Morris,* edited by May Morris. London: Longmans' Green.
Circa 1913	*Ecclesiastical Dress and Vestments. [Burlington Magazine* excerpts 1905–13. Publisher and date unknown. Located at Los Angeles County Museum of Art.]
1917	William de Morgan: Recollections. *Burlington Magazine* XXXI (August): 77–83, 2 plates.
1917	William de Morgan: Art. *Burlington Magazine* XXXI (September): 91–97, 2 plates.
1919	Weaving and Textile Crafts. In *Handicrafts and Reconstruction,*

	41–52. London: J. Hogg for the Arts and Crafts Exhibition Society.
1921	Preface in J. Bruce Glasier, *William Morris and the Early days of the Socialist Movement.* London: Longmans, Green.
1934	A Talk on William Morris. *Philobiblon.* March: not paginated.
1934	Reminiscences about My Father. *Philobiblon.* March: 169–72.
1934	William Morris, 1834–1934: Some Appreciations (Limited edition [350] of 1 pg). Walthamstow Antiquarian Society.
1936	*William Morris, Artist, Writer, Socialist,* edited by May Morris. Oxford: Basil Blackwell (2 vols.)
1973	*The Introductions to the Collected Works of William Morris.* New York: Oriel Press.

Bibliography of the Works of John Quinn

1911	Lady Gregory and the Abbey Theater. *Outlook* (16 December): 916–19.
1913	Modern Art from the Layman's Point of View. *Arts and Decoration* (3 March 1913): 155–58, 176.
1913	*A Plea for Untaxed Contemporary Art.* New York: Assoc. of American Painters and Sculptors, 1913.
Circa 1915	*Memorandum Against Taxing Sales of Works of Art* [Londraville private collection].
Circa 1915	*Senate of the United States Committee on Finance in the Matter of the Protest of Munition Makers Against the 8 Per Cent Excess Profit Tax* . . . [Londraville private collection].
1916	"Sir Roger Casement: Some Notes for a Chapter of History by a Friend Whose Guest He Was When the War Broke Out." *New York Times Magazine* (13 August): 1–4.
1917	An American Opinion. In *The Irish Home-Rule Convention* [by Quinn, George Russell (A. E.), and Sir Horace Plunkett]. New York: Macmillan Co.
1921	*Memorandum Against the Imposition of Any Duty on Original Works of Art* [Londraville private collection].
1983	*The Letters of John Quinn to William Butler Yeats.* Edited by Alan Himber. Michigan: UMI Research Press, 1983.
1988	John Quinn's 'An Evening in New York with W. B. Yeats' [1920]. Edited by Richard Londraville. *Yeats Annual* #6: 166–85.

General Bibliography

This bibliography lists books and articles that contain significant information about May Morris or John Quinn.

Anderson Galleries
1924 *The Library of John Quinn.* 2 vols. New York: Anderson Galleries. [Republished in 1969 in 2 vols. by Lemma Corp as *The Complete Catalogue of the Library of John Quinn].*

Art Center
1926 *Memorial Exhibition of Representative Works Selected from the John Quinn Collection January 7–30th, 1926.* New York: Art Center, 1926.

Anscombe, Isabelle
1984 *A Woman's Touch: Women in Design from 1860 to the Present Day.* New York: Viking Penguin Inc., 1984.

Blackwell, Sir Basil
1962 More about Miss Lobb. *The Bookseller* (October): 1736.

Brummer, Joseph and Weyhe, E.
1926 *John Quinn: 1870–1925, Collection of Paintings, Water Colors, Drawings & Sculpture.* New York: Pidgeon Hill Press.

Callen, Anthea
1979 *Women Artists of the Arts and Crafts Movement 1870—1914.* New York: Pantheon Books.

Carlano, Marianne
1993 *Early Modern Textiles from Arts and Crafts to Art Deco.* Boston: Museum of Fine Arts.

du Cann, C. G. L.
1963 *The Loves of George Bernard Shaw.* New York: Funk and Wagnalls.

Dunlap, Joseph
1980 The Infernal Triangle. *The Independent Shavian* 18 #2: 35.

Fielding, Una
1968 Memories of May Morris 1923–1938. *The Journal of the William Morris Society* (Winter): 2–5.

George, J. Anne and Campbell, Susan
1987 The Role of Embroidery in Victorian Culture and the Pre-Raphaelite Circle. *The Journal of Pre-Raphaelite and Aesthetic Studies* 7 #2 (May): 55–67.

Holroyd, Michael
1988 *Bernard Shaw: The Search for Love.* London: Chatto and Windus.

Horton, Margaret
1982 A Visit to May Morris. *The Journal of the William Morris Society* (Winter): 14–19.

Leary, Emmeline
1981 William Morris and May Morris. *Embroidery* (Summer): 47–49.

Lock, Teresa
1982 The Morris Family Remembered. *The Journal of the William Morris Society* (Summer): 9–15.

Londraville, Janis
1992 May Morris's Editing of 'So Many Stories Written Here'. *The Journal of the William Morris Society* (Autumn): 31–34.

1993 The Private Voice of May Morris. *The Journal of Pre-Raphaelite Studies* New Series II: 2 (Autumn): 28–37.

1995 *Lady Griselda's Dream:* May Morris's *Man and Superman. The Independent Shavian* (April): 6–14.

Londraville, Richard and Janis Londraville
1990 Two Men at War with Time: The Unpublished Correspondence of Wyndham Lewis and John Quinn. *English* 39, nos. 164 and 165: 97–145 and 229–51.

1991 'A First Class Fighting Man': Frank Hugh O'Donnell's Correspondence with John Quinn." *Eire Ireland* XXVI #3 (Autumn): 60–81.

1991 The Stage Irishmen and Pseudo-Celtic Drama: Selections from the Correspondence between Frank Hugh O'Donnell and John Quinn. *Yeats: An Annual of Critical and Textual Studies* IX: 66–86.

1992 The Mighty Quinn. *Irish America* (May): 34–38.

1994 No Idle Singers of Empty Days. *The Journal of Modern Literature* (Summer): 89–114.

Manning, Elfrida
1980 A Visit to May Morris, 1925. *The Journal of the William Morris Society* (Summer): 18–19.

Marsh, Jan
1985 *The Pre-Raphaelite Sisterhood.* New York: St. Martin's Press.

1986 *Jane and May Morris: A Biographical Story 1839—1938.* London: Pandora Press, 1986.

1987 The Defence of Janey. *The Journal of the William Morris Society* (Autumn 1987): 18–22.

Masterman, Elizabeth
1984 May Morris: Some Notes for Book Collectors. *The Book Collector* 33, #2: 163–78.

Murphy, Daniel J.
1987 Dear John Quinn. In *Lady Gregory: Fifty Years After,* edited by Ann Saddlemyer and Colin Smythe. Gerrards Cross, England: Colin Smythe.

Murphy, William M.
1978 *Prodigal Father: The Life of John Butler Yeats.* New York: Cornell Univ. Press.

Peters, Sally
1990 From Mystic Betrothal to *Ménage á Trois:* Bernard Shaw and May Morris. *The Independent Shavian* 28 #1–2: 3–16.

Reid, B. L.
1968 *The Man from New York: John Quinn and his Friends.* New York: Oxford University Press, 1968.

Saarinen, Aline
1958 *The Proud Possessors: The Lives, Times, and Tastes of some Adventurous American Art Collectors.* New York: Random House.

Scanlon, Dennis P.
1975 *John Quinn, An Irish-American in Conflict with his Culture.* New York: City College of the City University of New York: MA Thesis (October).

Shaw, George Bernard
1966 *William Morris as I Knew Him.* London: The William Morris Society.

Simmonds, Harvey
1968 *An Exhibition to Mark the Gift of the John Quinn Memorial Collection.* New York: New York Public Library.

Sloan, Helen
1989 *May Morris, 1862—1938: An Exhibition at the William Morris Gallery 10 January—11 March 1989.* London Borough of Waltham Forest: The William Morris Gallery.

Waugh, Evelyn
1976 *Diaries,* edited by M. Davie. London: Weidenfeld and Nicolson.

Zilczer, Judith
1978 *'The Noble Buyer': John Quinn, Patron of the Avant-Garde.* Washington, D. C.: Smithsonian Institution Press.

Index